THE
KOREANS

BY THE SAME AUTHOR

The Light and the Shadows
(short stories)

Behold, the City
(a novel)

Theirs the Darkness:
A Journey Through Equatorial Africa

Black Star Rising:
A Journey Through West Africa

Black Africa
Vol. 1 *From Prehistory to the Eve of the Colonial Era*
Vol. 2 *The Colonial Era and Modern Times*

The African Revolution

Along the Afric Shore:
An Historic Review of Two Centuries of U.S. Relations with Africa

The Power Peddlers:
How Lobbyists Mold America's Foreign Policy
(with Sarah Hays Trott)

Weapons:
The International Game of Arms, Money and Diplomacy

Mata Hari—The True Story

Witch Hunt:
The Crucifixion of "Tokyo Rose"

Russell Warren Howe

HARCOURT
BRACE
JOVANOVICH

San Diego
New York
London

THE KOREANS

Passion and Grace

HBJ

Copyright © 1988 by Russell Warren Howe

All rights reserved. No part of this publication may be reproduced or transmitted in any form or by any means, electronic or mechanical, including photocopy, recording, or any information storage and retrieval system, without permission in writing from the publisher.

Requests for permission to make copies of any part of the work should be mailed to: Permissions, Harcourt Brace Jovanovich, Publishers, Orlando, Florida 32887.

Library of Congress Cataloging-in-Publication Data
Howe, Russell Warren, 1925–
   The Koreans: passion and grace/Russell Warren Howe.—1st ed.
     p. cm.
  "A Harvest/HBJ book."
  Includes index.
  ISBN 0-15-647185-X (pbk.)
   1. Korea (South)—Civilization. 2. Korea (South)—Social life and customs. I. Title.
DS922.27.H69   1988
951.9'5—dc19   88-984

Designed by Dalia Hartman
Printed in the United States of America
First edition
A B C D E

To Yŏng-ja

*Korea, once a bright light
Of the golden age of Asia,
If it is relit, it will be
The Light of the East*

—*Rabindranath Tagore*

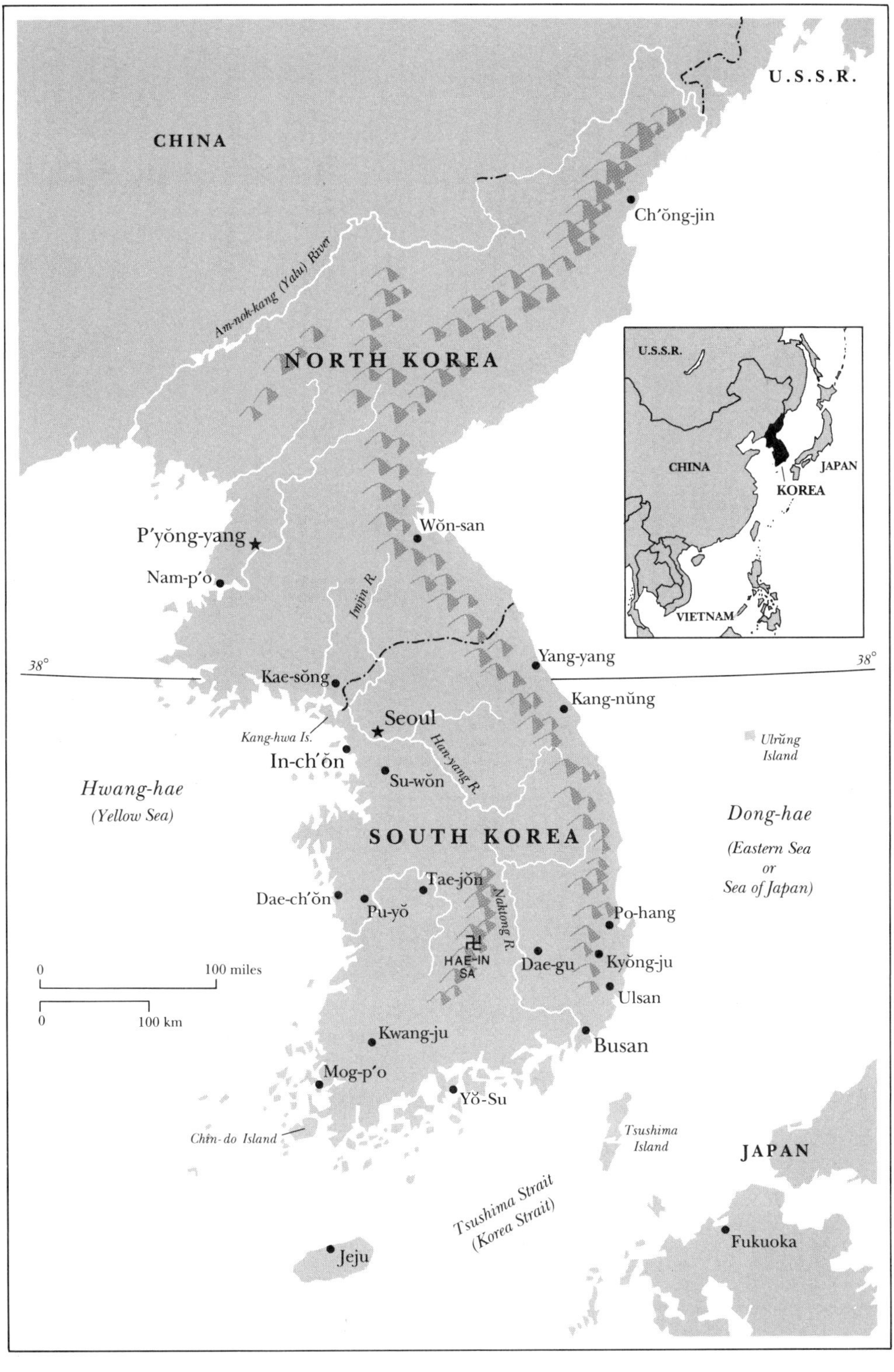

U.S.S.R.
CHINA
Ch'ŏng-jin
Am-nok-kang (Yalu) River
NORTH KOREA
U.S.S.R.
CHINA
JAPAN
KOREA
VIETNAM
Wŏn-san
P'yŏng-yang
Nam-p'o
Imjin R.
38°
Yang-yang
38°
Kae-sŏng
Kang-nŭng
Seoul
Kang-hwa Is.
Han-yang R.
Ulrŭng Island
In-ch'ŏn
Su-wŏn
Hwang-hae
(Yellow Sea)
Dong-hae
(Eastern Sea or Sea of Japan)
SOUTH KOREA
Tae-jŏn
Naktong R.
Dae-ch'ŏn
Pu-yŏ
Po-hang
HAE-IN SA
Dae-gu
Kyŏng-ju
0
100 miles
Ulsan
0
100 km
Kwang-ju
Busan
Mog-p'o
Yŏ-Su
Chin-do Island
Tsushima Island
JAPAN
Tsushima Strait
(Korea Strait)
Fukuoka
Jeju

CONTENTS

Prologue *xvii*

1. A Life in Contrasts *1*
2. A Life at the Crossroads *33*
3. A Life in Words and Rules and Graces *72*
4. A Life with the Spirits *105*
5. A Life with the Sea *150*
6. A Life in Alchemy *173*
7. A Life in Art *192*
8. A Life in Leisure *213*
9. A Life in *Mi-rae* *238*

Guide to Reading Han-gŭl *257*
Acknowledgments *259*
Select Bibliography *261*
Index *263*

Photographs follow pages 67, 145, 187, and 233

AUTHOR'S NOTE

WITH A FEW EXCEPTIONS, transliteration of Korean words from *han-gŭl* to the Latin alphabet follows McCune-Reischauer, the officially adopted system. Most exceptions are on personal names, which their owners often transcribe in a bewildering variety of ways.

Where possible, hyphenation has been eliminated. It has been preserved where required by convention, notably in given names, and where needed to facilitate pronunciation for foreign readers (i.e., *yŏ-gwan,* to make it clear it's not *yŏg-wan*).

R.W.H.

PROLOGUE

SŎ MAN-JUNG TURNS OVER ON the thin *yo* where he has been sleeping and folds back the ornate *ibul,* the duck-feathered quilt which is the only cover. He rubs his eyes and tries to guess the weather from the color of the daylight through the translucent clouded glass of the house door. He rises to his feet and performs some brief calisthenics, then goes to the bathroom. His wife Jae-mi, usually known to everyone as Hyŏn-du's mother, has begun to stir on the other side of the *yo.* Her first instinct, as she hears her husband close the bathroom door, is to switch on the bedside light of the clock radio, beside her organdie pillow, and to go to the wall mirror, where she closely examines her face for any telltale spots, however minute. Hyŏn-du's mother is convinced that she has an allergy of some sort, and she is trying to determine what it is; she is sure only that it is something basic in her diet, such as garlic or one of the shellfish, or perhaps her *in-sam* (ginseng) capsules, and every time she finds a minute spot on her cheek, she eliminates one of these from her regimen for a few days. She has not confided her problem to her husband, since there is no cause for disturbing another's *ki-bun,* or mood, except in matters of life and death.

PROLOGUE

In the bathroom, Mr. Sŏ is squatting near the drainage outlet in a slightly lower portion of the mosaic floor and is washing himself from head to toe. Finally, he fills a plastic basin with mostly cold water and douses himself with it, then rises to brush his teeth and shave. He can hear Hyŏn-du's mother making coffee in the kitchen and arranging small bowls of pickled vegetables, kippered eels, and pine-nut porridge. She is calling to the younger child, a daughter, Su-na, in an imperative tone, urging her to get up at once or she will be late for high school. Mr. Sŏ can also hear his wife talking in lower tones to their daughter-in-law, Hi-suk, who lives in the third small bedroom of the crowded house with the oldest Sŏ child, Hyŏn-du. Hyŏn-du is a junior manager in a large store and does not have to be at work until ten o'clock. From Hyŏn-du and Hi-suk's room comes the sound of a baby complaining. This is Hi-jong, the Sŏs' sickly granddaughter.

Sŏ Man-jung, a civil servant, is soon dressed in a conservative suit with white shirt and gray tie. He and Hyŏn-du, who is still in night attire, sit on cushions at a low, black lacquer table in the small living room, and the women serve them breakfast. Su-na is in the bathroom, which she must vacate by the time Hyŏn-du finishes breakfast. Soon, she is breakfasting in the kitchen with her mother and sister-in-law, apart from the men. Her sister-in-law is suckling the baby. As Su-na hurries off to catch the crowded bus to school, her mother calls after her with some errands she should perform on her way home in the afternoon and which she will probably forget.

Once the men have gone, the house becomes the empire of Hyŏn-du's mother, for her daughter-in-law is also her domestic servant in all but name, just as Su-na will become to some other woman when she marries. Although Hyŏn-du's mother is not a tyrant, she is no better than other women of her generation, and she tends to revenge the problems she had with Hyŏn-du's father's late, domineering mother by exacting

PROLOGUE

an emotional price from her own daughter-in-law—who, of course, she has never been completely convinced is good enough for Hyŏn-du. Hi-suk, in the fashion of the day, is as thin as a reed, and Hyŏn-du's mother is convinced that she will never have healthy sons.

Hyŏn-du's mother is the Sŏ chancellor of the exchequer, to whom both her husband and son bring their pay packets every week. She gives them what they need for their out-of-pocket expenses. Today, she gives Hi-suk money for marketing, issuing specific instructions as to what the young woman may buy.

"If the pig's cheeks do not look fresh, get some oxtails instead. If you cannot find the sort of large *chog-gye* clams which Hyŏn-du's father likes . . ."

"*Ne, ne . . .*"

The conversation goes on against the competition of the television, which offers a mawkish melodrama set in Lyi (or Yi) dynasty times, occasionally interrupted by high-volume advertising for instant noodle soup or backache medicine. After Hi-suk has gone to market, with the baby on her back in a carrying blanket, Hyŏn-du's mother goes to the apothecary for some professional advice about her real or imagined allergy.

Since Hyŏn-du married, Hyŏn-du's mother's life has become much easier, with Hi-jong's mother, as her daughter-in-law is usually referred to, doing the entire family's monstrous hand laundry on the bathroom floor, the larger share of the house cleaning, and the preparations for the cooking, while also caring for her little daughter and seizing any odd moments when her mother-in-law is not at home to telephone the young women who were her high school classmates, whom she rarely has time to see any more.

Hi-jong's mother is also worried—concerned that her baby's evident frailty must be caused by a malevolent spirit,

xix

probably that of Hyŏn-du's paternal grandmother, whom everyone seems to agree was a very difficult woman. She would like to ask a witch to hold a *kut* for the little girl to propitiate the spirits, but this would cost about two months of her husband's salary and is sure to be a cause for discussion in the house. So she is waiting for Hi-jong to be a little more sick before broaching the subject.

Mr. Sŏ has arrived at his office in the Ministry of Agriculture, where he is a medium-level bureaucrat, a section chief, about the equivalent of an army captain. He expects one more promotion on the grounds of seniority, which will improve his pension before he retires at sixty. As he enters the long room, with its fourteen small desks surrounding his own larger one, and the long table of the typing pool, everyone rises and gives a short bow. The bow is not short because it is perfunctory, but because a more impressive obeisance is made whenever Mr. Sŏ's superior enters the room, thus leaving the possibility for a real ninety-degree affair if the Minister or his senior civil servant should ever repeat their one-time inspection call. On such an occasion, Mr. Sŏ would jackknife impressively along with his minions.

Short of a record flood destroying a whole Korean province, no subject that might disturb Mr. Sŏ's well-being is ever likely to be raised during the morning, and he goes to lunch at noon with a clear conscience. Formerly, Hyŏn-du's mother brought his food to the office, warm, in metal bowls, but this practice is dying out, and Hyŏn-du's mother now gives Hyŏn-du's father enough cash for a noodle soup or a plate of *saengsŏn ch'o-bab* (sushi) or *man-du* and some *in-sam cha* (ginseng tea).

Later, a colleague tells him over the phone that the Minister is in a foul mood, and Mr. Sŏ worries that his supervisor may be on the receiving end of this, and may pass the bile on to him. But this isn't likely, because Mr. Sŏ is now so senior in age and in service in the ministry that his serenity is rarely

PROLOGUE

challenged these days in the way it was when he was working his way up the bureaucratic ladder.

Hyŏn-du has arrived for work at the store in time to change into company uniform and take part in the ceremony of the opening of the store's doors at 10:30. His boss, the awesome general manager, gray-haired, bull-necked, and with all the spirit of a Foreign Legion sergeant major, heads the parade, bowing to the first customers at ninety degrees, alongside the pretty greeters in their high-fashion uniforms. Behind this group, all the managers, junior managers, and salesgirls are standing beside their counters, making obeisance to the invading housewives. The approaching gift giving and festivities of the lunar new year mean that it will be a busy week, followed by post-new-year sales which will make the store busy again.

Meanwhile, Hyŏn-du's mother has settled for only some of the medicine recommended by her traditional apothecary, and for a long and sympathetic chat with a friend she meets in the street. Her friend confides that she too is suffering from a mysterious allergy, which is bringing spots—*O, wa!*—to the insides of her thighs. This is enough *in-yon* (fate) in common for them to go to a coffee shop together. They order scotch with their coffees and pour it into the beverage, asking the *kŭp-sa* to take the whisky glasses away so that no one will know they are drinking alcohol.

When Hyŏn-du's mother gets home, her daughter-in-law has prepared the contents of the evening meal, and it remains only for Hyŏn-du's mother to put it on the fire and claim the credit for cooking it. The daughter, Su-na, is doing her homework as she watches the fate of an actress playing a girl only slightly older than she who is in the throes of a three-way love affair and consequently spends at least part of each daily sequel in a state of *nun-mul*—sobbing. Like her mother, Su-na loves *nun-mul* soaps. Her mother shouts to her to shut off the little black-and-white television in her room and says Su-na will not get the color set she wants for her lunar birthday if she insists on turning the TV on while she is doing her homework.

By the time Mr. Sŏ comes home, he has clearly had a pint of *so-ju* in a *sul-jip* with some of his cronies, because his voice is a crotchet higher than normal and he is complaining in an incipiently argumentative tone that he is very hungry. The two women soon attend to his gastronomic needs, but Hyŏn-du's mother has bullied him into not drinking alcohol with his meals, which he says is what makes it necessary to go to the *sul-jip*.

After he has finished eating, she reminds him of their promise of a color TV for Su-na's birthday, which is, like everyone else's birthday in Korea, on the day of the lunar new year. This leads to a general discussion of family finances, and Hyŏn-du's mother flatters her husband by asking his advice on where she should invest the three hundred thousand *wŏn* which she will shortly draw as her dividend in her *kye,* or women's thrift group.

Hyŏn-du's mother has had her dinner in the kitchen while her husband was finishing his in the living room. Her daughter-in-law has said that she is not hungry and prefers to wait until Hyŏn-du comes home. Since department stores do not close until 10:30 P.M., he will not be home until after eleven o'clock, when the rest of the family will be in bed. Hyŏn-du and his wife can thus break the rules by eating together, American television-style—but in the kitchen, of course, since Hi-jong's mother would not dare eat in the living room; that would be upstaging her mother-in-law.

Hyŏn-du's father travels to work by subway train, and the commuter crush daily assaults every fiber of his Confucian temperament, so that in summer he often elects to forgo the twenty-minute ride in favor of a ninety-minute walk; but Hyŏn-du comes home each night in a half-empty bus, made even quieter by the fact that half of the passengers are sleepily inebriated. Hyŏn-du arrives home tired and a little out of tem-

PROLOGUE

per, but Hi-jong's mother produces a bottle of *so-ju* which she has kept hidden from Hyŏn-du's mother. Hyŏn-du drinks, and soon the young couple are on the best of terms. They go to bed about a half hour after midnight, and before long the only sound in the Sŏ household is of Hyŏn-du's grunts and his wife's suppressed giggles as they make love. Even the baby has ceased to whimper.

THE
KOREANS

1

A LIFE IN CONTRASTS

THERE IS NO SUCH THING as a rest day in Seoul. You are being driven in from Kimp'o airport. Your white-gloved taxi driver is sweeping you over wide new bridges on the Han-gang and, perhaps, if he takes that route, across an artificial island that serves as a concrete tray for Asia's tallest building. You go on past the walls of commercial canyons that grow progressively taller as the city center fills the windshield, past a mounting hubbub of voices and vehicles and pushcarts and activity. There is no such thing as a rest day in Seoul.

Captured four times in the Korean War—twice by each side—Seoul's devastated ruins were patched together, growing to house refugees both from the north and the scorched countryside. When this writer first saw Seoul in 1968, it was a bustling metropolis of 600,000 souls, about the size of Stuttgart or Baltimore, trembling with purpose; its new commercial buildings were the usual Third-World matchboxes of gray surpassing ugliness. Today, Seoul houses ten million—nearly a quarter of the South Korean nation—and has been almost totally rebuilt to create a handsome version of the vertical architectural culture of our time. Only Houston and Singapore and the goddesses of the silver screen have had their faces rebuilt so quickly.

Han is the name of the country in Korean, and the city was originally Han-yang, the suffix being the Chinese and Korean word for the male synergy. Seoul (pronounced *Suh*-ool) essentially means the place where the ruler lives. Although the monarchy has gone, and rule has given place to government, the name remains. It was a capital originally chosen, after others, for its frontier status between rival princedoms and also for its suitability for rural warfare—protected to the north by jagged, granite hills and in the south by the forested Nam San, or South Hill.

Today, the northern crags, festooned with radar, are a barrier to urban sprawl in the direction of the border; but Nam San has been pierced by three toll tunnels, and the city itself has breached its other defense, the shallow moat of the Han-gang. The river rises in the mountains to the east, but flows turgidly into the sea north of Inch'ŏn, Seoul's outport on the Hwang-hae, or Yellow Sea. Across the Han-gang, often shrouded in winter drizzle or summer haze, stand the serried ranks of suburbia, like a thousand off-white walkie-talkies with windows in them, stretching to and beyond the great sports complex, built to host the 1986 Asiad and the 1988 Olympic Games.

Seoul, once the royal seat of an agricultural nation that had few real towns—and more hamlets than villages—is now the fourth or fifth largest city in the world. Size has become a factor in its importance as a trading and banking center, a site for international conferences and conventions and functions such as the Olympiad. Cities of less than a million souls such as Washington and Frankfurt, Geneva, or San Francisco, could not absorb 300,000 visitors at a time; there are just not enough buses, trains, hotels, or taxis. The wooded village of Seoul, emulating the precedents of Tokyo or New York or London, has evolved into a great amorphous concrete sponge that fights to preserve its identity.

So, the Koreans are a people who live with the contrasts of their cultural past, their cultural present, and their cultural infinity. They are an urbanized rural people who have retained much of their rural graces and politenesses in the maelstrom of the concrete jungle, along with their peasant excitabilities which belie the three-piece suit and the Pierre Cardin office dress.

Many Koreans have the same physiognomies—although not the same facial expressions—as Japanese. Many look like Chinese, especially northern Chinese. Although there are specific Korean features rarely seen elsewhere, it is obvious that Koreans have the same Siberian and Manchurian origins as the Mongol people of Manchuria itself or the Nipponese islands. But Koreans are different in personality from Manchurians and especially from Japanese, despite the many qualities which all East Asians have in common.

As your taxi brings you into the downtown area, the driver impatiently pushing between two buses with an inch or so to spare on either side, you wonder about what you've heard—that street accidents are rare. The reason is concentration. Koreans take things seriously. Even reckless driving must be done recklessly well. And then you see a minor fender-bender occur, anyway. Were this Japan, there would be a cool exchange of cards and a wait for a policeman. Even more than the British islanders at the western end of the Eurasian continental mass, the Japanese islanders at the other end favor harmony over discord, and are reluctant to make fools of themselves in public. But already the two Korean drivers are doing just that; they are barking like *chindo* hounds and soon even pushing and shoving each other, while onlookers laugh and a cop rushes to separate them. Fortunately, however, this is not Los Angeles or Chicago and the officer of the law bears no weapon with which to make things worse: his main protection is his knowledge of *t'aekwŏndo,* a martial art which bears some similarity to Japan's judo or China's kung-fu, in that it requires more brain than brawn.

At the hotel, however, much will remind the visitor of Japan: the taxi driver and the doorman refusing tips, the elaborate politeness of the front desk staff—people who earn their living by that skill. There is the preference for the bow over the unhygienic habit of shaking hands. Unlike, say, America or Africa, Korea is not a *touching* culture. The son returning from six years of study in the West will greet his family at the airport by bowing deeply. From three or four yards away, the family will do the same. A tear is beginning to form in Mother's eye, but the only other detectable sign of deep emotion on both sides is that son and family bow to each other twice instead of once. At the hotel, however, the wide smile is even more overt than Tokyo's—it is the face of the countryside in the city.

When I first came to Korea two decades ago, my host, the Food and Agriculture Organization of the United Nations, took me around the country to see projects connected with the peasant society which Korea was then still expected to remain. This afforded me a view of Korea which is disappearing and which, for the casual visitor, has disappeared already. Agricultural and fishing projects tend to be in remote places far from towns, places where there were then no modern hotels, in most places no traditional inn—*yŏ-gwan*—and sometimes not even a real *yŏ-in-suk,* or mom-and-pop guest house. My FAO escort and I would sleep on a thin *yo* of artificial sponge or on mats on the wood-heated floor, our heads on tiny *pe-gae* pillows filled with dried beans or barley husks. We would breakfast on a dozen or so minuscule traditional dishes, which nearly always included grasshoppers in a black-bean, sesame, garlic, and chili-pepper sauce. At the projects, the local official on whom we called would receive the visiting reporter with the self-abnegating grace of a West African chief; but instead of tumblers of schnapps he would offer barley tea, a beverage even more bland than American office coffee. Almost everyone wore traditional dress of white cotton.

Sometimes, I would be left to travel on my own, and once when I doubted my driver's ability to hurl a Toyota wagon through a mountain stream two feet deep, he promised to resign if he stalled in mid-current. He did it all in reverse—out of consideration for me, so that getting out of the torrent, if he failed, would be easier than getting in. On the other side, he checked the chassis and found no damage, bowed, and apologized for the discomfort. I bowed and apologized for doubting his skill and obvious experience. Today, the perfume of that sunset afternoon comes back; one surveys Seoul's cityscape conscious that this is a population made for the graces and also for the risks and relaxations of country life, yet inhabiting a megalopolis—not exactly unwillingly, but with reservations.

Other apparent contradictions abound: a high-fashion secretary with a poodle cut and Lancôme makeup waits at a yellow taxi shelter along with some elderly peasant from the countryside in his loose, off-white *chŏ-g'i* waistcoat, white raffia hat and pantaloons, or perhaps a long gray *paji* tied with a bow. Each understands the other more than each cares to admit. Close by, an expensive French restaurant run by Koreans with *cordon bleu* diplomas is neighbor to a noodle stall. A business administration graduate of Seoul National leaves his skyscraper office to prepare for his promotion interview with the boss by going to a *han-yak,* or traditional apothecary's shop, for a concoction that will make him, he hopes, alert or even brilliant. Both he and the high-fashion secretary, as well as the rice farmer in his country clothes, may have postponed everything from the day before—a fourth or thirteenth or twenty-second of the lunar month, therefore an unpropitious day for action. The young executive's boss may even have stayed away from the office the entire day, to avoid being led by his *in-yon,* or karma, into dire misfortune.

To prepare for his meeting, the young man has read W. Edwards Deming, Dale Carnegie, Galbraith and Schumacher (in pirated Korean editions, of course) and has prayed to Buddha and Jesus and conferred with his late father in meditation; and in order to go to a *han-yak,* he has had to resort to a thin subterfuge. Although it is the lunch hour, his immediate supervisor has stayed at his desk, meaning that none of his staff can decently leave their desks either. It is, however, acceptable to do so briefly if you stay behind in spirit, so the young executive has left his gabardine raincoat and umbrella on the office hatstand, even though it has started to rain.

In the *han-yak,* the apothecary takes down a few bottles with labels handwritten in Chinese ideographs, the Latin of traditional Korean medicine. He mixes chrysanthemum seeds with some tree bark and the grated brainbox of a frog. He pestles all this together and pours it into tamarind juice. The drenched young man pays and swills the potion down on the spot. Despite the expense, he also decides to ask for some deer horn gratings. He and his girlfriend are going dancing in a psychedelic disco that night; he has high hopes of what will follow, and wants to be at the peak of his sexual powers. He hurries through the rain shower, back to his office building, and is soon seated once more in front of his Samsung computer, working on the new import contract proposals from Philadelphia and Bombay.

His supervisor finally leaves at eight P.M., and the staff make a dignified rush for the door two minutes, or one elevator run, later. The young executive walks down a narrow street, pausing to watch a traditional cloisonné artist at work in his shabby shop, which bears the official sign that confirms that he is a government-recognized craftsman. The young man's attention has been attracted by the fact that the artisan is using a computer not much different from his own to compose a version of a traditional graphic design for a vase.

Continuing on his way, the young man comes to a street stall where he takes a seat along with other well-dressed businessmen, a housewife with a child, and a couple of van drivers, and orders a bowl of *mae-un-t'ang,* seafood and vegetables in a steaming broth. He drinks a pint of *so-ju* with his dinner, then chews a breath deodorant. Now, it is dark everywhere, but a department store is still open and he goes in to buy a gift for his girl. The store resembles its counterparts in Paris or San Francisco or Tokyo except that, as he steps onto the escalator, a sixteen-year-old maiden in traditional Lyi dynasty *han-bok* dress bows to him, and again to the woman customer behind him, thus completing her 5,137th bow of the day.

You could spend an hour at a Tokyo bus stop in a freak electric storm, and your sole neighbor in the shelter might never say a word to you. Only the British are as covetous of their privacy. There is, however, a logical reason preventing the Japanese from addressing a stranger: he cannot know *how,* because the person *is* a stranger. Koreans share the same necessity to know if you are superior, equal, or inferior; like the Japanese, they would prefer to know what you do and what rank you occupy in your company or profession. And in this, you cannot be too precise. There are, for instance, different words in both languages for *writer,* according to whether you write fiction or nonfiction. There is no word for *broadcaster;* one has to be more specific—radio? television? scriptwriter? anchorperson?

But the Koreans have a solution which few Japanese would attempt. They ask questions. They are curious. They *stare.* Other

Asian peoples may appear inscrutable to us, and us to them, but the Koreans are not inscrutable. They dare not be, because they *scrute*. Those of us who had mothers who wisely boxed our ears if we focussed our gaze on a passerby with only one arm, or an oriental face, or who had just fallen facedown in a puddle, are startled by the unabashed inquisitiveness everywhere in Korea, in spite of the general insistence on *mŏt*—manners, taste. Even shy sales assistants will ask about your work, your family situation, your age—the latter being an important determinant in societal rank. All Koreans go up one rank in prestige every year; they even start with a bonus—time in the womb counts as the first year of life, so that you are born at the age of one. Moreover, all birthdays occur on the lunar new year: if you are born in December, you are two almost before you can even gurgle.

Modern Japanese comedy films like *Tampōpo* or *The Family Game* are as daring in their environment as the first erotic photo-essay magazines in America a generation or so ago; but in Korea, humor is endemic. Although the slapstick of television kitchen-sink comedies and soap operas borrows routines from Tinseltown, the genre was always there. However, like most people who love clowning, Koreans are sad and stoical at heart; the vague-à-l'âme courses through every artery of Korean life. If your taxi driver switches on his radio, and you are not forced to listen to outdated Western rhythms, you will hear Korean pop music as sad as Portuguese fado. Understanding the words isn't necessary. The themes are those of American country music: lovers and mistresses are ever unfaithful, absent, or gone forever; and as the voice of the singer breaks with spurious emotion, you usually hear the word *nunmul* (eye-water). What other language has an onomatopoeic for sobbing? For that matter, in what other tongue do birds or bells weep instead of singing or pealing?

This is, at base, a Confucian society. The most important

relationship was always between father and son, followed by ruler and subject, then husband and wife, then elders and youth, then loyalty between friends. The first four are different forms of the same. The second relationship, that of ruler and subject, which successive militaro-republican regimes have sought to exploit in recent times, is increasingly challenged in an era when the taxpayer has ascended the throne and begun to assert that generals are nothing more than armed usurpers.

The quality of loyalty, as important to Koreans as to Turks or Scots, is commanded by more than blood and friendship. As in Africa, there is an automatic kithship involving loyalties between classmates—people of the same age who have gone through high school, military service, university and so on together. In 1987, a great debate emerged as to how President Ch'ŏn Du-hwan*, before he retired, would ensure that all his fellow-members of the eleventh graduating class of the Military Academy would have suitable civil posts to take care of their military retirement years.

However, social rank, including rank by age, is primordial. Superiors—or elders—go first. For instance, a husband enters a taxi, bus, or theater ahead of his wife. There are five different ways of saying he and she, according to whether the person is an elder or an employer or, at the other end of the scale, a child or a servant. As in French, the way an officer speaks to a soldier, or a farmer to his laborers, or a policeman to a pimp, is also the way you address a colleague when you finally recognize him as a close friend, or a member of the opposite sex when you want to convey a trembling heart.

For twelve and a half centuries, from 667 to 1905, when Korea became a Japanese protectorate, much of the battle for rank revolved around the annual civil service examinations,

---

*The approved transliteration. The American press mostly uses Chun Doo-hwan.

prepared for by rote learning, Chinese fashion. These examinations assigned literate Koreans to their rung on the social ladder. This Confucian concept of the *yang-ban* (member of the gentry) has given way to the global ethos of our meritocratic era; but militarism has often replaced Confucianism, and the university or military college entrance examinations are now the master keys of the career gate. Two-thirds of all who take them fail; there is usually only one second chance a year later, and that's it! And even passing successfully doesn't guarantee a place. The old Confucian exams could be taken over and over again, into old age, and people who never passed still pridefully noted their improved scores every year.

Chinese influence also remains in the ideograph, still used alongside the Korean *han-gŭl* alphabet in publications, because ideographs distinguish between different meanings for the same word and also make for briefer headlines and titles. As in Japan, a high school student must learn eighteen hundred Chinese characters to graduate.

These days, of course, he or she must also study English, from middle school on, with its vastly more illogical alphabet than *han-gŭl,* its often confusingly dissimilar "big" and "small" letters, its seven different ways of pronouncing *-ough,* its differences between Standard English and Indian English and American English, its galaxy of geographical accents, and so on. There are also lessons on how to use a knife and fork: Koreans must be the only East Asians who sometimes prefer to eat rice with a spoon instead of *jŏtgarak,* chopsticks.

All this is ancillary, however, and less demanding than during the Japanese colonial occupation, when Japanese was the *language of instruction,* and the only language permitted in public. Moreover, as in Japan, but unlike the West, study pressure at the university level is significantly less than it is in high school.

A LIFE IN CONTRASTS

Until recent times, just reaching adulthood was more of a challenge than what one did with it. A sort of clothesline adorned with phallic red peppers, hung across the entrance to a house, announces not only that Madame has given birth to a boy, but also that she is not receiving visitors, who might carry infection. Instead, she is suckling, and drinking bowls of *miyŏk-guk*—seaweed soup, strong in iodine. When a child reaches its hundredth day (which in the past more than half failed to do), there is a celebration. The infant is propped up to view the array of fruits, sweetmeats—notably the *ttŏk* rice-cakes—and other goodies, not forgetting alcohol, displayed before him for his older kith and kin to consume in his honor.

When he reaches the age of one (two or sometimes three by Korean count), there is another shamanistic fête, *tol,* with even more of an altar of gluttony, including special *susŏk ttŏk* ricecakes, flavored with mugwort. If it's a boy, objects are carelessly displayed to see which he will take up first, to predict his future calling. The commonest are a writing brush and money. Seizing the former indicates a future writer or intellectual. Grabbing the money does not indicate, as you might expect, a budding politician, but a businessman. If he takes the thread, that means long life. The future artist picks a flute. The choice is clearly limited, even weighted. Wouldn't most children, given the option, seize a strawberry or a banana, thus presaging a life of agricultural servitude, or a toy gun, thus indicating a career in the military and perhaps, eventually, in dictatorship?

At the age of fourteen, in previous centuries, the boy's long hair was plaited into a topknot, and parents, matchmakers, and *mudang,* clairvoyants, began thinking about a mother for *his* children. Indeed, they often married him then to a bride in her mid-twenties, who would tease the embarrassed child

11

spouse into lust by obliging him to undress her out of her complex bridal attire. This "suitable" wife, however mismatched in terms of age, produced his heir, and later ruled over his seraglio of more suitably-aged concubines. At the age of sixty—fifty-nine to us—*harabŏji* (granddad) and *halmŏni* (grandma) could contemplate another feast, called *hwan-gap,* with all or most of the family assembled around them. From then on, theoretically, they could depend on their children for shelter and sustenance.

Today, reaching sixty is no longer the achievement it once was, and such customs are beginning to die. It is hard to reunite a hundred or so relatives in an urban apartment about the size of an American hotel room. (However, just as there are wedding halls, *yesik-chang,* so there are now *hwan-gap* halls. Both ideas seem to have been copied from Japan, which has similar problems—but you have to know Koreans well before daring to suggest that Korea ever copies *anything* from Japan.)

Perhaps the clearest indication of how close Korea's present remains to its past may be seen in any telephone book, or wherever names are listed. As in medieval societies, there are only about two hundred different family names—and more than half of these are rare names associated with a particular province or section of it. There are only about fifty names you are ever likely to encounter. Nearly a quarter of the population is called *Kim,* which originally meant *metal;* members of the initial Kim clan even have an iron-colored birthmark, sometimes on the least likely parts of the anatomy. Over a fifth of the population share the names *Pak* and *I* (also written in the Latin alphabet as *Li, Lee, Lyi, Leigh, Yi, Ri, Ree, Rhi,* and, by the first president, *Rhee,* but pronounced, usually, *Ryi*).

Sons are usually given a generation name, before or after which is added the father's given name. Thus, President Kim Il-sŏng of North Korea has a son and heir apparent called Kim

Jong-*il*. Given names all have a Chinese character and, like Patience or Victor or Charity or Linda or Bruce, describe a quality. Korean women, like Ethiopian women—and Japanese women until after World War II—keep their father's family names. Apologists will insist that this was to show that an unhappy wife could always return to her family; but the real reason was to demonstrate that the children, who took their father's name, belonged to him, not her. This was a social necessity in bygone eras, when the *yang-ban* gentry had as many concubines as they could afford and "borrowed their wombs" (a Korean and Japanese expression) to create and briefly garage their offspring. The convention is not much different from the Western legal concept that the father of a married woman's children can only be her husband, even if she hasn't seen him for years. Since women, unlike their husbands, cannot confer names, they can usually receive any given names—unrelated, for instance, to their mother's. The situation is further complicated by the fact that many given names can be bestowed on both boys and girls.

Although Korea's agricultural centuries were synonymous with its long poverty, it is still in the countryside that one senses best its most pervasive values. Respect for elders, for instance, is an enduring delight of civilization. One remembers how, in childhood, the most friendly friends were the elderly, even in the West. Korea still retains this now largely Third-World trait. Even in the city, it is unlikely that anyone would speak loudly in the presence of an elder or even drink alcohol or smoke in his or her presence unless invited to do so.

It must be remembered that, while Buddhism teaches that one is reborn as a new soul after death, the shamanistic Koreans are not so sure—they feel the presence of the dead, so there are reasons to ensure that these wraiths remember you well. Splendid burial tumuli are to be seen all over the countryside. They do not subside with rainfall, like the forgotten mounds over Western graves, but are carefully padded up with fresh soil every year.

In our advanced societies, the golden years may be principally gilded with the rust of neglect, but in Korea the sunset has an authentic glow. The old men, more evident in public than the old women, squat at low tables on the porches and play *chang-gi,* the ancient form of chess brought to China from Baghdad about four and a half millenia ago, or *paduk,* the slightly less sophisticated game which is popular all over Japan under the name of *go.* This is only two thousand years old and is more indigenous to eastern Asia. For the more intellectually lazy, there is *yut,* a board game that resembles ludo, and *kol-p'ae,* a variation of dominoes. Mostly the elders read, buying all manner of books at the "three for a thousand *wŏn*" stalls in lunar festival fairs. In Korea as elsewhere, however, television is beginning to challenge literacy.

If the old women are less visible, secluded in the "inner room," teenage girls may still be spotted enjoying two lusty toys which their ancestors invented—the seesaw and swings. The former, once known as *nŏl-dwi-gi,* has now taken the English name of *si-i-so-o.* Both are tackled standing; energizing a swing with one's buttocks in the Western way would look indecent in Asia; and by jumping on a seesaw one can rise quite high in the air, so that in olden times one could glance rapidly over the wall, to glimpse the great wall by father's room and the trees beyond.

Less often observed is *yŏn,* the boys' pastime of flying kites, including fighting kites with ground glass on the string to sever the line of a competitor.

As the seafood diet, "insular" culture, and naval traditions imply, Koreans are a seafaring people like the Japanese and the British. They have been so for about five thousand years, when their Altaic ancestors arrived in the peninsula, largely displacing or interbreeding with the paleolithic aborigines, thousands of whom fled north across the icy waters to what are now Sakhalin and Kamchatka. Some of the Altaics pressed on across more temperate seas to colonize Japan. In all these places, a maritime culture imposed itself. Although both Koreas together (North Korea is larger) measure only six hundred miles from north to south, from the Soviet and Manchurian border to Mogp'o, the jagged peninsular shoreline measures about five thousand five hundred miles, and the shoreline of the islands, a similar distance—eleven thousand miles of beach and tide in all.

In the countryside, traditional mores are more evident. As in Japan and, until recently, the West, the father's role is discipline; the mother's, tolerance. Sons are spoiled. They are the future heirs. In return, they must support their parents in old age. Where there are no sons, a redundant nephew or a son-in-law may be adopted.

Homes also are more traditional: single stories, dictated by the *ondol* heating system, under tiled, tilted roofs with upswept corners—ski ramps for goblins. Today's city houses are often cluttered; they have become a great depository for consumer goods, both useful and useless, justifiable or just plain ugly, indicating perhaps how Japanese homes will look in a generation's time, when the government in Tokyo ceases to subsidize the weekend "dude" paddies and turns them into housing land for larger dwellings. But in the countryside the Korean home retains the roominess and grace of an older era, the floor a polished living space, the walls decorated with calligraphy and brush drawings, the screens embroidered with flowers, birds, and fish. A low black lacquer table serves for meals. More affluent dwellings may add a hexagonal table inlaid with abalone shell, also tracing similar nature motifs.

Korea, then, has gone from being agriculturally proud but poor to industrialization and comparative wealth in two decades; but it tries to preserve its traditions. City wedding halls with hired costumes have replaced village nuptials with the groom arriving on mule or pony, and his bride carried in a palanquin. Both bride and groom, however, are still allowed to wear the costumes of the traditional gentry for one day in their lives, and little else has changed: the ceremony, a mixture of Buddhism, shamanism, and superstition, is the same. As in Japan, many marriages are still "arranged," even among the educated. Matchmakers continue to make a very good living, and the *hojuk dungbon,* the family registry or doomsday book, is still the determinant of birth, marriage, death, provincial origin, and nationality—one of many Korean concepts inherited by Japan.

As will be explained in the next chapter on the peninsula's history, there was a two-and-a-half-century interregnum before the Japanese imperium when the Koreans, in reaction to the great Chinese, Mongol, Manchurian, and Japanese infestations of their country, became the "Hermit Kingdom," forbidding foreigners, withdrawn from the world and almost from world trade; this may well explain Korea's unique gregariousness and extroversion among East Asian peoples today. The repressed Koreans emerged from hermitry to be the most eager to lead Asia into the twenty-first century. Here again, at the risk of going against the grain of Korean sensibility, Japan must deserve some credit. As the Japanese moved into the last stages of decay of the Lyi dynasty, taking over the country completely in 1910 for thirty-five years, they stepped into a vacuum. They imposed a system of administration and education which was, and remains, largely Japanese, even down to the soldierly school uniform for the boys and the sailor uniform for the girls (the former has been preserved). Foolishly rejected by France and Britain at the turn of the century, Japan had been forced to turn to Germany in its Prussian era; this influenced the Japanese military and, in turn, Korea's military today.

The Koreans had always seen themselves as squeezed between their two bigger and more powerful neighbors, the Chinese-Mongol-Manchu and the Nipponese, just as it sees itself today as the unfortunate rope in a tug-of-war between two far more exotic and powerful superpowers. This factor has helped to mold the Korean character still further—both mettlesome and nettlesome. The Koreans are often described as "the Irish of Asia"; but, given their role as the heirs to Chinese culture who passed it on to the Japanese—who have now left their Chinese and Korean preceptors behind—Korea can perhaps more accurately claim to be Asia's Rome.

The Korean id is a medley of Buddhic patience and intemperate extroversion; the latter is combined with an apologetic recognition that raising one's voice is graceless and even shameful. Koreans are both rigid and adaptable, cunning and frank, stubborn and sentimental, stoic and soulful. As will be looked at in a later chapter, religion sits lightly on the people, but superstition does not. How many American high school pupils know what "intuition" is? In Korea, *nun-ch'i* is a word which almost every small child understands. Throughout centuries of travail, this Siberian faith in the occult, in extrasensory perception, in telepathy, has been a haven of the spirit and the emotions.

Much else can be explained by the recent trauma of the Japanese occupation, from 1910 to 1945, even though this is no longer recent enough to be remembered by most living Koreans. Polls constantly show that the Japanese are the foreigners whom the South Koreans distrust or dislike the most, followed by the Russians and the North Koreans (who are not, strictly speaking, foreigners). Because the Japanese repressed

Christianity, thus associating the missions with nationalist resistance to the colonial power, the churches became almost as much a candle of hope to Koreans as the Catholic Church is to Poles. Largely owing to this resistance image, a phenomenal fifteen percent or more of Koreans are now Christians, compared with less than one percent in Japan and China, and this in turn has spawned a crop of syncretisms—of which more later. Korean Christianity may conceivably be, as so many insist, a veneer, with Koreans fascinated by its mysticisms, such as the Trinity or the supernatural character of Jesus, rather than by its canons. However, just as the missionary priests and pastors in Korea emulated Jesus by their anticolonial and antibourgeois attitudes, so today the churches and their syncretistic foundlings are a rallying point against the militaristic legacy of the Confucian system, while offering a form of family discipline more adapted to the modern age.

Despite the Korean tendency to exteriorize feelings, Koreans share the conviction of other Buddhist societies that conflict reflects a failure on all sides. America is dichotomous on this question. In most societies, nearly everyone will see a doctor sometime, but only a small proportion will ever see a lawyer. In contrast, the fact that America has fifty percent more lawyers than doctors—meaning that Americans are expected to see attorneys one and a half times as often as physicians—respectabilizes disagreement, to feed the legal eagles. Most, perhaps all, African societies see conflict as normal, and extol the role of the mediator, who deflects blame from the adversaries onto himself. The Koreans, however, believe in biorhythms. They speak of *ki-bun*—roughly, mood. This concept, which informs life in most of Asia and, to a lesser degree, Western Europe, has apparently seemed exotic to many American writers.

Not only does it make sense to preserve a good *ki-bun* for oneself: it is even more important to create a good *ki-bun* for others. The best people are those who do this instinctively—who have what Arabs would call *barakha,* which is preferable to mere charisma. The sort of Western assistant or secretary who waits for your arrival at the office to pounce on you with the news that something has gone wrong, some catastrophe has occurred, some problem is waiting on your desk that you need to know about before you have even taken off your coat, does not exist in Korea. The opposite extreme prevails. Bad news is put off to the end of the day or week, or longer—even to the point, Paul Crane says, of leaving really bothersome communications out of the morning mail. This surely makes sense, since it militates against impatience.

Where there is good *ki-bun* and instinctive *nun-ch'i,* how could there not be taste—*mŏt?* Not only in clothes and furniture, but in everything. Few compliments are more flattering to a Korean than to say that he or she has taste. Working-class Koreans, for instance, appreciate classical music—their own, and ours—far more than the plebeians of Louisville or Lyon or London. A shipyard welder gathering flowers on a mountain hike, and arranging them carefully in a vase at home, is neither rare nor considered effete.

Korean men, even more than Japanese men, tend to drink to excess. According to a recent international survey, only Icelandics drink more degrees of alcohol per head per year; and if *in vino veritas* means anything, we see the Korean's character best when his guard is down. In his cups, the Japanese is usually joyful, often effeminate. He loves everybody, and if somebody would only bring a brush he would write some dreadful poetry. But the loaded Li or the pickled Pak is invariably gloomy. Although both peoples have the same frenzied approach to pleasure, in Korea the Falstaff of the dusk becomes the midnight Hamlet. It is then that he likes best to sing sad, nostalgic songs.

However stoic, he is less so than the Japanese in grief. Just as he laughs more easily, even when sober, so the Korean, even the male of the species, permits himself to weep quietly in public, for instance at a funeral. Like the British, he would regard an unrestrained, florid, or noisy display of misery as lacking in taste, and perhaps in sincerity; but unlike the Japanese, he can shed one distinguished tear at a time without losing the face he sheds it on.

Inevitably, a round-eyed demon like the author finds himself contrasting Korea's contrasts with Japan's, since Japanese culture, like the Japanese "race," is so obviously an insular and highly successful offshoot of the Manchurian Riviera culture of which we speak. Just as India was enriched by the British raj, so living under the Japanese was like thirty-five years of boot camp for a soporific, even decadent Lyi society. It introduced a new, slightly Germanic discipline (even the drinking songs of Japan sound as German as the national anthems of West Africa sound decadently Northern English). It also enforced adaptability. Whatever it was that enabled the Japanese to go from making brittle dentists' drills which snapped in half in the patient's mouth to building the best fighter aircraft of World War II seems to have helped the Koreans go from the pitchfork to the fifth-generation computer overnight.

It can only have been the Japanese imperium—it certainly wasn't the Eighth Army—that laid the groundwork for transforming a backward agricultural economy, based on rice and worm-infested bok toy *kim-ch'i,* into the fastest industrial development the world has seen. Thus, the Koreans were able to correct most of their societal deficiencies while hanging on with a mixture of pride and obstinacy to their heritage.

Of all Koreans, the ones male Western writers come to understand the most are Korean women. There is nothing mysterious about this: the Westerner is physically attracted to the petite, flowerlike Asian woman, and she to him, but the inverse does

A LIFE IN CONTRASTS

not apply; amazons from California are not flocking to the Orient to tuck Asian males under their shaven armpits; and although Western bar hostesses would probably have the same success in Seoul as they have in Okinawa (where impoverished U.S. servicemen's wives fulfill the role to make pin money), anything more permanent would make most Asian males uncomfortable. Again, Western and especially American males who are refugees from the feminist phase in world history find Asian women extremely feminine; the latter in turn find Western males less macho, in the contemporary era, than Asian males. Throw in the attraction of the Westerner's relative wealth, and it's a fact that most Western males who arrive in Korea unaccompanied spend longer hours with Korean women than with their Korean male colleagues.

Not surprisingly, Korean women are as much a salad of contrasts as the men and as everything else in the country. To begin with, there is the tradition of subservience to males—to father, husband, husband's parents, and, in old age, to one's son. As elsewhere, physical frailty is one pretext for inferiority. Again as elsewhere, fidelity was a requirement of women but not of men, because only women could bear children. In the later Lyi period, when women's rights were virtually suppressed for two centuries, men alone could divorce, for the seven reasons cited in Confucian *ch'il-gŏ chi ak* doctrine. Most of these resembled conditions for divorce that were common to the West: failure to produce a son (which we now know depends on the prospective father's chromosomes), infidelity (euphemistically referred to as "wanton behavior"), theft, mental or physical incapacity, and nagging (described as garrulity). The other two were specifically Confucian: jealousy (surely a variant of nagging) and—second in importance to not bearing sons—disobedience to one's parents-in-law.

The only exception was that a woman could not be divorced if she had no family to which to return. In 1918, under the Japanese, women were also given the right to divorce, but there were restrictions which made it very difficult: to begin with, she had to obtain her husband's parents' consent.

Much importance was placed on *pu-dok,* female virtue. Curiously, Korean widows, far from having to marry their brothers-in-law as in so many other societies, could not remarry at all; presumably, there was a shamanistic fear that the dead husband would be jealous and cause all sorts of mischief. If a widow broke this taboo, her sons and male descendants for seven generations would be forbidden from taking the all-important Confucian civil service examinations.

Traditionally, women could not speak first, or contradict a man, especially their husband, father, or father-in-law. In the house, they could not stand in the presence of a man. Facial expressions were constrained by the rule that they should not display their teeth in front of males, but this requirement could be satisfied by raising the hand to cover the mouth when laughing—a delightful reflex which endures. Even after King Sejong introduced the *han-gŭl* alphabet and gave women the means to be literate, learning to read was usually the only education which they received—although it could be argued that once you have learned to read, there is nothing you cannot learn by your own efforts.

The single most important consequence of all this repression is that Korean mothers-in-law take it all out on their sons' wives. One major attraction of the Western husband is that the Korean wife will not have to live with her mother-in-law; and even if the newlyweds do live temporarily with his parents, the bride will be regarded as another daughter, not a domestic servant.

In 1948, under President Yi Sŭng-man (or Syngman Rhee), who had a Western wife, a new constitution gave both sexes equality; but legislation doesn't make it so, overnight, and such reforms are harder to bring about in poor countries. Korean women are still underpaid and underpromoted. Most mothers do not take jobs unless financial circumstances necessitate it, and—as in Japan—most women would still rather be well-housed, well-dressed mothers than sales managers or journalists.

But the husband who was—and still largely is—king in his little castle always brought home his pay packet unopened to his wife, and still does wherever this is a practical possibility. It is she who pays the bills, opens the savings account, decides if they can afford a car, and so on. This, of course, gives rise to arguments; but it is a very different situation from that in the West where the male, if he is the sole source of the family's income, has nearly total control.

The Korean wife gives her husband what he needs for fares, lunch, and so on. She is the treasurer of the rest. This relative financial independence has its offshoot in the *kye* clubs: a group of women will contribute an equal sum every month to a fund. Each member in turn receives all the money. For instance, if there are ten members and each contributes fifty dollars, then each in turn, over a period of ten months, will receive a bonanza of five hundred dollars. Of course, any one of them could simply save fifty dollars a month in a piggy bank or savings institution and take it out after a year; but the *kye* imposes discipline. Short of disaster, one *must* contribute. If such an institution existed in most Western countries, each housewife, as her bonanza week arrived, would go out and buy a designer dress, an exercise machine, or a week in the Bahamas; but Korean women have always been the family bankers, and in most cases Mrs. O or Mrs. Chung takes her jackpot and invests it, if only in a savings account.

How is the Korean woman of the eighties? Not surprisingly, a wide gap has opened up between the generations, between mothers and daughters. Since three-quarters of all these traditionally rural people now live in cities, and since most remaining rural people envy city life with its acclaimed opportunities, the young woman of the city is perhaps the most "typical" of the present female generation. By and large, she remains conventually disciplined yet sentimental, loyal and moody. She laughs and sobs easily, and one senses that she gets almost equal satisfaction from comedy and tragedy. She accepts many of the old traditions of inequality, since this makes failure more difficult, or at least an abstract concept; but she resents much of the tradition also. She is influenced by American television, which reassures her that people can succeed materially and even live quite happy lives while being hopelessly mediocre in their work ethic, manners, and general self-discipline. (The Korean ideal is probably not so much to emigrate to the West, as to colonize it and lick these poorly behaved but materially endowed societies into shape.)

One American professor in Seoul maintains that the driving force behind the "Korean miracle" is the Korean woman, whom he sees as controlling men through a devastating femininity which no feminism could match in authority. A Korean professor says his nation is one of witches and concubines and determined male juveniles—implying that Korean women are the mature element in the national concoction, and naive male synergy the fuel. What is most evident in the Korean woman is what the Korean professor calls her role as *mudang,* as witch. If *nun-ch'i,* intuition, is a national characteristic, it is above all a female one.

The Royal Asiatic Society reports that, since 1967, its most popular publication has been the work of an American medical missionary, Dr. Paul Shields Crane. Yet today, his *Korean Patterns,* although still containing a few timeless truths, is principally interesting as a reflection of how much Korea has changed in the past two decades, and of how wrong the more Kiplingesque Occidentals can be about a culture that is not so much mysterious as intentionally trying to be.

A LIFE IN CONTRASTS

Crane's Koreans are full of black-and-white characteristics in bold relief, and his observations are infested with old-fashioned, missionary homilies. The importance of good *ki-bun* seems more curious to Crane than it really is, because he fails to appreciate how catholic is this trait, with America one of the odd exceptions to the pattern. Korean efforts to avoid needless disharmony and preserve good *ki-bun* are merely more dutiful than those of Europeans. When enmities rise to the surface, Koreans are supposed to give their adversaries, in Julius Caesar's words, a "golden bridge across which to retreat."

Crane cites as examples of the desire to preserve good *ki-bun* the Korean greeting "Are you in peace?" and the farewells "Stay in peace" and "Go in peace." Most other languages recommend that you go in peace, or with God, or that you fare well, or something along these lines. Even Americans, however abstractly, will enjoin others to "have a nice day." Koreans, in contrast, also have a greeting, "*Yŏboseyo!*" (Listen, please!) which is almost as peremptory as "Hi!" and is the way one answers the telephone.

In Korean society as a whole, people tend to tell their superiors only what they think the latter want to hear. In America, I think, this is mostly a characteristic of the political world, the bureaucracy and large corporations. Koreans are more class-conscious than Americans and perhaps even Europeans, and until recently you could almost never climb the social ladder from the rung onto which you were placed by birth. America, being a nation of economic refugees, is essentially a plutocracy in which money is the principal symbol of distinction; but in traditional Korea, merchants ranked only slightly above the soldiery, prostitutes and grave diggers in a complex caste order, with—as in most settled societies—the scholar at the top. Korean society is now more flexible than it was, but it is probably only among Korean emigrants to the West that business is seen as a truly desirable class to join. Loyalty to the nuclear family and to the clan has the same importance in Korea as in Africa and most of Asia, contributing to problems of nepotism and corruption, as Crane emphasizes.

The medical missionary is at his avuncular and ethnocentric best when briefly discussing Korean sexuality, which broadly resembles that of all Africa and Asia, including Russia. Since most of the world's men make love from behind and on top, the breast culture is a new phenomenon in Korea, as indeed it is in neighboring cultures, in the measure that it exists at all; the nape of the neck, which is where a man's gaze rests in the act of passion, is the most titillating feature of her anatomy that a woman can reveal. Our culture has forgotten that décolletage (bare neckline) referred to the back of the neck until the turn of the century, when Parisians discovered the Kama Sutra and started making love face to face. Traditionally, Korean women never concealed their breasts except for reasons of fashion or warmth, although a maiden always did—she would bind them, like a nun, to conceal the fact that she had reached maidenhood. In Crane's account, Korean sexuality is *sui generis*.

The Korean nation is symbolized by its unusual flag, the *taeguk-ki*, which was invented on shipboard in 1822 by two royal envoys, Kim Ok-kyun and Pak Yŏng-hyo. These men were sent to negotiate a treaty of peace with Japan, later signed at Che-mul-p'o (modern Inch'ŏn), to end the war of Toyotomi Hideyoshi's invasion of the peninsula three centuries before, in 1593. It occurred to them that a couple of ambassadors should have a flag, so they painted one on a white sail from a ship's locker.

The white background, they explained the following year (when the flag was officially adopted by the Korean court), represented the land. The circle in the middle stood for the people: the upper section of the circle, in red, represented the *yang* (male) element, and the lower, blue segment was the *ŭm*, or female element, which the Chinese call *yin*. Red and blue were chosen to symbolize the complementarity of male and female, fire and water, heat and cold, day and night, lightness and darkness, action and passiveness, construction and destruction, plus and minus.

The surrounding signs signify balance and harmony in a changing human world. The three unbroken lines in the flag's upper left quadrant represent paradise; the three broken lines in the lower right are earth; in the lower left, the two lines with a broken line between them stand for fire, and their opposite in the upper right symbolizes water.

If you meditate on this, it reveals much about the Koreans, a people who not only celebrate obvious things such as Buddha's birthday, Christmas, "Liberation Day," and Chu-sŏk (the harvest festival), but also *Han-gŭl* Day, in honor of their alphabet, and Arbor Day, when everyone should plant trees.

Kim and Pak, with their flag, sought to honor their court—their government; but, despite centuries of Confucius, the Korean of today is thoroughly modern in regarding government as a disease, an infestation of bureaucrats. Like the French, Koreans usually go into government only if they fail to establish themselves in some more prestigious activity, such as playing the violin, or fear to fail if they tried. However, since the Korean word for a central, regional, or local administrator means "magistrate," bureaucrats, although despised, were also feared and therefore placated. They were bribed with money, booze, or girls. Just as French colonial police were allowed to keep part of the fines they imposed, so traditional Korean bureaucrats were expected to supplement their incomes by extortion. East Asians are no different from the rest of the world in this regard; but East Asia was probably closer to Africa in this, than to the West, where the bureaucrat was traditionally seen as a sorry fellow, a "Pickwick" rather than a junior "officer" or a magisterial infliction.

For most of this century, Korean bureaucracy has been, and to some extent still is, controlled from the top by espionage. Like their Japanese equivalents, senior Korean bureaucrats keep files on their subordinates. Just as a libel defendant challenges the plaintiff to put his entire life and moral fiber on trial, so a disgruntled junior civil servant in Korea, arguing against being passed over for promotion, may find himself confronted by the defendant—his supervisor—with all sorts of sins of long duration: the exact number of times he has been late for work in twenty years, the three tasks he never completed, the inadvertent insult he visited one day upon a superior, the five times he came to work with stains on his jacket, and so on. It is, in the end, easier to lick the boot that fate has imposed on your face, this time around. In counterpoint, dismissal is rare, and never occurs without careful determination and the certainty that a dossier exists to justify it. Normally, it is accepted without protest, because to contest the matter could bring about more serious sanctions, such as loss of pension.

In modern times, as Dr. Crane notes, a dossier of misdeeds can be leaked to the press unless superior palms are greased. By the same token, the journalist receiving the leak can either publish or forget, with the minister's prospective victim paying the purchase price of the amnesia. In short, much the same balance of power exists as in Washington, but there are more alternatives. Perhaps the single most beneficial thing about South Korea's adoption of a private enterprise economy instead of a socialist one is its restraints on the growth of an already bloated bureaucracy, dating from Japanese times. The number of official seals required on a single document is ample reflection of the number of functionaries' hands through which it must pass. Efficiency virtually requires using bypasses wherever possible. In Korea, as elsewhere, it's not what you know but who you know.

Much in the Korean culture remains Japanese, notably education, banking, and the legal system. Defendants, as under the Napoleonic Code, are considered guilty until proven innocent. As in Japan and Africa and other shamanistic cultures, an innocent party in an accident (for instance, a driver who hits a pedestrian who crosses the street without warning) is seen as the instrument which an evil spirit possessed to achieve its ends. However innocent in real terms, such a person is *guilty of misfortune* and must bear the consequences of this, much as our ancestors felt that all who were touched by the occult, however insane, deserved to be burned.

However, Koreans have certain significant differences from the Japanese, notably in everyday things. They are more earthy, and therefore more assertive. To eat, Koreans sit in the lotus posture, while the Japanese kneel. Koreans rarely bow more than once—two or three times would be a maximum, even for a very special occasion. There is no maximum in Japan. Dr. Crane, rejecting the notion of Chosŏn as Asia's Rome, calls the Koreans the Palestinians of the Orient, with the invading Chinese as the Greeks and Romans, and the colonizing Japanese in the role of the European Jews. The Koreans, he implies, undergo invasions and spit them out, however much they may borrow from them. One could equally well compare this long-suffering people to the Irish or the Eritreans or to any other nation too proud to be overruled—yet overruled, nevertheless, for a moment in history.

The travails of the Koreans have not yet resulted in a real code of human rights. Accused persons, once arrested, are defamed by the press. Interrogation of a suspect is painful and humiliating. Although most diplomats attribute modern Korean interrogation methods to the same sort of Israeli "technical assistance" teams that helped the Shah, in fact degrading forms of torture existed under the Japanese, and even before that. The Israeli contribution seems to have been mainly in the area of sexual torture, which did not exist before. The police are part of government, and no one is expected to cooperate with them voluntarily. Opposition to government is a natural reflex, going back centuries, and opposition to that opposition perhaps naturally leads to harsh interrogation methods. Fortunately, crime, while not as rare as in Japan, is much rarer in Korea than in the West.

The public ways of opposing government are stylized—demonstrations that are, essentially, violent in appearance only. This is largely borrowed from the Japanese model. So important was the "demo," rather than real violence, that this lighthearted abbreviation from the English entered the Korean (and Japanese) languages before it became American slang in the 1960s.

Historical events in recent decades have inevitably introduced a deep American influence into Korea, one that goes beyond television. Naturally, Koreans have borrowed most easily those American characteristics which reinforce or exaggerate their own—such as the love of ceremony. The sort of Fourth of July celebrations which make European immigrants cringe go down well with Koreans. When Myŏng-dong, once the boutique center of Seoul, felt it was losing its edge to new downtown districts, it staged a "Myŏng-dong Festival" in 1987, complete with oompah band and teenage pompom majorettes. It's hard to imagine such fare going down in Piccadilly or the Faubourg Saint-Honoré. School festivals and lunar holidays are flush with unbridled rhetoric and festooned with children dressed up in special clothes and playing bad music, in Mog-p'o as in

Mud Springs. As in America, the holding of a ceremony is more important than whatever purpose might have been used to justify it when it was planned. And Koreans, like Americans, are protagonists of overconfidence. If anything, Koreans are even more foolhardy.

Today's Korean soldiers are taught the team spirit of defending each other, even if they come from different regions and are not acquainted. This ethic, which is if anything more Buddhist than Christian, nevertheless conflicts with karma. If you dived into the sea to save a drowning maiden, you might well be expected to marry her, since you would have interfered in her fate—probably because of supernatural guidance of which you were unaware—thus making the prolongation of her life your responsibility. Crane related that Western surgeons like himself were sometimes asked to pay the costs of the operations they recommended, when these were successful in prolonging life—the exact opposite of the American malpractice suit.

Koreans, although ranking behind Japanese in this regard, are superior to Westerners in their acquisition of patience—as in finding the propitious moment for, say, discussing a business proposal. They are most unlikely to discuss it simply because they have just arrived from a long way away for that very purpose—as Westerners, and especially Americans, might brashly and naively do. Waiting a month or two, they know, is better than negotiating at once and losing.

Any culture poses a problem to those foreigners who live in it. Under pressure, the American, European, or Australian will often "revert" to what he knows best, thus failing to acculturate. Koreans, like Japanese, tend to understand Western culture better than Westerners understand eastern Asia. However polite, they are very conscious of the flip side of Western and especially American culture, and aware of many things that they would like to avoid. Yet they remain, even more now than in history, a nation of contrasts, confused by their own changes, and by the challenges of their new prosperity and importance.

2

A LIFE AT THE CROSSROADS

THINK OF THE KOREAN PENINSULA as the Manchurian Riviera, the warm-water projection of Mongolia and Siberia. Inevitably, it became a crossroads of East Asia, a conduit, between Manchu China and Japan, for everything from Buddhism, Confucianism, Asian medicine, and all the arts—plastic, performing, and martial—to *in-sam* (ginseng) and geishas.

Today's visitor can rediscover Puyŏ, the old capital of Paekche, as well as the museum-without-walls city of Kyŏngju, capital of Silla (pronounced Shilla). If he is fortunate, he may even get a visa to visit P'yŏng-yang, capital of Ko-gu-ryŏ and later Ko-ryŏ (Korea), which is today the capital of North Korea and, like former Han-yang (now Seoul), heavily concreted.

The story of Korea is, like the story of much of the world, a saga of epic battles; but, perhaps more than most, it is a history of invasions. Living, as it were, on a causeway between Japan and the mainland territories of the Mongols and the Manchu, the Koreans inevitably saw a lot of two-way traffic—pointed directly at them. The peninsula was the scene of great martial encounters, especially naval ones. When Korea finally chose to become the Hermit Kingdom, it was not until it had proved itself in battle many times over, finally seeking to withdraw from a world of violence.

It is in the last hundred years that history suddenly spins out of control at terrifying speed—the Japanese imperium, World War II, the happenstance that divided the peninsula, the slaughterhouse of the Korean War (which, given the short duration and small geography of the conflict, made World War II and Vietnam seem almost moderate in their demands on human life), and the astonishing reconstruction.

The Korean character, which impresses, bewilders, amazes, and excites those who come into contact with it today, was forged in two millenia of stylized life and savage conflict. This contrast has left the peninsula people both more stubbornly insular than most islanders and more gregarious than almost any other people east of the Urals or north of the Himalayas.

Conscious, like Greece, Italy, Turkey, Portugal, and Spain, of having been overtaken by its former satraps, Irishly sensitive about past humiliations, but Confucian in its work ethic, contemporary Korea has achieved a victory of brain and brawn over natural resourcelessness. On the other hand, political development has been hobbled by these same traditions—Confucian subservience to authority and acceptance of the nation-saving role of the military.

Except for the country's unnatural division in 1945, which there seems no prospect of undoing in the predictable future, the countryside one sees today is what has changed least over the centuries; it is rural Korea that gives meaning to its history.

To begin with, there is its compactness. South Korea is about the size of Virginia or Sri Lanka. North Korea is comparable to Tennessee or Greece. But the peninsula as a whole—commensurate with Oregon, Ghana, or Britain—is now home to over sixty million people, and the biggest change has been its urbanization and industrialization. South Korea's climate and seasons are about the same as New York State's; North Korea's are more like Quebec's. When you look at events in the country's history, you envision deep snowdrifts on Kŭmgang-san (Mount Diamond) in North Korea or on Sŏlag-san (Mount Snow), today a ski resort in the South. You think of hot, humid summers. With a general's eye, you see the rivers mostly flowing to the Yellow Sea in the west, providing plains and valleys for moving troops, and water for men and pack animals. To the east, where the mountains descend sharply to the Dong-hae, the Eastern Sea (known to most of the world as the Sea of Japan), the coastal scenery is more impressive, less suitable for maneuver.

Despite the growing incursion of human beings, the countryside remains a surpassing delight for nature lovers. A few decades ago, Koreans tended to blame Japanese lumbermen of the prewar era for the country's diminishing forest reserves, and the sheer firepower of the Korean war for adding to the problem. But in truth, centuries of wood-burning underfloor heating, *ondol*, was the real culprit. A massive reafforestation program, begun with a pilot project on 2.5 million acres in the mid–1960s, along with the rise in popularity of oil-fired *ondol*—a necessary accompaniment of high-rise architecture and urbanization—have replenished the country's trees to as many as there must have been at the dawn of time. Evergreens are predominant—pine, poplar, spruce, elm, and bamboo—along with many deciduous species, such as willow and oak.

In the shelter of this leafy canopy, there has always been a feast of fruit for history's rampaging legions—huge pears and apples, wild persimmons, and in the southern provinces, tangerines (mandarin oranges), grapes, and today (under plastic) bananas and pineapples. The abundance of nuts—pine nut, gingko, walnut, chestnut—must have been one of the attractions that lured Manchurian nomads into the peninsula thousands of years ago. The medley of brilliant flowers in Korean art reflects their profusion in the country. The national flower is found all over Asia. Its name originated in Palestine—the rose of Sharon. The Koreans call it *mu-gung-hwa*.

Contrary to its name, the roughly five-mile-wide Demilitarized Zone (DMZ) which bisects the peninsula is the most heavily armed and mined region of Korea. As a consequence, it is where the conditions are least friendly to man and where modern wildlife has flourished best. It is rich in deer and boar. In the mountain sections, there are bear—mostly miniatures—and leopard, and the latter roam beyond the Zone as far south as the region near Daegu. Both bear and leopard must be commoner in the more rugged, less densely populated north; but the national beast, the Siberian tiger, apparently no longer lives on the peninsula at all. On Jeju Island, the *cho-rang-mal*—Mongol pony—roams wild, and Chin-do Island has the *chin-do-gae* dog, an intelligent and lovable canine. It is now a protected species, and cannot be exported even to the mainland.

The national bird, the crane, may still be seen, along with ducks of every hue and feather, swans, pheasants, quail, and, on the coast, herons.

This potential Eden not surprisingly has a legendary origin—two, in fact. The more colorful of these dates back to the year *wu-chen* of *tang-yao*, which everyone seems to agree was 2333 B.C., when the king of heaven, Hwan-in, sent his son Hwan-ung to earth. Hwan-ung alighted on T'ae-baek-san, a peak of 9,100 feet (2,800 meters), now located in North Korea and called Myo-hyang-san (Mount Sublime Perfume). There, this human son of God discovered a she-bear and a tigress who, the legend says, each wished to become a woman. (A skeptical mythologist will inevitably speculate that this transformation may have been Hwan-ung's desire more than theirs, since he was the only animal around at the time without a mate.)

Koreans have ever believed in natural remedies to cure all physical problems, and Hwan-ung may have been the first of that ilk. He recommended that the female bear and the tigress retire to caverns for one hundred days, with twenty garlic onions and some mugwort each. The tigress grew bored with the dark and gave up the retreat, but the she-bear stuck it out and emerged a woman.

Then, the legend says, Hwan-ung "married" her—although some frankly more bawdy word might be more convincing. The results were twofold: first, Tan-gun, who as the only boy on earth must have had a severe identity complex; and second, the Korean people—which suggests that, after Tan-gun, the happy celestial and his unusual bride must have had at least one fertile daughter.

Another version of the legend has him arriving on the mountaintop with a heavenly host of three thousand, presumably of both sexes, thus founding the nation and avoiding the Genesis-type implication of a few generations of incest. Hwan-ung, however, is still believed to have "married" his bear/woman, and with her to have founded the Korean royal family.

It was young Tan-gun, according to the myth, who founded Chosŏn, with its capital at P'yŏng-yang, now North Korea's capital—although history contends that this name was conferred much later, in honor of a royal princess. Chosŏn approximately means "the Land of Dawn." (Korea's tourist authorities have always maintained that a better translation is "Land of the Morning Calm.") The celebration of the founding of the nation still takes place very October 3 on Kang-hwa Island in the Yellow Sea, not far from Seoul.

Less fanciful historical accounts reveal that Altaic nomads from Siberia, Manchuria, and further west penetrated the peninsula somewhere around 3000 B.C., encountering Paleolithic forebears who had first arrived some thirty thousand before. Chinese chroniclers reported that a Manchu tribal chieftain named Ki-ja came to Chosŏn in 1122 B.C., conquering what must then have been an essentially Mongol nation, and that he and his Manchurian successors ruled the conquest until 194 B.C. This seems to correspond to known factual evidence—even though nobody at the time kept written records, so that it's all oral history or "history written by a committee." Ki-ja is even said to have taken as his queen a local maiden whose tribe had the bear as its totem, thus opening up a pragmatic explanation of the Hwan-ung legend. But why spoil the best story that the garlic industry ever had?

It seems to be a fact that in 1122 B.C., when the Chu dynasty replaced the Shang in China, a prince called Chi Tsu (could *Ki-ja* be a Korean form?) took over "southern Manchuria" and called his fief Chosŏn. Eventually, according to the Chinese, fate caught up with Chi Tsu's descendants, as China itself conquered Chosŏn in 108 or 109˙ B.C. and ruled it until 313 A.D. We are talking of a vassal state of seminomadic people, but with a centralized government of sorts that paid tribute to China. Eventually, the dynasty changed its name to Han—implying a Korean empire in part of northern China. The people must have been a Mongol-Manchurian mixture, which could today be called Korean-Chinese.

If the people now have such a high reputation for intelligence, one reason may be a secular attachment by law to exogamy, the absence of which law accounts for so much retardation in European royal families. Since Koreans are forbidden even to marry distant cousins, anyone called Kim theoretically cannot espouse about a quarter of the members of the opposite sex whom he or she sees in the street, unless they come from other parts of the country.

Exogamy was originally required, however, not as a mental hygiene precaution, but to promote peace, much as West

38

African chiefs were succeeded, not by their possibly oedipal sons, but by a sister's son, selected after his uncle's death.

Under China, the vassal kingdom changed its name, becoming Ko-gu-ryŏ in 73 B.C. It survived under that name for seven centuries.

Three other kingdoms also developed in the peninsula. To the southeast, facing Japan, Silla was founded in 57 B.C., while way down in the southwest, a few hours' sailing time from the Chinese coast, the smaller realm of Paekche appeared in 18 B.C. In between was the smaller sovereignty of Gaya or Kaya, a federation of tribal principalities.

Ko-gu-ryŏ, culturally and geographically closest to Manchuria, was to introduce Chinese ideographs and other cultural baggage of the Manchu: Buddhism, which had spread through China from India, becoming the court religion in 372 A.D.; the doctrines of Kung-fu (called *Kong-ja* by the Koreans but eventually known in the West by the Latin name *Confucius*); and the philosophy of Lao-tzu. A Chinese-style university for the sons of the nobility was founded in the Ko-gu-ryŏ village of T'ae-hak.

Ko-gu-ryŏ grew in power and, in its turn, came to occupy Manchuria as far north as the Liao, making it nearly twice the size of present-day North Korea. By then, Parhae, as it became known later, also occupied a pocket of what is now South Korea northwest of Seoul, as well as a goodly chunk of modern China and a sliver of the contemporary Soviet Far East, including modern Vladivostok.

Paekche, to the south, was the more intellectual state, the place where Buddhism took root the most firmly in the peninsula (from 384), and the kingdom whose emissaries introduced Buddhism and Chinese script to Japan in 552. As early as 369, however, the "horse riders of Puyŏ" from Gaya had already initiated a conquest in Japan.

That story also has the stuff of legend. There is a beautiful princess, Jin-gu, married to Gaya's patriarchal king. One night, she dances for him and is possessed by "three gods," with whose voices she speaks. They command that King Chu-ae and his queen take their horses across the sea and occupy new territory. The king, a peaceful old fellow—he was, it's said, idly playing the *kayagŭm* for his dancing consort at the time—refused to take the spirit messages seriously. Then, quite suddenly, and a little suspiciously, he died; but his wife kept his death secret.

According to the *Nihon Shoki,* a Japanese chronicle, Jin-gu then became the mistress of a high military official of her husband's court, a man to whom the chronicler gives the Japanese-sounding name of Takeshiuchi. The warrior-courtier and the wanton widow, now pregnant, set out across the Tsushima Strait with their soldiery and horses, to fulfill the god's command.

The witch-princess brought forth on Honshu, proclaimed the child—a boy, of course—to be the son of King Chu-ae, and also to be the "Emperor Ojin." He is now buried near Osaka.

It had, in short, become time to reveal Chu-ae's death. Jin-gu herself thereby became the Empress-Mother. The seductive Korean *mudang* seems to have given her name to Japan's national animistic faith, Shinto.

Meanwhile, back in Korea, Puyŏ—which appears to have taken its name from a Manchurian region whence its people originally came—had become part of Paekche, the Korean kingdom which ultimately had the most influence, in medieval times, on Japan. Nippon's first monastery was built and peopled by monks from Paekche and later from Ko-gu-ryŏ. The coarse islanders of Honshu were soon importing artisans, especially for temple building, from Paekche; the dark ages began to lift from the archipelago, putting it a century or so behind Korea but nearly a millennium ahead of Europe.

Korean scribes, bringing with them the first books seen in Nippon, became the court historians of the Japanese rulers. Korean preceptors were hired to teach the Japanese princes literacy and religion, and Korean women were soon in great demand at the Japanese courts, admired for their velvet skin, trim figures, and their courtly arts, such as embroidery. By 815, according to Japan's own doomsday book, fully a third of all names of the Japanese nobility were Korean.

In alliance with T'ang China, Silla, which already stretched north as far as Han-yang (Seoul), and which had royally converted to Buddhism in 528, captured Paekche in 660. Together, the two kingdoms marched on Ko-gu-ryŏ eight years later to establish what the history books call "Unified Silla." The peninsula was one nation for the first time, 1,320 years ago.

The victorious Sillan court, however, was rent by dissension. The Kim clan unseated the Pak clan as rulers. Then, Silla and its Chinese allies fell out. China invaded, and occupied the nation for three generations until being ejected in 735.

Silla's capital at Kyŏngju had by then become almost as great a Buddhist center as Puyŏ and the other main Paekche villages, exporting its own teaching monks to China and even India. The alliance with China had also prompted the adoption of the Confucian system of government and life—as complete a social system as Islam, and without the burden of a faith.

Kyŏngju, now the capital of the whole peninsula, became a great Asian center for architecture, painting, ceramics, sculpture, music, silk, other fine cloth, gold and silver jewelry, lacquerware, and ironware. Indeed, for nearly three centuries, all the arts blossomed there and exerted a massive influence on the dynamic culture of Japan, with a rebound influence on China

41

as well. Kyŏngju grew to the size of an important city, by the standards of the age, with reputedly 180,000 households and six miles of covered paths.

However, although Silla sent students to T'ang China, where some remained as court scribes, the Korean kingdom resisted the full meritocratic spirit of Confucianism. The "civil service" examination which determined status and promotion in society was limited to the *yangban* class which had emerged with land ownership—often determined by success in battle by the *hwa-rang,* a literati of religious warriors.

Silla's was a civilization in which the royal literati were resented by the true warrior caste; both were despised by the *yangmin,* or "good people," as the taxpaying yeomanry were flatteringly called to try to keep them docile. Both groups were also despised by the peasants, tradesmen, and artisans, and by the laborers and slaves who worked for these groups—many of the slaves being descendants of prisoners of war.

The *yangban* were subsidized by taxes exacted from the *yangmin.* As years went by, the privileges of the gentry naturally led to ever greater disaffection among the yeomanry—the forerunners of the petite bourgeoisie who foment all revolutions, and eventually create new countries such as the United States, Nigeria, or Singapore. Regional dissent naturally flourished also. Paekche—incidentally, the seat of most opposition today in contemporary Korea—yearned to recover its separate identity. On the other hand, the enormous advantage of monolingualism in the peninsula remained a factor for unity.

The period of flux ended in 936 when a northerner, Wang (King) Kŏn, seized power and transferred the capital to Kaesŏng, restoring the dominance of Ko-gu-ryŏ over the unified kingdom. The name was shortened to Ko-ryŏ, from which we get the three-syllabled transcription *Korea.* By this time, the Korean ruling class in the kingdom of Parhae, farther north, had been chased out by the Khitans of Mongolia and had returned to Kaesŏng. Wang Kŏn was the first ruler to take the title *t'aejo.*

The class system, if pernicious in itself, encouraged leisure pursuits. With their love pavilions and lotus ponds, the courts were lively centers for art, notably the form of poetry known as *si-jo,* and celadon ceramics—which were pillaged like gold in warfare. The greedy, lascivious Buddhist divine entered popular Korean literature, acted out in masked mimes in which the common people expressed their discontent in mute but musical satire. In reaction, a "reform" movement of *Ch'an* Buddhism arrived from China and established a dissidence in the Korean mountain fastnesses, where it became *Sŏn,* later spreading to Japan under the name *Zen.*

In 994, the Khitans invaded Ko-ryŏ, eventually capturing Kaesŏng in 1011. They were finally defeated in 1018 in the epic battle of Kwiju, and were driven back. Ko-ryŏ then built a wall across the peninsula, from the Am-nok-kang (Yalu) mouth in the west to Ti-ryo-p'o on the east coast.

For two centuries, Ko-ryŏ prospered, and its fame reached Europe, resulting in the country's being universally known as Korea today.

In 1213, the Mongol soldiery of Genghis Khan invaded, installing a puppet government in Ko-ryŏ under a monarch called Ch'ŏng-yol, who was ordered to marry a Mongol princess. Ko-ryŏ then became an ally of Mongolia against the rising outside threat, Japan.

A custom developed of sending young Korean noblemen to Beijing to take Mongol brides. Their half-Mongol sons were also sent to Manchu China on the same errand, producing new *yang-ban* who were three-quarters Mongol, and so on. Across the sea of generations, Korea's aristocracy became virtually Mongol. Tribute to the Mongol rulers of northern China was paid in gold, silver, horses, *in-sam,* artisans, and concubines.

As in Japan, some of the latter rose in influence, one of them becoming queen of Mongol China.

Civilization persisted in this amalgam of effete nobles, bawdy priests, and sturdy Mongol warriors. In 1234, more than two centuries before Gutenberg, a group of Korean artisans perfected the world's first movable metal type, with all its implications for the spread of literacy and culture. Nonmobile bronze type had emerged a century before, using the same technology as for coins, while woodblock printing was centuries older. Wood printings uncovered in recent times during the restoration of a pagoda in the Bulguk-sa near Kyŏngju have been identified as the Dahrani Sutra, dating from the first half of the eighth century.

One early Tripitaka Koreana (Korean Buddhist canon) on wood was damaged in 1126 when the father-in-law of King Ki-jong set fire to the royal palace and burned hundreds of precious books. Genghis Khan's Mongols finished the destruction of the Tripitaka in 1238.

When what came to be known as the Ming dynasty overthrew Mongol rule in Beijing, the allies of the Mongols in Koryŏ shared in the sufferings of this defeat, but soon began to cultivate favor with the new Chinese rulers. In 1392, with Chinese support, General Lyi (or Yi or Li) Sŏng-gye, who had been the real power in the country for the past three years, ascended the Korean throne with the title of *t'aejo*. He barred Buddhist priests from the court, and decreed Confucianism to be official state doctrine. Still sheltered behind rigid class barriers, the elite became more dour and serious, but no less oppressive. Nothing seems to provoke great art so much as suffering—or at least discontent. It was in the early years of the Lyi dynasty (which lasted until 1910) that the development of satirical folk drama and mask dances flourished. The fourteenth century also saw the introduction of cotton seeds and gunpowder, both from China, brought by an invasion of tribes from the north. These "Red Turbans" had captured the capital in 1361 and had finally been expelled by Lyi.

The bluff general-king restored the name of Chosŏn and moved his capital to Han-yang, which later became Seoul—like Washington, chosen as a southern (Silla) town that lay on the border with the north (former Ko-gu-ryŏ). It was also easier to defend than Kaesŏng. *Han,* it will be recalled, was the ancient Chinese name of the country, and *yang* is the male element. Lyi strengthened the alliance with Ming China against Korea's former Mongol allies and, now, aristocratic forebears. Together, the Chinese and Koreans turned their attention to the problem of Japanese pirates, then as much a plague as Barbary pirates in the late eighteenth century or Thai pirates today.

The man usually regarded as Korea's greatest ruler was Lyi's intellectual-looking successor, King Sejong, who was *t'aejo* from 1418 to 1450. His most distinguished achievement was to appoint a committee of scholars, which he himself directed, to devise a form of writing that would not be accessible only—like Chinese calligraphy—to a few monkish intellectuals and the male court literati. From this committee emerged what has been described by Professor Edwin Reischauer and others as the world's most logical alphabet, *han-gŭl,* consisting of thirty-five consonants, vowels, and diphthongs. Any reasonably intelligent person could learn it during the time it takes to fly from America or Europe to Korea.

Thanks also to Sejong, scholars produced a 265-chapter compendium on Chinese medicine and, in 1433, compiled a similar manual of native *han-yak* remedies in eighty-five chapters; these were transliterated into *han-gŭl*. Sejong promoted the science of astronomy and sent traveling doctors through the countryside. He encouraged use of the pluviometer, water clocks, maps, and even written music. He instituted land reform.

Soon, however, the Mongols were at the gates again, followed by the island warriors of Japan. In 1592, under the great military Shōgun Toyotomi Hideyoshi, Japan invaded Korea, reportedly massing one hundred fifty thousand troops on Tsushima Island in the strait between the old Sillan port of Busan and the main Nipponese island, Honshu.

Using muskets supplied by another breed of empire builder, the Jesuits of Nagasaki (who also brought red pepper to Asia, where it made more converts in Korea than Japan), the Japanese spread through the country, conquering Han-yang. Mindful of their long supply lines, they bought huge quantities of rice everywhere they went. When the time for counterattack came, the Koreans either recovered the rice for which they had already been paid or, if the Japanese tried to take it with them, their slow, weighted columns were harassed to the Koreans' advantage.

Driven out on that attempt, the Japanese returned again in 1597. Interestingly enough, we are now only three years away from the beginning of the influence on Japan of Will Adams, immortalized by James Clavell as John Blackthorne in *Shōgun,* and of the rise of Shōgun Tokugawa (Torenaga in Clavell's book). What rings particularly true in the novel is the spurious scorn with which Torenaga and other Japanese military nobles speak of Koreans, a reflection of Japan's recent humiliation on the peninsula. This indeed was the era of Korea's greatest hero, the nation's equivalent of Nelson.

Admiral Yi Sun-shin's statue is found today in all sorts of places, the best-known being on Seoul's Champs-Elysées, the Taejong-no, which shows him twice as tall and twice as broad as any Korean man. Yi invented turtle boats, the world's first armored ships. The idea of building ironclads had been mentioned in court chronicles as early as 1413, but it was under Yi that the prototype was actually launched in 1592.

The turtle ships were about one hundred feet long and

twenty-five feet wide. Like Japanese vessels of the time, they were rowed by slaves. Their originality lay in covering their vulnerable topsides with iron, which deflected fire arrows and cannonballs, and in embellishing them with spikes, so they could not be swarmed. Twenty-six cannon fired broadsides through portholes, and a bowsprit in the shape of a turtle's head contained a wood-fired generator which enabled it to spew sulfur smoke. This clouded the entire ship during maneuvers to approach, fire on, or board the Nipponese vessels, and probably intimidated superstitious enemy sailors.

These Mephistophelian feats of ingenuity were grouped in a fleet which Yi kept at Yŏsu, on the inland sea now known as the Hal-lyŏ Waterway. In the short period from May to July 1592, Yi is said to have sunk two hundred fifty Japanese men-of-war and supply ships. He cut Hideyoshi's supply lines in the Tsushima Strait. He then sailed into occupied Busan harbor and, presaging Drake's feat at Cadiz and Nelson's on the Nile, burned the enemy fleet at anchor. Korean history books insist that this military genius put five hundred ships on the bottom there.

In 1596, the Japanese sued for peace. The next year, however, they were back again with one hundred thousand men, thirsting for revenge. History records that the current ruler in Kyoto demanded proof of his men's victories by requiring that they cut off the ears of captured Koreans and send them, pickled, to the Japanese capital. No less than thirty-eight thousand ears, it is claimed, duly arrived in barrels and were given a proper burial, far from home.

Admiral Yi, alas, had another trait in common with Nelson. He had an ego as big as his fleet, and soon fell out of favor at court. Banishment followed.

His successor lost battles as regularly as Yi had won them. Capriciously restored to command, Yi was given only twelve ironclads—either because that was all that remained, or be-

47

cause it was feared that he might stage the world's first naval coup d'état. He once more defeated the Japanese at sea before, like Nelson again, falling victim to a sharpshooter's bullet in his hour of glory. What he was doing on deck has never been satisfactorily explained.

The Japanese, politically afflicted by Hideyoshi's death in 1597, retreated once more from Korea, taking with them shiploads of celadon and thousands of books, which in turn helped to instill Confucianism more firmly in the islands.

In the seventeenth century, the Manchu Chinese overthrew Korea's Chinese ally, the Ming court, and sent a punishing force into Korea. When this invasion was over, Korea, devastated and looted by countless wars, concluded that it was, as one Korean author wrote, a "shrimp among whales." The country withdrew into itself with a determination that led to its being known as the Hermit Kingdom.

For two and a half centuries, it even limited trade with China and Japan. Some intellectual ferment, however, did continue. Sixteenth-century contact with Europeans in China had introduced new books and maps and rekindled an interest in science. An updated manual of Korean medicine had appeared in 1610.

In 1627, three Dutchmen, led by Jan Janse Weltevree, either landed or were shipwrecked on a southern shore of Korea. They were prevented from leaving, and were forced to produce weapons and train troops against future invasions. Eleven years later, three other European seamen of undetermined origin were stranded on Jeju Island; they also were taken to Seoul where they became, probably unwillingly, mercenaries for the king; they died in battle.

On August 16, 1653, the Dutch ship *Sparrowhawk* was blown ashore in a typhoon at Mosŭlp'o, on the southern littoral of Jeju. The ship was on its way to the great Catholic port of Nagasaki, already the main Japanese center of Christianity. Captain Hendrik Hamel and twelve of his crew survived. Ashore, regarded as spies, they became virtual prisoners, eventually being taken to the mainland, whence they escaped to Japan and returned to Holland. In 1668, Hamel wrote a fascinating book about his experience.

For all intents and purposes, Korea was, from 1632 onward, a vassal state once more. It was sinking, like its European equivalents, Ancient Greece and Ancient Rome, into decay. But it continued to produce books, maps, and art, and experienced the first whiff of Christianity. This was, above all, a great age for the literati.

Many of this aristocratic group lived frugally as book readers and "intellectuals," painting and writing poetry. Their only "serious" option was the civil service. They were exempt from military service. If convicted of an offense, they could pay a serf or nominate a slave to serve the sentence or absorb the blows. In return for these privileges, they were constrained to a rigid Confucian code of behavior and unquestioning loyalty to the sovereign. Says Yi Kwang-rin, an historian: "A scholar was supposed to live for ceremony and righteousness."

The goal for most was to pass the civil service examinations. By turning the intelligentsia into government servants, the system encouraged decadence. (Conversely, probably nothing has so encouraged sophistication in modern times as the development of an adversary vernacular press.)

Professor Kim Tong-wook, who teaches Korean literature at Yonsei, has outlined the life of the young literati at Sŏnggyun-gwan School, where they prepared for the civil service tests and for their future life as aristocrats:

> Those who followed vernacular styles or rhetorical flourishes would be expelled from the school and those who did not write properly would also be punished. . . .

49

Those students who indulged in tall tales and heresy, spoke ill of those who studied harder, talked [about] wine and women, and fawned upon the rulers as a means of getting state appointment were punished. . . .

Those students who were conceited on account of talent . . . family power [or] wealth, the young who humiliated the elder, [those who] dressed unlike others and flattered . . . were expelled; some would be readmitted, however, when they mended their ways.

Those students who traveled often at the expense of the state treasury . . . not writing compositions and not reading books but going around on horseback and violating curfew were punished.

The students were allowed to go home every eighth and twenty-third day to wash and change clothes, but those who . . . went shooting arrows, played card games, went hunting or fishing . . . were also punished.

If a student met his teacher on the road he had to stand still with folded hands on the left side of the road until the teacher rode by. A student who hid himself from the teacher or covered his face and did not pay respect . . . was also punished.

The students rose every morning before dawn at the toll of a drum, and at the second toll they put on the full dress attire and began to read and at the third toll they entered the dining hall in the order of their age and sat on the east and west face to face. After eating, they walked out of the dining hall in the order in which they entered. Anyone who violated this rule or made a noise was punished. . . .

During the first ten days of every month, the minister of the board of rites and the president of Sŏnggyun-gwan met to review the academic records of each student . . . and selected five excellent students . . . to apply for the civil service examination. For the students in the lower dormitories and in the four schools in the capital, [certain dignitaries] met during the first ten days of every month in one of the schools to test the students on the Four Books and selected ten most excellent students, allowing them to apply for the preliminary examination to become first-degree licentiates. . . . Those who were lazy and could not finish the courses . . . were punished.

Dr. Kim describes a student assembly which was a sort of trial:

The servants escorted the president into the place . . . carrying the case of inkstone . . . ahead of him. . . .

When everything was readied, the president declared the names of the crimes. The severest punishment was to strike the culprit's name off the student roll, and the next was a temporary suspension. . . . The number of characters used in describing the names of crimes was set at eight. . . . [These were] pasted on the outer wall of the West First Room.

When it was a matter of great importance, the drum was sounded and the culprit was apprehended at the mealtime drum toll by the servants, who beat him and called him by name and dragged him toward the village. The purpose was to give maximum humiliation. If the matter was grave, his expulsion . . . was announced, and the servant was required to write down the whys and wherefors and report it to the chief of the village and the members of the student council.

When the punishment (*sic*) was to be absolved, the

list of crimes would be taken from the wall and crossed out by the youngest student. . . .

The students of the upper dormitory could punish those of the lower dormitory and punishment took two forms: a few days' abstention from eating at the dining hall for a minor case, and expulsion for the worst case. In the event of the latter, someone would be brought in to replace the one expelled.

The students were also, however, permitted and expected to petition the sovereign with popular grievances, and propose solutions, sending a "memorial" to the court. Professor Kim describes this procedure:

> After the procession of memorial presenters started for the court, it was a common practice from olden times that the boy servants and rascals of the village would riot and loot. This was why the common people, on hearing that the memorial presenters procession was on its way, would close up their shops and houses and go into hiding.
>
> When at last the procession reached the palace gate, the students, after placing the memorial boxes on a red table in front of the main gate, would sit on the ground in two groups. The students from the Four Schools were seated behind. A servant was despatched into the palace to inform the royal secretariat of their arrival. At this point, even a state minister could not pass before the procession on horseback. If there was a trespasser, the chief of the boy servants gave a warning and then, if the warning was not heeded, they roughed up and flogged the footman. . . .
>
> If the royal answer proved unsatisfactory, [the presenters] plotted to offer another memorial.

One solution was the *kwŏn-dang,* which Dr. Kim calls a "walkout or strike." It was used as a "last resort." For instance, "In 1551, the Confucian students of Sŏng-gyun-gwan presented memorial after memorial in condemnation of High Priest Pu," and when their repeated request was denied, they walked out.

> King Myŏng-jong despatched a minister of the royal secretariat and an official chronicler to persuade the students to . . . stop protesting. When the students refused, the court mobilized the fathers of the students, but this too ended in failure. Thus the students walked out of Sŏng-gyun-gwan for a few months. A few such incidents occurred thereafter, which subsequently helped heighten the morale of the students. On such an occasion, the royal court customarily despatched an officer of appeasement. The origin of walkouts was said to have been in Sung China. . . .
>
> When the students presented their [request] in written form, the doyen presented a synopsis to the court and then gave them an official answer, enjoining them to go back to the dining hall. If the answer proved satisfactory, they obeyed his order, but if not, they did not.

An excellent chronicle of upper-class life under the Yi dynasty, the *Yangban chŏn,* was written in the eighteenth century. Pak Chi-wŏn, its author, led a life of elegant poverty until finally being made mayor of Yang-yang, a pleasant fishing town on the Dong-hae coast. He died in 1805. Pak, who has been called Chaucerian, was critical of his own class and the limitations of Confucianism, and encouraged by the new ideas entering China from the West.

In the story, a *yang-ban* sells his title to a merchant, who is informed of his new duties:

> [The *yang-ban*] must call his servants in a firm, dignified voice. He must walk in a dignified manner, stepping lightly with his feet turned outward. In copying the Chinese anthology and the T'ang poetry, he should be able to write so small as to put one hundred characters on a line.
>
> He must not grasp money in his hand, nor ask the current price of rice. However hot the weather, he must not remove his socks; when seated at the dinner table, he must always be properly attired. When dining, he must not eat his soup first, and when he eats it he must not make a noise. He must not poke about and play with his chopsticks. He must not eat raw onions. When drinking wine, he must not suck on his beard; when smoking, he must not suck on his pipe so strongly as to make the flame die out.
>
> No matter how exasperating his wife may be, he must not beat her. In anger, he must not kick the furniture. When rebuking servants, he must not use abusive language or unseemly insults such as "base knave who should be put to death" or "lowly slut." When reprimanding livestock, he must not speak ill of their owner.
>
> Even though an illness should afflict his house, he must not call the *mudang*. When the time comes to pay homage to his ancestors, he must not call a monk to perform the rites in his stead. Even though the weather be cold, he must not warm his hands before the brazier. When talking, he must not splutter his saliva in another's face. He must never slaughter a cow. He must never gamble.

> If he does not abide by these standards of conduct, bring this document [his title] to the government office and litigation will be begun against him.

The new *yang-ban* was then informed of some of the advantages:

> Even though a scholar be poor and rusticate in the country, he is still a law unto himself: a man who can demand his neighbor's cow so that his fields may be plowed first, and who may require the people of the district to weed his fields. Should someone slight the *yang-ban*, the wretch will be seized and lye poured down his nostril, and he will be tied down by his topknot and his beard will be torn out hair by hair, and no one will attend his grievances.

On hearing this, the wealthy trader thereupon refused to use his new rank, crying: "It is more than I bargained for! You would make me into a thief!"

Imperialism, like nature, abhors a vacuum, and the Jesuits, having persevered and survived in Nippon, were anxious to save the souls close by across the sea. Their brief incursions, although tolerated at first, received little encouragement. In 1839, one hundred thirty Catholics, European and Korean, were executed. Out of respect for their religion, however, the senior prisoners were not decapitated in the traditional way, but were crucified. More exactions against missionaries followed in both Korea and China. In retaliation, a British and French expeditionary force captured Beijing in 1860, and sacked the city.

Over the next decade, nine French Catholic priests and an estimated eight thousand Korean converts allowed themselves to be put to death rather than renounce their faith. The French navy responded by bombarding Korean ports. It was an era of massive xenophobia, and when an American freighter, the *General Sherman,* sailed onto a sandbank in the Taedong River, approaching P'yŏng-yang, the citizenry responded by burning the vessel and putting the crew to death.

Undaunted, Frederick Low led a U.S. trade mission to Kang-hwa Island five years later. He took with him a squadron of marines, who appear suitably dissolute in a surviving photograph. The party had to fight its way back to their ship.

The nation most exercized over Korea's unwillingness to join the world was Japan, who also resorted to gunboat diplomacy. A trade agreement with Edo (Tokyo) was finally signed in 1876. Pacts with the United States, Russia, France, and Britain followed. A Korean legation was established in Washington in 1887 under Pak Chong-yang. It presented its letters of credence in *han-gŭl* only, and was soon sending home American cattle and seeds for Kojong's model farm.

The first American minister to Seoul was Lucius Foote. He had been preceded, in 1883, by U.S. military advisers and an American palace school for the royal family, known as the *Yŏng-yuk Hakwŏn,* as well as by Seoul's first postal, telegraph, and telephone service, a Seoul-Inch'ŏn railroad, and tramway streetcars. The latter were fitted with people-catchers in front, to clear aside roadway sleepers without seriously harming them. The first hospital was opened by American missionaries in 1884.

Korea was still the crossroads. In 1882, China and Russia schemed to remove the patriotic regent, Tae-wŏn-gun, who was made a prisoner in China. The pro-Chinese, pro-Russian, anti-Japanese Queen Min was made the virtual authority over her husband, Kojong. The Chinese again intervened in 1884 to keep Queen Min in control. Other powers were also active: in 1885, the British briefly occupied Kŏ-mun Island.

Japanese troops crossed the country to attack China in 1894, defeating the "Middle Empire" the following year. At the time, Chosŏn was involved with the *tong-hak*, popular revolution, particularly in Ch'ŏlla province. China, seen by Edo as the cat's-paw of Russia, had landed troops at Kang-hwa-do that year, giving the Japanese a pretext to occupy the island with five hundred elite cavalrymen, brought by ship. These were soon followed by twenty thousand troops, who proceeded to seize the capital in the name of defending the peninsula from Western imperialism.

The Japanese took advantage of their occupation of Hanyang to force reform on the Korean emperor, as the diminished monarch was now euphemistically styled. Slavery and child marriage were banned, for instance, with the Japanese proclaiming such reforms to boost their argument that, like Britain, France, Portugal, Holland, and other colonizers in Asia, theirs was a civilizing influence. Clearly, they had some reason on their side. If Chosŏn was too weak to resist colonization, a neighbor-culture like Japan's was probably preferable to absorption into the Czarist empire.

In 1895, the Japanese legate, Miura Goro, convinced that the Empress Min was the head of the "Russian faction" at court—favoring the Czar over the Emperor in Edo—had her assassinated by a posse of officers who burned her cadaver with kerosene. The assassins faced a mock trial in Hiroshima and received only light sentences. This episode strengthened the resolve of her ineffectual widower, Kojong, to resist, but not very impressively: he took up asylum at the Czarist legation.

The Russians underestimated their adversary. In 1896, St. Petersburg rejected a Japanese plan to recognize a Russian sphere of influence in the peninsula north of the thirty-ninth parallel, with Japan controlling the southern portion. By 1903, the Japanese were offering a harder bargain: Russia could now have only Manchuria; Japan, the entire peninsula. Again, the Czar said no. In 1904, the Japanese invaded Port Arthur and delivered a stinging defeat to the Russians the following year. At the peace treaty, signed at Portsmouth, England, in 1905, Korea was internationally recognized as a Japanese sphere of influence. Edo then had the equivalent of a political adviser at the court of Seoul, and became responsible for Korea's foreign affairs—much the same situation that Britain was acquiring in Egypt.

Meanwhile, in 1896, a Korean physician trained at George Washington University in the United States capital, Sŏ Chae-p'il (who preferred to be called Philip Jaisohn), had returned home and founded Korea's first political party, the Independence Club, with reputedly ten thousand members. His newspaper, *The Independent,* was published exclusively in *han-gŭl.* But he fell foul of both the Japanese and the nervous Korean court, and was forced to return to exile in the U.S. with his American wife.

On November 18, 1905, the Emperor Kojong accepted a plan which made Korea a virtual Japanese protectorate, matching similar rights about to be given to France by the Sultan of Morocco. There were street demonstrations, but these only led to Japan's extending its powers to include "law and order" and other domestic issues.

Kojong was then persuaded to abdicate in favor of his retarded son, Sun-jong, in 1907. The Japanese settler population in Korea rose to one hundred twenty-six thousand the following year. Resistance movements spread. Japanese officials were assassinated—most notably, the Resident-General, elderly white-bearded Ito Hirobumi, at Harbin railroad station on October 26, 1909, by a Korean patriot, An Chung-gŭn.

On August 22, 1910, Japan and Sun-jong made it official: after five hundred nineteen years and twenty-seven Lyi kings, Korea was taken over as a Japanese territory, but more with the status of a colony than as part of Japan itself. By the following year, the Japanese presence had grown to two hundred ten thousand. Land expropriation began, in favor of imported Japanese farmers.

Colonization usually requires a sharp differentiation between the colonizers, who are first-class citizens, and the colonized, who form an inferior or a set of inferior classes. In pursuance of this, the measures taken have often been quaint and have reflected the simplicity of the ruling caste. In the Philippines, for instance, the Spanish insisted that only a European could wear his shirt inside his trousers; Filipinos must wear theirs outside—which has now become an aspect of "national dress." Johannesburg Air Terminal once had two entrances to the same ticket hall. The Japanese in Korea were just as silly, but did it all in infuriatingly backward order.

All Koreans eventually had to take Japanese names, like those of their overlords. Only Japanese could be spoken in the streets, and after some time it became the language of instruction in the schools—which were forbidden to teach Korean history.

The Koreans proved about as easy to reduce to serf status as the Palestinians in our time. On Sam-ril (the first day of the third month) in 1919, a group of Korean intelligentsia staged a quiet protest under the bravely raised *tae-guk-ki* flag. The event was timed to take place three days before the date set for the funeral of the former emperor, Kojong, who had just died in exile. Decked out in their best clothes, the group met in a city restaurant and issued a manifesto calling for the withdrawal of all Japanese troops and officials. They then waited to be arrested.

What followed was a massacre which brought thousands more (Korean history books say two million!) into the streets to protest—and to be shot down in their turn. It was Korea's Amritsar. Ironically, hundreds of women, only recently released from centuries of purdah by the Japanese, took part in this resistance against the island overlords. One seventeen-year-old, Yu Kwan-sun, cruelly put to death after arrest, became the nation's Joan of Arc. Unfortunately, the Japanese, like most colonizers, had never studied the colonized. Official Korean history, which may embrace some hyperbole, claims there were seven thousand killed and many more thousands wounded on Sam-ril.

As Japan pushed its Great East Asia Co-Prosperity Sphere program into China, there were a few relaxations in Korea, whose support was clearly needed in what was going to be a long campaign. However, when Japan subsequently found itself at war with the United States and its allies, and in a state of desperation, conditions hardened once again. By then, all but one of Japan's governors-general in occupied Asia were military. A total of 4,146,098 Koreans were placed in forced labor in Korea itself; 1,259,993 Korean workers were shipped to Japan to replace Japanese in the factories, and Korean girls were shanghaied into a concubine corps for the Nipponese soldiery. Other Koreans were taken to China, to Sakhalin, or to guard prisoner-of-war camps in Southeast Asia.

Korea's fissiparous exiled opposition had formed a government in Shanghai in April 1919, under Yi Sŭng-man. Yi had appealed to President Wilson in 1918 to help put his country under the League of Nations. He later moved to Hawaii and continued to lobby Washington. Korean resisters loyal to him harried the Japanese in "Manchukuo" (invaded by Japan in September 1931) and in the north of the homeland peninsula. A Princeton graduate with a Western wife, Dr. Yi seemed a likely choice to head Korea after emancipation.

Japan's bombing of Pearl Harbor in 1941 was as beneficial to Korea's position in Washington as it was to Western Europe's hopes for survival, succored until then by another piece of good news that year—Hitler's mistake in invading the Soviet Union.

A LIFE AT THE CROSSROADS

Yi Sŭng-man, however, did not have a seat at the table of the masters. In Cairo on December 1, 1943, President Franklin D. Roosevelt met Prime Minister Winston Churchill and Generalissimo Chiang Kai-shek: one of the decisions they took was that Korea would be independent "in due course" after the war. Marshal Josef Stalin was not present, but later at Yalta he agreed on the principle of independence for the peninsula.

On August 6, 1945 (August 7 in Japan and Soviet Asia), the atom bomb was dropped on Hiroshima, and Japan showed signs of imminent collapse. On August 9, Stalin suddenly remembered to declare war on his Pacific neighbor, and sent forces into Manchuria. In London and Washington, fear mounted that the Johnny-come-lately Red Army would occupy the entire Korean peninsula. A hasty agreement on joint liberation was drawn up, with American and Soviet forces due to meet and divide at the thirty-eighth parallel. This line was chosen as the approximate neck of the country, having the shortest possible land border between the two zones of occupation.

The Russian soldiers were in position by late August, but the U.S. Eighth Army took until September 8 to get there. The seventy-three-year-old Yi was brought in from Hawaii, reminding everyone he met that he had been in prison under the Japanese and would now introduce democracy. There was, however, ominous talk of a twenty-five-year transition to independence.

On December 15 in Moscow, Truman, British premier Clement Attlee, and Stalin agreed on a trusteeship for Korea by their three countries, plus Chiang's China. Kim Il-sŏng's legions in North Korea acquiesced, but South Korea staged protests. Finally, at the U.N., it was decided to dispose of liberated Korea in the same manner as liberated Libya, just delivered from Mussolini's Italy: there would be a five-year trusteeship. In Libya's case, the mandate power was Britain. In Korea, it was to be an unlikely condominium of the Soviet Union and the United States.

Needless to say, the two liberators agreed on nothing; but while the Russians were installing the leaders of the Communist resistance in power, the Americans, under the artless General John Hodge, were using Japanese officials as administrators and treating the population as coolies who should be grateful that the right overseers had won the war. As hope for nationwide elections, called for by the United Nations, diminished, the U.S. authorities went ahead with a poll in the South on May 10, 1948; Dr. Yi Sŭng-man, who now styled himself Syngman Rhee, became the first president of the new republic. He was installed on August 15, three years after the Japanese surrender.

The Russians hastily organized their own elections in the North in December, and 99.9 percent of the populace magically voted for Kim Il-sŏng, who has governed—or virtually ruled—ever since. The following year, the U.S. withdrew, leaving ninety-six thousand South Korean soldiers with five hundred U.S. instructors. The Soviet Union also moved back over the border, leaving one hundred seventy-five thousand North Korean troops with two thousand five hundred instructors, along with two hundred combat aircraft and about five hundred tanks.

In a speech made on January 12, 1950, the Secretary of State, Dean Acheson, defined the perimeter of U.S. interests in Asia as running from the Aleutians to the Philippines, via Japan—somehow omitting the Korean peninsula. Many were to die for this slip of the tongue. Mistaking a mistake for a signal, Kim Il-sŏng soon flung his forces across the border, officially to accommodate the U.N. decision to reunify the country.

It was on June 25 that year that about seventy thousand

A LIFE AT THE CROSSROADS

North Korean troops and seventy Soviet-made tanks crossed the thirty-eighth parallel and started the most devastating war the often devastated country had ever seen.

Fortunately, the Soviet Union was then boycotting United Nations debates, in protest against the admission of the delegation of the (by then) defeated government of Chiang Kai-shek. This enabled Acheson to recoup by getting a resolution passed that mandated a U.N. force under an American general to restore order in the peninsula. General Douglas MacArthur sent the Eighth Army over from Japan, and the Americans began the task of stiffening the resistance of the under-armed, largely untrained South Korean army, and shipping in reinforcements from the United States.

Fifteen other countries also sent expeditionary forces to fight under MacArthur—who was to spend most of the war at his office in Tokyo. Veterans still recall the extraordinary courage of some of these small units, fighting under often Arctic conditions against a large and determined enemy. The Turks and the Ethiopians are most often singled out for especial praise.

However, before much of the organized battle plan could be put in place, the North Koreans had overrun Seoul in just four days and swept south. By September, the South Koreans and their American allies were penned inside the hilly perimeter around Busan, the country's main port, in the extreme southeast.

A professional military history of the war as seen from both the North and South Korean sides, as well as from the vantage point of the United States forces and the other fifteen armies involved, remains to be written. But the broad details are well known.

In a reckless drive to pincer the enemy, MacArthur ordered a landing at Inch'ŏn, the outpost for Seoul, famous for its twenty-eight-foot tides. With a soldier's luck in a sailor's operation, he was almost undeservedly successful, and his forces somehow got ashore and marched on Seoul. Then, instead of driving across the country's neck, he shipped his forces out again and all around the peninsula to take Wŏnsan, on the eastern shore—only to find that the South Korean army had already liberated that town.

Nevertheless, in spite of MacArthur's limitations as an absentee general, Seoul had been liberated on September 28—and of course, in the process, devastated once again. The U.N. then authorized MacArthur to press into the North. P'yŏngyang was taken on October 19, and by late October the U.N. and South Korean forces had reached the Am-nok-kang (Yalu) River border with China. MacArthur was talking of getting the boys home for Christmas.

It was not to be. It was now North Korea's turn to call for help. China brought troops across the Am-nok-kang, and the U.S. X Corps scattered, abandoning virtually all its weaponry and equipment (some of it sold, thirty-five years later, by North Korea to Iran for its war on Iraq).

Seoul fell again on January 4, 1951, and the South Korean and American forces continued to fall back. Reinforcements finally arrived, and the situation was "rectified." Seoul fell for a fourth time on March 12, once again to its own and U.S. forces.

The war settled down to random skirmishing and two years of erratic truce talks, which began at Kaesŏng in July that year and were moved to Pan-Mun-Jŏm in November.

Stalin's death in early 1953 left North Korea less certain of Soviet support. Finally, on July 27, 1953, an armistice was signed, setting the new artificial frontier approximately where the old one had been. MacArthur had been fired two years earlier, and the victor of the day was General Matthew Ridgway. Two million North Korean refugees had already fled south, never to return. A "Neutral Nations Supervisory Commission" was established, consisting of a handful of officers from Czechoslovakia, Poland, Sweden, and Switzerland (the latter, or course, provided the mess chef). Peace, however, has never been signed, and the quadripartite bridge party still continues almost daily.

The rugged country of mountain ridges and exposed valleys, with its frigid winters in the north, had proved an expensive place in which to fight a largely infantry war. Although only one year of the three-year conflict was devoted to set-piece battles, the South Koreans lost one hundred forty-seven thousand killed, plus sixteen thousand in the police force, the Americans 33,629, the other units over three thousand. A staggering three hundred thousand troops were wounded, of whom one hundred eighty-three thousand were South Korean. Eighty-five thousand, mostly South Korean, were missing or captured.

The dubious roundness of these figures indicates how approximate they are. Many people just disappeared. Civilian casualties included one hundred thirty thousand who were said to have been executed, two hundred thirty thousand wounded, three hundred thirty thousand "missing." South Korea's military and civilian dead, wounded, and missing amounted to about fifteen percent of the population. Every family had a story.

North Korean casualties—dead and wounded—were put at five hundred twenty thousand, and the Chinese admitted to losing nine hundred thousand, including thousands who literally froze to death at their guns.

After the firing ceased, it was more of the same on both sides. Kim Il-sŏng developed a regime of Marxism, monarchy, and magic, based on a cult of devotion to himself and, eventually, to his son as well. Other religions were discouraged, while shamanism was discreetly encouraged. In the South, President Rhee (or Yi) became more and more autocratic. He was reelected in 1960 in a ballot marked by overt fraud. Student protests mounted. Eight persons died—always a political catalyst in a country in which demonstrations are largely symbolic, however big. Rhee was forced to retire in disgrace on April 27. He returned with his wife to Hawaii and died there five years later, on July 19, 1965.

He was replaced in an election by Chang Myŏn, a Christian who styled himself John M. Chang. Chang, however, proved ineffectual and was replaced in a coup led by Major General Pak Chung-hi (also often written Park Chung-hee), who ruled through a junta. In 1963, Pak won an election of dubious propriety, and he was reelected in 1971 and 1978. In 1971, however, he came close to losing to a popular tribune, Kim Dae-jung, who subsequently claimed that he would have won, had the balloting been entirely honest.

Whatever his autocratic ways, Pak revitalized the country's economy, starting its great industrial revolution, and forcing reforms through a rubber-stamp parliament. North Korea, having most of the peninsula's natural resources and only half of South Korea's population, had made a swifter recovery; but President Pak successfully drove his country into high gear. Historically, he was a fairly benevolent dictator, less democratic than Atatürk but more intelligent than Cromwell, and he put his stamp on Korea's emergent success enough to be assured a distinguished place in his country's saga. However, the martinet made many enemies. On October 26, 1979, he was assassinated by Kim Jae-kyu, the director of the Korean Central Intelligence Agency, an unusual background for a reformer. Kim was later tried and executed.

The Prime Minister, Ch'oi Kyu-ha, became acting president, then was elected by an electoral college; but the military was unconvinced that he would have the necessary authority to keep the accelerated economy's throttle open, and de facto power passed more and more to the generals. These were headed by Major General Ch'ŏn Du-hwan. Ch'ŏn subsequently took over leadership of the government, and was elected president for a single seven-year term beginning in February 1981.

Economic growth continued at a rate of about ten percent per year, except during the brief period of the international oil crisis. However, even this helped Korea: one hundred fifteen thousand workers went to the Gulf for the construction boom, sending home $5.7 billion in remittances. Per capita income, which rose from $45 in 1953 (on a par with Ethiopia) to about double that, $86, nine years later, soared to $2,900 in 1987.

Efforts to negotiate with the North for reunification, set back by the discovery of North Korean invasion tunnels, seemed finally defeated in October 1983, when North Korean commandos killed twenty-one persons in Rangoon, Burma. Most were Korean officials, including four ministers.

The next year, Ch'ŏn made the first Korean state visit to Japan since liberation. He received an expression of regret from the Emperor for Japan's misdeeds of the past.

The time had come for Korea to move to a more democratic constitution, with a president and legislature chosen by direct election. A series of stylized demonstrations in 1987, with minimal casualties, brought this about. Korea was put to the acid test of how well it had caught up with its one-time disciple, Japan.

THE KOREANS

1. Seoul by night [Korean Overseas Information Service]
2. Korean couples still marry in traditional yang-ban clothes [KOIS]
3. Traditional birthday celebration [KOIS]
4. Flute player in traditional Confucian court dress [KOIS]
5. Playing the kayagŭm [KOIS]
6. Modern celadon ware [KOIS]
7. Brushing han-gŭl, *art and literature combine* [KOIS]

4.

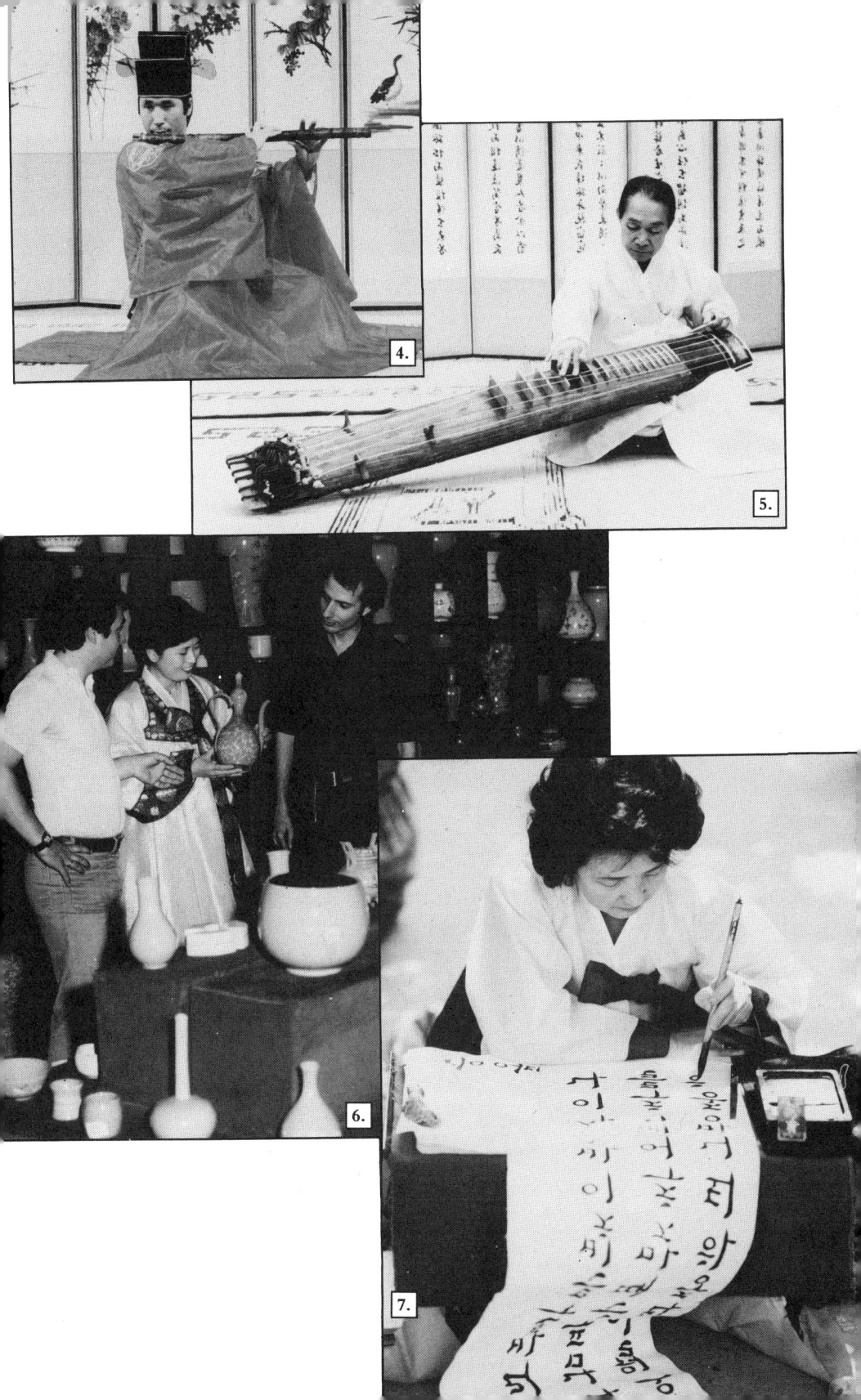

5.

6.

7.

THE KOREANS

1. *Elders at a celebration* [KOIS]
2. *A fishing family at Hae-un-dae, near Busan* [Russell Warren Howe]
3. *Weeding* in-sam [KOIS]
4. *Sitting at an outdoor café in downtown Seoul* [KOIS]
5. *Shopping alley* [Russell Warren Howe]
6. *Frontier guards at the "demilitarized" zone* [KOIS]
7. *Korean war graves* [KOIS]

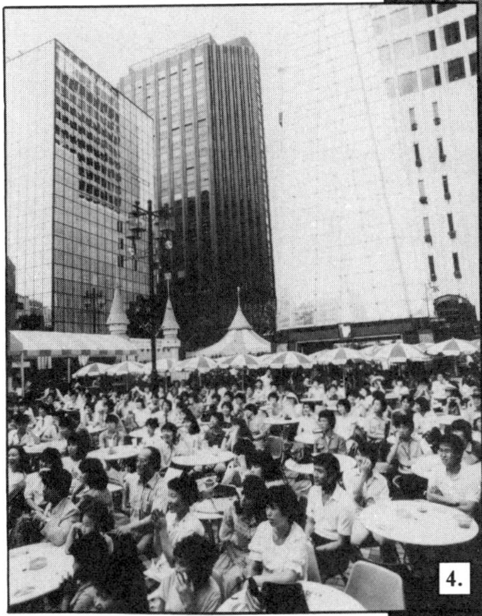

4.

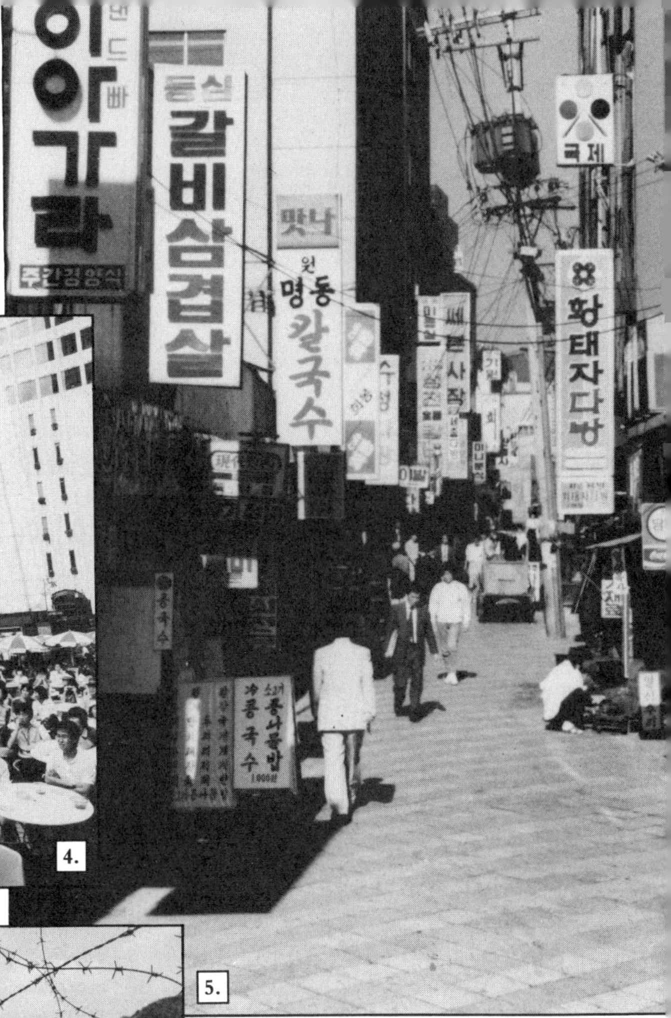

5.

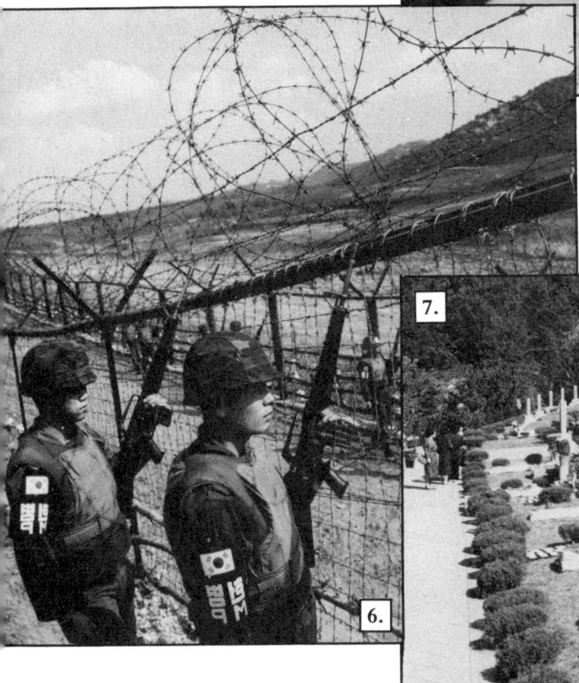

6.

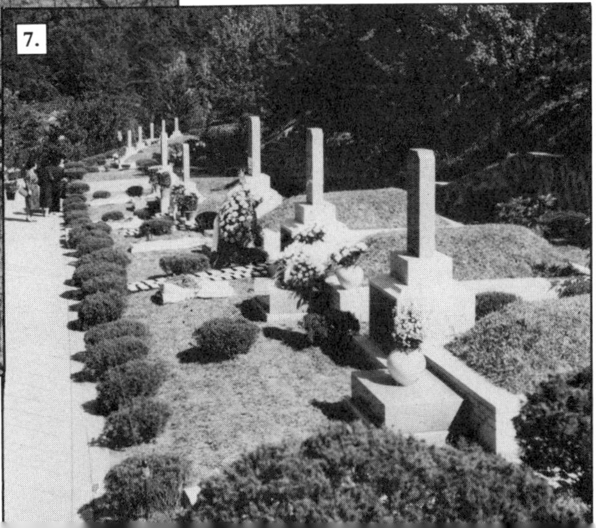

7.

3

A LIFE IN WORDS AND RULES AND GRACES

PROFESSOR PAK BYUNG-RO returns the bow of his class as he enters his lecture hall at Seoul National University. His parched features, lined by gallons of *so-ju* and *jŏng-jong* lovingly consumed during years of devoted reading of literature, are dominated by humorous eyes sheltered by beetling brows and epicanthic lids. He speaks with a mixture of asperity and jocularity as he enunciates the gist of the lesson of the day. Meanwhile, the students have lifted their heads and resumed their seats.

Dr. Pak writes a few lines on the blackboard. More accurately, he draws—for the Korean alphabet can only be written respectfully with a brush. Presented in utilitarian, sans serif form over a shop or a billiard hall, it can look crude, even ugly; scribbled, it possesses an arcane spirit of reduction like that of shorthand; but calligraphed with artistry, with the feel of a brush—even in pen or chalk—it takes on a beauty of its own, as graceful as Arabic letters or Chinese ideograms, more pleasing than Japan's kana syllabary. Professor Pak, as well as being an expert on Korean literature, is justly proud of his *hangŭl* calligraphy, which can appear just as aesthetic as the graceful words on a Chinese tomb or an Arab scroll.

A LIFE IN WORDS AND RULES AND GRACES

Having summarized the lesson he proposes to teach, he begins by reciting poetry. As his tongue tumbles on a fortuitous match of male and female sounds, he cannot resist the temptation to inscribe the harmony in *han-gŭl* on the board. The students will thus remember it photographically, in their minds.

The language and its writing are the keys to Korean thought and culture. The language reflects Korean life, with its brisk imagination and taut politeness, its view of the spiritual nature of the universe. It reflects the mores. Long before the Japanese, Koreans had a passionate devotion to literature and the written word—which was why *han-gŭl* had to be invented, and perhaps explains why movable metal type (still then in Chinese characters, of course) was invented here so much earlier than elsewhere. The oldest complete surviving work from Korean metal type that remains in good condition is a collection of Buddhist sermons printed in 1377 and now in the Bibliothèque Nationale in Paris.

Given the high skill of the Koreans in metalwork and jewelry, their pioneering of metal type is not surprising. In contrast, the *han-gŭl* alphabet is recent, only five and a half centuries old—but it is a phonetic alphabet, not a collection of characters. King Sejong said that a clever person could learn *han-gŭl* in a morning, a foolish one in ten days. *Han-gŭl* brought reading—and thus, eventually, all education—within reach of virtually everyone, three centuries before the notion of popular education entered the West, China, or Japan.

But the love affair with words dates back to before Sejong, to the days when the Koreans had only Chinese characters, which corresponded to things and ideas, not verbal sounds, and which can be read in different languages, but which cannot reflect those tongues.

A tiny elite of royals, near-royals, and eminent monks spent a lifetime embracing the memorization of Chinese pictographs. There are about fifty thousand of them in all, involving anything from one to fifty-two strokes of the brush. Some idea of the effort and grace of this art form can be realized on a visit to Hae-in-sa, the main monastery of Sŏn (Zen) Buddhism in Korea, which houses the *polman daejung kyung*, or Tripitaka Koreana; this consists of 81,137 or 81,258 woodblocks (accounts vary) over seven hundred years old, in classical Chinese. Seeing the reverence with which the monks handle these ancient Buddhist blocks, or pull a proof from one for you, enables one to journey back in time to the age when they were made.

The first tripitaka, or Buddhist canon, was carved in Ko-ryŏ in the eleventh century, from 1011 to 1087; as noted earlier, it was burned by a royal father-in-law, and its destruction was completed by the invading Mongols in 1238. The present, larger set, carved when the court of Ko-ryŏ was in exile on Kang-hwa Island, was ordered in 1236. According to Dr. Jon Covell, wood was soaked in the sea for three years, then dried for three more years; then, the six-year process was repeated before carving began. The first printings were made in 1251, meaning that hundreds of monks must have spent only three years carving the tens of thousands of blocks on both sides, in spite of the necessity to carve in reverse for printing purposes. For safety, the treasure was moved to Hae-in shortly afterward, and it has since survived two great monastery fires.

Many Confucian works had been printed earlier, as well as a saga of the three Korean kingdoms, published in 1145, and a fuller book on the same subject which appeared in the next century. These two venerable sets of texts still remain our main source of knowledge of the peninsula's early golden age.

By then, movable metal type had made its incursion on the scene, and by the time of the *sir-hak* (practical learning) movement in the sixteenth century, which sought a modernization of Confucianism, the great Chinese philosophical classics could be published in *han-gŭl*, including a valuable seventeenth-century geographical study of the country. As *sirhak* devoted itself more and more to the promise of human rights and equality (at least, among males), the revolutionary role of *han-gŭl* and printing grew. There were "seditious" works—for land reform, popular education, and even, in the nineteenth century, a treatise on smallpox vaccination. More histories, medical volumes, political tracts, and even extraordinarily accurate maps, followed.

Han-gŭl calligraphy remains a serious art form, as Chinese calligraphy has been and still remains in Korea. Korea produced such great calligraphers as Kim Chŏng-hui, whose *ch'u-sa-ch'e* style is prized by collectors. *Ch'u-sa-ch'e* was used to brush for eternity the *han-si* poetry of China, and both Chinese and *han-gŭl* calligraphy recorded the short, sonnetlike *si-jo* (pronounced shi-jo) of the Korean language. *Han-gŭl* also popularized narrative poetry, such as that of the sixteenth-century writer Kim Sat-kat.

However, at the time of *han-gŭl*'s introduction, the Korean nation still remained largely illiterate, like hundreds of other peoples across the world. Many tongues were to embrace already existing writing systems that represented sounds, such as the Latin alphabet or Arabic script. Turkish eventually went from the latter to the former. Sejong's decision to create his own alphabet was genial.

Korean is a Ural-Altaic language, about five thousand years old, related to Mongolian, Turkish, Finnish, and Hungarian. Although it has absorbed Chinese words, much as English has absorbed Greek, it is linguistically unrelated to Chinese. Using Chinese ideographs to write a language with a different syntax or grammar—a different word order—was and is clumsy.

Korean has the same syntax as Japanese, with the verb at the end of the clause; Japanese presumably developed from common origins and partly from Korean itself.

As Chinese is still, Korean was once tonal. Today, like French, it is a monotone tongue, making it considerably easier to pronounce without mistakes. It has no articles, few particles, only a simple selection of tenses (for most conversational purposes, the present tense will do), no plurals, and none of the subject-verb agreement, gender or case problems of Indo-European tongues. On the other hand, there are, as in Japanese, different ways of speaking according to one's sex, age, and social rank, which in turn may reflect age and sex. Korean is harder to pronounce than Japanese, although not as difficult as English.

The great attraction of Korean, for a linguist, is the extraordinary logic and simplicity of *han-gŭl*. In dictionaries, telephone directories, and the like, the alphabet groups consonants first, then vowels, then diphthongs. Nothing in the Latin alphabet tells a child that *A* is a vowel and *B* a consonant, but in *han-gŭl* consonants look different from vowels.

Originally, there were twenty-eight letters; now, there are thirty-one: fourteen consonants, ten vowels, and seven diphthongs, which are simply obvious marriages of two vowels. (There are also four compound diphthongs, formed from the seven.) There is no lowercase form, so that thirty-one is the total number of letters to be learned. Each group of letters forms a syllable. A syllable can have from one to four letters, but single-letter syllables are of course vowels, and these must be preceded by a silent consonant—an *ng*.

Traditionally, writing was vertical, as in China, and syllables are still formed, not only from left to right but also vertically, from top to bottom; but today *han-gŭl* titles and sentences are written horizontally as well. Indeed, the horizontal is more commonly used in newspapers, letters, advertisements, and anything typed.

Han-gŭl not only diffused knowledge throughout the population; it conferred its own personality on the people by instilling a sense of logical order over appearances. In this respect, it may well have been the single most important thing that ever happened in Korea. The difference between Koreans and everyone else is in many ways summarized by *han-gŭl*.

It is not strictly speaking necessary to know how the letters were chosen to represent the sounds, because this knowledge provides virtually no aid to learning them today; but what looks at first like shorthand is actually both scientific and, in intention, spiritual.

Theoretically, the symbols for the consonants represent the shape of the speech organs. The letter *ga* (the hard *g* sound) illustrates the tongue blocking the throat. Its inverse, *na* (the *n* sound) is the tongue curling around to touch the upper gums. The *ma* (*m*), although square, represents joined lips. The circular *ng*, which is also the mute consonant in syllables beginning with, or simply consisting of, a vowel, outlines the tube of the throat itself. Some of the other letters are less obvious, but all, while entirely phonetic, borrow from the Chinese tradition of pictography in writing. (Readers are referred to the *han-gŭl* guide on page 257.)

Pak's literature students at Seoul National know all about the letters' resemblance to parts of the mouth. But Pak's hooded eyes twinkle as he goes on to remind them that Sejong's committee also wanted an alphabet based on cosmological principles—another inheritance from China.

There were thought to be five cosmological forces: water, wood, metal, earth, and fire, the latter being the dragon's-breath element capable of transforming all the others. Sejong's scholars decided that the throat, being moist, represented water; the molars, being plentiful and uneven, were the wood; the incisors were metal—hard and cutting; the lips, being joined to each other, were the earth, and the tongue was fire, for it was ever-mobile, and was shaped more or less like a flame.

The students watch, fascinated, as the professor draws simple vowels to show how the literati of Sejong's court thought these vowels related to paradise, earth, and man: *a*, *ya*, *u*, and *yu* have extensions on the outside of the syllable onto which they fit, so therefore they are *yang* (male) vowels; *ŏ*, *yŏ*, *o*, and *yo* have their "excrescencies" internally, so they are *yin*, female. He cites poetry again—"*Yŏrum hanami!*" (fruit abundant) mixing *yin* and *yang* (or, as Koreans say, *um* and *yang*) in words to show how this felicitous copulation makes for ecstatic vocal harmony, notably in poetry or song. Pak grins, reducing his avuncularly hooded eyes to slits, and his students titter, catching the concupiscent flavor of his reasoning, the girls with their hands to their mouths.

The three tones of old Korean appear in early *han-gŭl* scripts as diacritic dots, like the *the* and *a* of our shorthand, and originally the outward and inward extensions of a *ya* or a *yŏ* were brushed in dots. The dashes that replace them now indicate the hurried modern writer's reluctance to remove his pen from the paper any more than is necessary.

Professor Pak went to school under the Japanese occupation, and speaks Japanese, in which Chinese ideographs—*kanji*—still dominate. He is not averse to comparing the *han-gŭl* version of a poem to its Chinese-character form, then to Chinese words. This helps to illustrate to the students how different their own language is from Chinese in sound and texture, syllable structure, word formation, and syntax. The great challenge of creating beautiful sounds in an atonal tongue, with the absence of any syllabic stress, cannot be met by pictographs, and further justifies *han-gŭl*.

Before Sejong, Chinese was the official written language of the three kingdoms, Silla, Paekche, and Ko-gu-ryŏ, and later of Ko-ryŏ and early Lyi-dynasty Chosŏn. The impure Chinese used was called *idu* (clerical writing), which was systematized by the Sillan scholar Sŏl Ch'ong. Although the court literati could brush classical Chinese, the language of the village magistrate or apothecary was *idu*—an approximate equivalent of the "dog latin" of our lawyers, doctors, and priests.

Chinese script survives today, notably in literature and journalism. Where a single word-sound has more than one meaning—as with our *bough* of a tree, *bow* of respect, *bow* of a ship—the Chinese pictograph or ideograph distinguishes. In newspapers, Chinese characters say more than *han-gŭl* in less space. In both Japan and Korea, a high school pupil must learn eighteen hundred Chinese ideograms to graduate. It remains a literary snobbism to use Chinese-Korean words in preference to "plain" Korean. To Koreans, Chinese is what French was to the old aristocracies of Hungary and Russia. Moreover, the same Chinese signs represent the same things, spoken as different words, in the three great nations of East Asia; Japanese reporters could read the wall newspapers in Beijing during the Cultural Revolution, for example, even though Chinese bystanders could not understand the words that the Japanese read out.

Returning to a comparison of the Korean and Chinese languages, Professor Pak stresses that it was precisely this consciousness of the immense linguistic difference between the two tongues that prompted King Sejong, in 1443, to order the scholars of his *jip-hyŏn-jŏn* academy to produce his famous *hunmin-chŏng-ŭm* (roughly, "everyman's correct sounds"). Sejong, who took an active part in his committee's work and who is also noted for other intellectual achievements, could hardly have guessed that, five and a half centuries later, Korea would be a much poorer country than the then obscure barbaries of Japan and Europe, or than the sparsely populated American continent beyond Japan, and yet be more literate than any of them, or than China; 99.6 percent of Koreans can now read and write.

When the *jip-hyŏn-jŏn* had finished its labors, three years later, Sejong, Pak recalls, announced it to his people in an eloquent little speech which excused *han-gŭl's* simplicity compared to the classical script of Cathay; then, he ordered that the two hundred forty-eight poems and one hundred twenty-five cantos of the famous *yong-bi-ŏ-ch'ŏn-ga*, or Flying Dragons' Songs, be rewritten in the script of the people.

The scholarly monarch had his critics, notably the literary star of the day, Ch'oe Mal-li. He and others complained that *han-gŭl* lacked the sophistication of Chinese script and said that using it would reduce Koreans to the level of the Japanese, with their sixty-letter *kana*, or of the Mongol "barbarians" and the tribal people of the Asian interior.

For three more reigns, Pak reminds his students, the literati clung to Chinese ideograms, regarding *han-gŭl* as "womanscript"; Sejong's own son, Sejo, who ruled from 1445 to 1468, eventually forced his father's achievement on the nobility and the priesthood, who agreed to use *han-gŭl* as well as Chinese characters, but professional writers still shunned the new system.

Korea's repression by the Japanese in the first half of the present century was the deciding factor that finally convinced even members of the young intelligentsia, like the future Professor Pak, that *han-gŭl* was the soul of the nation. *Han-gŭl* Day—October 9—dates only from 1945; and it was shortly afterward that the first *han-gŭl* typewriter appeared—sure evidence that one could write anything in Korean without using Chinese.

Korea's language and alphabet reflect the culture, the style, the graces, the restraints—many of which remain astonishingly unchanged in the era of the skyscraper. Human relations remain Confucian, albeit Koreanly so, in both the positive and negative aspects of Kung-Fu's reasonings—the age and sex rankings, sibling diplomacy, the matriarchy of mothers-in-law, the complex interplay of relations between man and woman.

The structure of family relations overflows into the office, where ranks take on a sort of Confucian significance, cross-referenced, as it were—as everywhere else in the Confucian world—by age. As in Japan, few white-collar workers take their full vacation entitlement—although this may change in the current flux period of political spring. For the moment, much as Koreans love to travel and to play, talk of vacations still sounds frivolous. Except for honeymoons, many clerks prefer to forego vacations as such, then feign a visit to a sick relative—who happens to live near a beach, of course.

The stoicism of the Confucian work ethic, inevitably more male than female, is used to rationalize the belief that women are less suited than men to managerial and other responsible positions. Indeed, given the culture and the feelings of contemporary East Asian women, this argument is at least partly true, and the rare exceptions tend to prove it. A man would not go home before his boss, but a woman can do so, because she has household and perhaps maternal duties to fulfill which no male boss would dare expect her to set aside.

The stranger within the walls of the Korean nation is permitted a little leeway, because before he became the country's erstwhile rescuer and preceptor in technology, he was traditionally a *sang-nom*, a nonperson. But he must for the most part abide by the prevailing cultural mores. Change, perhaps reform, is not the stranger's business, here as elsewhere. Only when West meets East and marries does a compromise evolve, particularly when—as is almost invariably the case—the

Western element is male. There will probably be separate checkbooks, for instance, rather than the wifely ministry of family finance; and few Western husbands would want the burden of taking all family decisions alone. It would make little sense to marry an Asian woman if one wanted a home run on Western principles, and little sense for her to marry a Westerner if she wanted the sort of life her mother lived.

Whatever pertains within his walls, the transplanted Westerner must accept that, without, Confucian life is a little like army life: rankings must not be disregarded. Just as you bow and concede to superiors, so you do not inflict your comradeship on inferiors. As in our own world a few generations ago, everybody knows his place. Just as the glass partition in the Rolls Royce protects the chauffeur from patronizing monologues more than it maintains the secrecy of business conversations in the back seat, so caste has its compensations. After all, must officers not ask permission to enter the messes and clubs of sergeants? Would one not want to discourage them from coming too often? Job titles are important in Korea. In our own world, they are often meaningless: "vice president for marketing" may simply mean senior salesman; "executive assistant" may mean manager's typist; "director of human resources" is probably chief personnel clerk; the shameless hype is often used to compensate for inadequate salaries. In Korea, job titles are as accurate as rank markings—protective devices, useful guides to the avoidance of face-losing errors.

The touchstone is humility, possession of which precludes humiliation. Everyone's dignity must be preserved, even in defeat; Koreans are almost as good as Japanese in not vulgarizing their victories or personalizing their disagreements, although this skill was pressed close to breaking point in the course of the overlong 1987 electoral campaign. A culture which can put a hundred thousand demonstrators into the streets, and suffer only one death—then call fresh demonstrations to denounce that single breach of demo etiquette—also produces authoritarian leaders and opponents who sting each other in phrases that are almost gentle, and who rebound with genuine horror when a careless epithet slips through. The emphasis is on grace, but—given the Korean blend of grace with passion—grace is not always passive. There have been slugfests in the august Korean parliament which provoke justifiable scorn in Nippon, and street squabbles are now all too common. The stress on harmony is not as great as in Japan; but it remains the ideal.

There is much bonhomie among Koreans, but little or no spurious geniality which in the West is a style of politeness. Meetings between strangers begin, as do meetings between family or friends, with the peaceful exchange of mutual respect—the bow. Useless conversation about spelling and telephone numbers and uncertainties as to who does what is circumvented by the simple exchange of cards. Just as a Westerner who is not functionally illiterate would feel naked without a pen, so one does not venture far in Seoul without a substantial supply of visiting cards.

From there, a meeting of business associates proceeds slowly and surely—with equal emphasis on both words. The Western style of negotiation resembles a dirndl skirt, constantly turning back on itself in seemingly predetermined pleats and, even though making progress, using more yards of time than are necessary. In contrast, Korean negotiation moves cautiously but inexorably, and only when it is not going to succeed does it shift into neutral; it soon becomes apparent that this is to save the face of all concerned. Anything causing humiliation could serve no useful purpose, but might easily do indelible harm. Because a negotiation has not succeeded does not mean that one party or the other has failed; rather, it signifies that both sides have failed, so that no one has any advantage in advertising the fact. In Europe, it is said that if you dismiss an employee, it means not only that he has not worked out, but that you were guilty of misjudgment in persuading him to take the job when he might have been more successful somewhere else; this old Latin axiom has its parallel in many Korean matters besides employment.

Except when dealing with criminals, one never directly accuses someone of a fault, such as incompetence or dishonesty. One never reprimands anyone in front of others, especially that person's inferiors. There is as much need for a good mood, *ki-bun*, in the workplace as in the home.

Once a functional relationship exists, loyalty is as important as other forms of integrity. Where friendship exists, loyalty is naturally even more of a requirement. This in turn requires as strict a rein on the emotions as possible; and when this breaks down, Koreans are at least aware of their shortcomings. Women are allowed to be more emotional than men: it is one of the privileges of inferiority within any system.

When a Korean presents you to friends or colleagues, it is unlikely that he will mention your name. This is not because he's afraid of pronouncing it wrong, but because names are considered very private things, not to be distributed to third parties by others. He will probably gesture politely to invite you to introduce yourself, which is always done with visiting cards at the ready. Even if they don't normally carry cards, foreigners traveling alone—including women—need them in Korea. Japan Air Lines, if given sufficient notice, will supply visiting cards printed in Japanese, with the traveler's own language on the reverse side, but as yet no such service exists for visitors to Korea; so it's a good idea to have cards printed in *han-gŭl* and your native tongue before you depart. If you live in a country with a Korean community, there will be *han-gŭl* printing facilities somewhere.

A LIFE IN WORDS AND RULES AND GRACES

Who speaks first in introducing themselves? Naturally, it is the older or more senior in rank or class, if this is detectible. To be correct, you should step one pace back and bow, mumble your name, and modestly offer your card with your right hand to his left. The other person will do the same. There may be another semblance of a bow. If both parties are already seated when all this takes place, it is enough to shuffle slightly in reverse to indicate that you would have stepped back apace if you had been standing.

If you are meeting a complete stranger, rather than someone you had planned to meet for business or social reasons, it's a nice touch if you draw breath with awe when you read his card, with the implication, "A real assistant manager? How impressive!" Of course, always be ready for the Korean who, after a steady diet of *Dallas* and Hollywood movies, seeks to impress watching Koreans by grabbing your arm and saying "Hi! I'm . . ."

Names are not used much, for anything except documents. They are personal property, to be handled with respect. One does not usually sign documents, which would be too extravagant a gift: one takes out one's *to-jang* and appends one's chop. Modern life has made more frequent use of names inevitable, and the military, wearing nameplates on their breasts like French grocery tags ("Pure pork"), have helped in this vulgarization. In classy hotels and restaurants, it is now customary for the staff to wear such plastic labels, although it is noticeable that many omit their given names: they would be even more offended than a European to be addressed by a stranger using their given names, even though some Korean family names are so frequently encountered as to make given names a distinguishing necessity. In such cases, use all three names.

Names may, of course, be used to identify persons not present; but once again, one should try to stick to family names or full names and, if possible, avoid using given names alone. For instance, you would refer to your fiancée not as "Mi-na" or even "Ryi Mi-na-*ssi*," but rather as "Ryi-*ssi*," or "Miss Ryi." And when you arrive at the office, don't say "Peace be with you, Mr. Pak." Just "Peace be with you" is more polite. Even better would be: "Peace be with you, Deputy Assistant Training Manager." After all, in our own culture, we would rarely greet an armed services officer without adding "Colonel," or whatever. Koreans, more like Britons than Americans, dearly love a title.

In the confines of the home, a man will begin speaking to his wife by saying "*Yŏbo*," but the meaning is more in the tone than the word. Don't attract her attention in this way outdoors, however, because the inevitable rise in tone makes it an imperative: "Listen!"—about as subtle as, say, calling a porter. If you are dealing with an idiot who is wasting your time, you can "put him in his place" without resorting to colorful epithets, by simply announcing "*Yŏbo!*" in a raised voice. This implies: "Now shut up and listen to me!" (This is not recommended if the idiot is a black belt in *t'ae-kwŏn-do*.)

Koreans, like Americans, are enormously deferential to powerful politicians. The head of government is referred to, *even behind his back*, as "his excellency," much as White House staff will mention "the president" with awe. This is in sharp contrast to, say, Britain, Canada, Australia, or India, where the top executive is called "P.M.," with no *Mr.* or *Mrs.*, to his or her face, by messengers, newspaper reporters, and ambassadors alike, and is referred to in his or her absence by the choicest nicknames. In a rowdy Korean campaign speech, the opposition can "put down" an incumbent president by referring to him by name, which has roughly the same connotation as an American policeman's referring to "the individual."

At least as much as in the West, flattery is legal tender in Korea. As in the West, it is only believed by fools—but equally expected, nevertheless. A Korean will smilingly call you *Yangban*, much as an American will say "Doctor," an Italian "Professor," or the stranger you meet in an English pub may call you "Squire." It is safe to call writers and teachers *Paksa* (Doctor). If you find yourself in disagreement with someone, you may get him to concede gracefully by addressing him as *Paksa*, since this virtually obliges him to show upper-class restraint. When two or more real *paksa* are gathered together, the younger professors will call their senior *Son-saeng*—elder. Professors call students *Kun*, as in *Ch'oi-kun*. They would address a male garbage collector in the same way. However, a child or the modern equivalent of a serf—say, a beggar or a shoeshine—is called *Yae*.

Given names are used in the family, where they belong—in private. They can be used between very close friends, with the addition of *ssi* (pronounced *sshi*)—much as if, say, two best friends in an American elementary school called each other "Mr. James" and "Mr. Leonard." Normally, great efforts are made to avoid the use of given names, much as polite Standard English requires the use of *one* rather than *you*, as in "One has to do one's best." It's all much easier once parenthood is achieved. Thereafter, Mom and Dad refer to each other in their absence as "Hwan-du's father" or "Hwan-du's mother." This is, in fact, how most Koreans, especially women, are referred to. In France, the colonel's wife is *la colonelle*, and later *la générale*, but in Korea she would remain "Jean-Pierre's mother," regardless of her husband's ascent through the hierarchy. However, as in French, children and household pets in Korea are treated familiarly by everyone of any class, much as slaves in the Old South could refer to young massa and his sister by their first names.

Servants, if young, can be called by their given names. Fathers use first names with children, adding *-ya*, a term of endearment which is also added to the name of the family dog or cat. Alternatively, *ya* can be used on its own. Much as toothless American geriatrics sometimes refer to their arthritic wives as "my bride," so Korean wives may refer humorously to their husbands, however mature, as "my groom" (*sŏ-bang-nim*). Because grooms are always expected to get drunk at their weddings, in Korea as in most other parts of the world, the village drunk may be known by this word, as in *Chung-sŏ-bang*—Chung the (eternally drunk) bridegroom.

Normally, as noted, a man refers to his wife as so-and-so's mother, naming the eldest son or, if there are no sons, the eldest daughter, while the wife will use a host of expressions to identify her husband without bandying his name about in public. The most popular means "the man of our house," but rural and older wives still say "the outside gentleman." This term, which originally referred to the occupant of the outside room of the traditional compound, has survived the move to city apartments.

A man forced to make mention of his wife to someone else will likewise use any of more than half a dozen words for *wife*, according to whether he is speaking to his boss, a colleague, a close friend or relative, or someone to whom one should "talk down," such as a deliveryman or bank clerk. The most flattering description is "mother of my children" (even if there are none, as yet). But you would not use this to the president of the corporation, nor would your driver thus identify his spouse, just as a British cabbie would probably not talk to his fare of "my wife" or "Mrs. Smith" but of "the missus" or "my ol' woman." Foreigners who have learned some Korean often make the mistake of referring to their wives by the most respectful term, thinking that this translates Western ideals of equality; what it is taken to mean, of course, is that the Westerner is treating the corporation president as though he were a waiter.

Naturally, in speaking of someone else's wife, flattery is in order. The boss's wife is *yo-sa*. The next most respectful term is *pu-in*. Once again, to speak of one's own wife in this way would be pretentious. *Samonim* is polite, but most ordinary working-class people modestly refer to their wife as "the aunt" or, eventually, "the grandmother."

Some of the worst mistakes that male foreigners make come from copying the vocabulary of their Korean wives. Not only are feminine expressions different from masculine ones, but the Korean wife may be of a younger generation. She may, for instance, call a waiter *ajŏssi* (uncle), which would sound silly coming from her husband—who should use a talk-down expression, as he would in most European tongues.

A person in a subordinate position may, however, address a client as "uncle" or even, if he wants to be truly flattering, *ha-ra-bŏ-ji* (grandfather). How could anyone not be well disposed toward his volunteer grandchild? Many Western women, however, find it difficult to feel honored by being addressed as *hal-mŏ-ni* (grandma) by young Koreans anxious to show respect to the American or European executive's wife. One addresses an elder who is a real friend (and, consequently, is equal in every respect but age) as *hyŏng-min* (elder brother). When speaking of him in his absence, it is preferable to add a polite *-ssi* at the end, like the *-san* in Japanese.

Not surprisingly, given all these complications (which are dying out), nicknames are especially popular—most of them being derogatory. They are never used to the person's face.

How does a more rough-and-ready society like America's, of predominantly proletarian origins, function in this rarified ether? Imperfectly, of course. Fortunately, the little discourtesies of foreigners tend to be forgiven. They are, after all, not outcasts but out-caste, which is convenient. Their loud voices—perhaps their most obvious irritant to a Korean—are scorned as risible rather than condemned for their vulgarity. Confucianism and Buddhism concur with Christianity or Islam that the "bottom line" in any religion is humanism.

Korea's life-style, its "system," is above all reassuringly predictable and logical. There are few well-intentioned bad surprises. For instance, the old joke about three blenders or four coffee makers among the wedding gifts is not told here, where no one would presume to decide what the newlyweds need in their kitchen. Korean weddings are a young couple's dream: all the guests bring money, left in envelopes marked with the donor's name and a greeting, on a table at the entrance to the wedding hall, or wherever the traditional ceremony is being held.

To add to the tastefulness of the system, gifts are not opened in front of the giver. The wine you bring to a dinner at someone's home will be appreciated—at some later date. If you happen to receive a gift for your birthday, express your thanks, not too profusely, and do not open the package. To avoid requiring recipients to feel grateful in the donor's presence, Koreans may simply leave gifts somewhere where the recipient will find them later. For instance, in hotels, although tipping is not customary, there is one exception: the thousand-*wŏn* bill (about a dollar) left for the grossly underpaid chambermaid. This modest bounty is not handed to her, which would force her to extend her right hand, with the left hand holding the right wrist, in acknowledgment; it is hidden under the pillow, where it will be found when she makes up the bed. As in Japan, where the gift is in proportion to the length of stay (and can be conferred in person, provided it is concealed in an envelope and you apologize for not giving more), it is given within twenty-four hours of arrival. In short, it is not a post facto gratuity, but an encouragement. This is, after all, a society in which businessmen exchange gifts in the expectation of profitable relations, in the same way that we in the West exchange hospitality.

The survival in the culture of what anthropologists call "reciprocity and exchange" inevitably raises the point, as it would in the West, of what sort of a gift constitutes bribery, in business dealings; but the extent of this problem in Korea has probably been exaggerated. The basic rule of thumb is twofold: think carefully before *refusing* a gift, since such a gesture must be insulting; and try only to accept a gift which you can more or less reciprocate. If someone gives you a beautiful scroll of calligraphy in the hope that you will give his son a job, you have a clear choice: either give the boy a job or give his father some reciprocal collectible.

Gifts should always be wrapped. The envelope containing your financial donation to a wedding should bear your name and the Chinese character for happiness. If it's a funeral, it should be the character for sorrow.

In the West, if one wants to say "no" without offense, one says "I'll think about it," which is true in a way, or "I'll call you," which may or may not be true. In Korea, one usually says "*Ne*" (yes) which, like "Yeah, yeah" and Japan's "*Hai*," means only that you have heard everything that has been said to you. As in the politer cultures of the West, there would be no more point in saying no than there would be in trying to think of a way to start an argument.

The real basis of all this is that everyone is beholden and no one should feel beholden: the poor do not simply receive, but give in return whatever is theirs to give—in the chambermaid's case, satisfaction, courteous and smiling service. American men often complain that European women never seem to offer to pay a restaurant bill; and since machismo and femininity are more evident in the Orient, one might expect a Korean woman to exploit her inferior status in the culture even more. This is not so. One consideration in giving gifts or even extending invitations is that they could be a burden, because they are sure to be matched in some fashion. Gifts are exchanged constantly. Korean life is a study in reciprocity.

In the West, we bring wine to a friend's house when invited to dinner, but we would not think of bringing a gift if we only went to his home for a chat. In Korea, one invariably brings something to every visit, as a souvenir of one's passage—flowers, food, a gadget. I remember a very poor man calling briefly on me once, and leaving a cheap ballpoint pen—something he knew a writer would always welcome. One of the safest small gifts to bring these days seems to be fruit juice. If one is bringing a real gift, something that has required some time and thought to buy, it is good manners to apologize for its insignificance, whatever its value. This is not arrogant false modesty—it is intended to relieve the recipient from feeling indebted. Thank-you notes—for a gift, a dinner, or anything else—are not sent. Gifts are, after all, only good manners, nothing more, and require no more than spoken thanks. A Korean bride and groom can gather up all those envelopes, take the money, and run.

One final point about gifts: if you visit friends or relatives at Chu-sŏk, the harvest festival, the appropriate gift is food or drink. Fruit is universally popular: where else in the world do groups of men gather to get drunk on Friday night, and order huge plates of cunningly carved pears and apples to munch as they tipple? Today, the "in" small gift is a bottle of whisky—scotch, of course.

In the West, children, like wedding couples, frequently get things they already have or don't especially want, but not Korean children: like brides, children are invariably given what they really want—money. For a housewarming, everyone brings candles and matches: but, there again, a bottle of scotch in addition would not be unwelcome.

Those who need a more thorough guide to Korean etiquette are recommended to read Paul Crane's *Korean Patterns*.

If one Korean virtue is more admirable than any other, it is the intense respect for privacy. Even in the days before the telephone, one never arrived at the house of another unexpected or unannounced, unless it was a matter of life and death. Today, privacy is respected as much as modern life allows, and *ki-bun* is left undamaged. For example, you call on your boss, and find him sleeping off a hangover. You cough and walk over to the window to admire the view. He winds himself up, straightens his clothing and combs his hair, then gives a cough of his own. Ah, there you are! It's true that this could also happen in the West; but in Korea something of this sense of respecting face is *required.*

Another virtue which seems to have survived is trust. As in Japan, it is the height of vulgarity to count one's change. True, there might be a mistake—but it might be in your favor, no?

As in Africa, entertaining of guests in Korea should always be—or appear to be—more lavish than the host can really afford. A Korean might hesitate to become involved in unnatural responsibilities by saving the life of a stranger, but he would not hesitate to go modestly into debt to entertain him. As in restaurants, any emptied plate will usually be replenished; if you do not want more, leave some food uneaten. If you are the guest, don't wait to be invited to do the obvious: serve yourself first. If you have enjoyed what you have eaten, take more. Your gluttony will be appreciated as praise. Waiting to be asked to take more implies that you are only taking a second helping out of politeness.

Cover your mouth to use a toothpick. If hot pepper makes it necessary to clear your nostrils, go to the toilet. Don't use your fingers to eat anything, unless Koreans present do so; almost anything can be eaten with chopsticks or a spoon, or by drinking it from a bowl, cup, or glass. Eat sandwiches with a knife and fork. As with wine, beer, etc., don't pour your own soy sauce; wait for someone else to do so—then pour his or hers.

As in France, invitations to a home are rare. Hosts usually prefer the expense of inviting you to a restaurant. Also as in France, there is a time for eating and a time for talking. Conversation at meals should be light and mostly about the food. Indigestible business discussions are not recommended at private soirées or in restaurants. Perhaps as a result of this, there are no prolonged musings over after-dinner drinks; dinner parties, like religious services, end rather abruptly.

Dividing a bill is considered coarse; only one person pays. The stylistic fight for the privilege of picking up the check is accepted, indeed fairly common, but of course the invited guest will not be allowed to pay. The next time will be your turn, after another mannerly dispute at the cash desk. (Even in quality *sik dang*, bills are not settled at the table; waiters and waitresses handle food and therefore need clean hands; money tends to be dirty, so waiters never touch the stuff.)

Because unexpected visits are very rare, invitations are carefully thought out in advance. Entertaining remains formal. You may even get a speech of welcome, which will include obligatory phrases about the inadequacy of the house and the paucity of victuals the host has to offer. Later, you can express your approval by slurping or even belching.

When Koreans relax, they relax. The hilarious scene in the film *Network* in which Faye Dunaway, as the ultimate business bitch, talks "shop" in bed up to the moment of orgasm, and resumes her line of thought shortly afterward, is unlikely ever to happen in Asia, if indeed it ever happens in Europe.

Before this century, the social pecking order in Korea was at least as varied as that of a military unit. The "good people" who ranked below the *yang-ban* were grouped into three main castes—the *chung-in*, or bourgeoisie, the *sang-in*, or yeomanry, and the *ch'ŏn-min*, or serfs.

The civilian or "eastern" branch of the *yang-ban* caste was itself subdivided into nine ranks, with each rank in turn divided into two. At each rank level, the military or "western" branch of the *yang-ban* was subservient to the civilian or "eastern" branch. Ranks were determined by the Confucian civil service examinations. Today's visitors to the K'yŏng-bok Palace in Seoul will see, in front of the great hall, the rank stones of the king's ministers, commanding the distance at which each of them were to stand from him.

With rank went land, whose peasantry provided food and taxes for their liege. The peasantry, the artisans, and the merchants composed the yeomanry. Both they and the serfs could be conscripted in time of war.

The yeomanry and the serfs, the two lower orders, contained much of the talent in the country, as well as genuine laborers. Like the literati at the higher end of the social scale, they wrote the poetry. They also built the temples. The lower orders were particularly extensive, and included priests and shamans, *ki-saeng* hostesses, other entertainers, butchers, grave diggers, and slaves, including slaves of the state acquired by war. Reducing monks to the lower orders was probably what most helped Buddhism to survive. (Our "princes of the Church" in their Dior gowns emulate Jesus and his dozen illiterate fishermen even less when they are viewed from a Buddhist monastery—which still shares Christ's distaste for the bourgeoisie.)

Sterling services to the kingdom could occasionally lead to a rise in rank, but for the most part status was hereditary. Like white South Africans today, the Brahmins of Chosŏn were not inclined to dilute their ranks. Exceptionally, someone of the *chung-in* class—and, very exceptionally, even a boy of lower birth—was admitted to the magisterial examinations. Intermarriage between castes was forbidden; when infringements occurred, the principal punishment fell on the lower caste. Virtually all social intercourse between castes was repressed— except, of course, between *yang-ban* and other gentry and the *ki-saeng*, whose children's rank was contingent upon whether their fathers adopted them or not; this in turn inevitably depended on whether the mother could irrefragably identify the father.

The clan was the source of strength of its members, and a patriarch, even of the lowest caste, enjoyed considerable respect from his legion. Genealogical studies were of great moment, especially among the higher orders, and clan members would establish a shrine to a common ancestor, if one was known. Because of exogamy, women always became the human property of different clans from the ones whose names they bore.

The magisterial examinations were essentially literary, devoted to memorization of the Confucian classics and history, thus encouraging rote learning rather than cerebral initiative. There were also tests of mathematics, astronomy, medicine, and Chinese. Many successful candidates were students of the Sŏng-gyun-gwan Academy, mentioned in the previous chapter; it was established by royal decree in 1398 and had numerous local branches. Private tutors established *sŏ-wŏn*, to which one proceeded from preparatory establishments called *sŏ-dang*.

Agriculture was the backbone of the system, the plasma of the ruling classes. Commerce was disdained. Although a monetary economy existed, with bronze coins, most merchants were peddlers, and for centuries, most markets relied on barter. Provincial markets opened every five days, but the larger towns had full-time bazaars. When the nation withdrew into itself in the Lyi era, some border trade continued with China, but there was little other foreign trade, with Japan or the rest of the world.

Where the caste system broke down, to some extent, along with the derogatory attitude to trade, was in the relationship between upper-class men and lower-class women. The *ki-saeng* houses of Korea, which are thought to date from the eighth century or even earlier, long preceded the creation of the *gei* quarters of Japan.

The extensive civil service spent much of their time on the road (more accurately, on the pony track), and the government set up *ki-saeng* houses one day's travel apart. The *ki-saeng*, like their better-known geisha imitators, learned to play musical instruments, sing, and dance. They wrote or read poetry, painted, drew calligraphs. They were sophisticated listeners. They were also, in earlier centuries, courtesans. A successful *ki-saeng* amassed savings and set up house on her own. Some were staked in these operations by admirers.

Professor David McCann and others cite the case of Hwang Chi-ni, a stylish writer of *si-jo* poetry in Ko-ryŏ. She signed her work Blue Mountain, comparing herself in verse to mountains past which rivers of men flowed ceaselessly. However, unlike rivers, some of this clientele clearly flowed back again; according to Jon Covell, her regular admirers included a governor of Kaesŏng, a learned Buddhist priest who had never before sacrificed his celibacy, and a noted philosopher named Hwa-dan. This was in an age when Buddhism held sway rather than Confucianism, and women were markedly freer in Ko-ryŏ than they were to become under the more rigidly Confucian Lyi dynasty. Hwang Chi-ni retired at thirty, as her physical assets began to wane.

It was not until the eighteenth century that Sin (pronounced Shin) Yun-bok, who sometimes signed his work Hye-won, was to match Hiroshige and Utamaro across the waters in depicting courtesan life in lithographs. Many of his pale-colored pictures are in the private Kam-song Museum in Seoul, but replicas often appear on the walls of modern hotels.

The *ki-saeng*, like the noble courtesans of Japan, played a major role in popularizing poetry. They were noted composers of *si-jo* poetry, and also wrote narratives, the best known being Hwang Chi-ni's *Tale of Ch'un-hyang*. McCann (in an essay included in the anthology *Korean Women*) has identified about thirty *ki-saeng* who wrote poetry and prose under their own names, along with many anonymous bedchamber poets. Asian courtesans, unlike most of their Western counterparts, tended to fall in love—usually of the unrequited variety, which inspired poetry and song, the forerunners of today's *nun-mul* music. Although *si-jo* are quite different in composition, they share with the *haiku* of Japan the three-line format and the preoccupation with scenes and seasons. But unlike the *haiku*, the *si-jo* are meant to be sung; singing remains, today, a more highly prized art form in Korea than in probably any other Asian country. Perhaps more than anyone else, it was the *ki-saeng* who helped King Sejong's drive for literature to be written in *han-gŭl*. According to Covell, it was not until Kim Manjung in the eighteenth century that male writers of any note abandoned Chinese ideograms in favor of *han-gŭl* script.

Today's *ki-saeng*, like Japan's geisha, are among the most independent women in East Asian cultures. Like the geisha, they have long ago ceased to sell sexual favors. Given the role of music and art in the *ki-saeng* houses, these can rarely have resembled the sordidness of France's *maisons closes* or Britain's stews. The work was servitude of a sort, and it had no future, in most cases; but it may well have seemed an attractive alternative to family life at the lowest levels, especially in the Lyi era. Today, however, the profession is dying out.

About three centuries ago, as the isolation of the Hermit Kingdom set in, Korean girls began to go into purdah early. Brothers and sisters were separated at the age of seven when, in the upper classes, male education began. Seven years later, a son or daughter was married, sight unseen, to a spouse selected by the parents. As the Lyi era advanced, it became the custom for the wife to move into her husband's parents' house, and into the purdah of the *an-bang*, or "inner room," that the womenfolk shared, far from the *sarang-bang* of the senior male members of the family, which was the only room in the compound directly accessible from the outside.

Often, in all classes, there was *min-myŏ-nu-ri*—child-bride marriage. Usually at the age of six or seven, the little girl would be taken from her family, her maidenhood still symbolized by the single hair-braid down her back, and placed under the tutelage of her often formidable future mother-in-law. In a few cases, after a betrothal ceremony (involving, of course, dowry payment to her father), she was allowed to return home. There, her mother would put her hair up in a *ch'ok* to signify that she was, in effect, already someone's wife. Most often, however, the bride-to-be became a prisoner in her new home, teased by the other children of the village because her mother-in-law had put her hair in a spousal *ch'ok*. The prospective groom was almost always adult already, sometimes middle-aged.

The late Professor Youngsook Kim-Harvey, in an essay also included in *Korean Women*, related how she had questioned many old women who still cried when they remembered their betrothal years, although sometimes the forced marriages had been happy ones. Ko-ryŏ had discouraged the practice of child brides, which some of the kings regarded as tantamount to slavery. Fiction about *min-myŏ-nu-ri* often has a Cinderella flavor—a beautiful family member treated as a servant, and treated badly. Administrative disapproval continued into the early Lyi period, when the permissible marriage age was raised to twelve. If this sounds like a normal age for puberty or adolescence, it must be remembered that Korean children are born at the "age" of one, and become a year older every New Year's Day, so that "twelve-year-olds" may be anything from eleven to just over ten by normal math. Grooms must have been impatient, and the pattern seems to have been that brides were wed and deflowered shortly after puberty.

It was in this later, hermit-kingdom Lyi period that divorce became more frequent, although the failure to bear sons could often be remedied by adopting one, sometimes a son-in-law. Adopted sons were usually adults, and the country's doomsday book indicates that the majority were in their twenties. According to Professor Mark Peterson, adoption was so common that fifteen percent of those taking the civil service examinations were adoptive sons. Curiously, an adopted son could do *chesa*—commemorating his nonbiological "ancestors," despite his different family name. Wives, although preserving their father's name, were buried with their husband's—who would, of course, need them in a shaman heaven. They were commemorated with their husband as the instrument for preserving his lineage. As with the Christian concept of heaven, a husband who died at thirty was expected to have no problem cohabiting with his wife who died at eighty.

Peterson says that Confucianism, after becoming state doctrine under the first Lyi *t'ae-jo* in the late fourteenth century, became the sole criterion for statecraft in the course of the century that followed. It was consolidated in the sixteenth century, but only really affected family life so completely in the seventeenth century, which saw the birth of the "hermit kingdom."

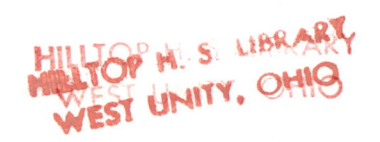

Before that time, all sons and daughters inherited equally, with no concern for sex or primogeniture. In the "hermit" era, women lost the right to inherit from their fathers who, if they had no son, would adopt one to ensure that they and their forebears would be propitiated by *chesa*. It was, indeed, the lineage factor that militated against the former, pragmatic practice of widow remarriage, since children under the same roof but belonging to different father-clans would produce a sort of Confucian confusion. In recompense, a chaste widow was rewarded after death by a *yŏl*, a memorial tablet, in her village. One attraction of Christianity (and subsequent syncretistic cults) to older women was removal of the barrier to widow remarriage.

In the traditional household, women served the males their food, leaving them to eat alone, dining themselves on what remained. In most Korean homes, this is still the case today—and with the older generations it is probable that the women would not want things changed too much. At night, a curfew was supposed to keep men off the streets, so that women could venture abroad and meet each other. They were, however, well advised not to do this too often, lest their husbands become suspicious. In Seoul, the great Chong-no bell was tolled at eight P.M. to clear the thoroughfares of men until daybreak. But aristocratic women could go abroad in daylight in their curtained palanquins, and their female servants could be observed walking barefaced beside them. Higher-class women, when outside, even at night, wore a shawl from head to toe that resembled a veil.

These Confucian principles weighed most heavily on the privileged women. The yeoman's wife and daughters worked the fields, unconcerned about being visible. Yeoman and serf women brought water from the wells, and lascivious Christian missionaries noted in their narratives that, when they raised their arms to balance the pitchers on their heads, the space between their short jackets and their pantaloons and skirts revealed their naked breasts.

Women were essentially, however—especially in the higher classes—under the thumb of their husbands and their in-laws. The higher the rank, the more hobbled they were. Today, similarly, it is the husbands of the middle or upper class who feel the most diminished if their wives take jobs. To some extent, the psychology of the "inner room" persists. Korean men probably work harder than any people on earth. They come home late, and expect to find the women waiting.

101

When Dr. Horace Allen of the United States first practiced medicine in Seoul in 1884, he acquired Queen Min as a patient; but custom forbade him to see her. To allow him to examine her, she passed her arm through a hole in a screen, but the hand was gloved, and ribbons bound her wrist except for the small area needed to feel the pulse. She put her tongue through another hole for the foreign medic to take a peek. Somehow, from this and from questions—through the screen, of course—Allen managed to be accurate enough in his diagnoses and prescriptions to be invited back.

In the first churches, the female side of the aisle was hidden from the male side by a curtain of blankets hung from lines, and the priest would preach from the male side. Girls were baptized through a hole in a cloth which revealed only the silky black dome of their heads. The obsession with the female anatomy invites obvious comparison with that of Islam and Orthodox Judaism.

A century ago, in 1886, what is now Ewha Women's University was a school seeking pupils. However, asking girls to go to school in Korea was about as respectable as asking them to dance the can-can in the West. Covell records that Ewha's first pupil was a royal concubine who wanted to be trained as the Queen's English interpreter. The second was a starving girl attracted by the free food and board; the third, a victim of cholera left by her family to die outside the gates of Seoul.

Ewha grew; but male teachers lectured from behind a screen until 1892, when it was regarded as sufficient if they simply turned their back to the class and addressed the blackboard. The girls turned their backs as the teacher entered the room, lest he be seized by lust at the sight of all those naked faces. He would take his seat, with his back to them, then cough to cue them that they could now turn around. The first "coed" classes in 1904 sparked angry editorials.

A LIFE IN WORDS AND RULES AND GRACES

Through the long centuries of Lyi purdah, while Korea awaited enlightenment on this point from the West, the *ki-saeng* represented feminine independence, and as did the witches, the *mansin*: although also of the lowest caste, they were the doctors and seers, their services in demand by all, from royals down. Their close relations with the dead and the gods made them people to be feared and respected, at all cost not offended. Says Professor Martina Deuchler: "The Confucian founders of the Yi dynasty confronted a strong shaman tradition. Confucian officialdom viewed the shaman as a dangerous manipulator who subjected the rational human world to the irrational, and therefore unpredictable, world of the spirits." The *mudang* were barred from large towns. But shamanism remained strong—as it does today, even under the successive juntas of South Korea and the rigidly ideological regime of the North.

Given the seminal role of the *mudang* in the culture, the geishalike importance of the *ki-saeng*, and the unconventional roles of Korean women in fishing communities—in a country with eleven thousand miles of coastline—it is not surprising that some have argued that Korea is a country of witches and concubines, in which power itself radiates from the *an-bang*, the "inner room" of the old compounds where only the women lived.

"In the palace," says Dr. Laurel Kendall, "women worked their wiles for good or ill from behind the scenes. . . . Scheming concubines . . . plotted sorcery with avaricious female shamans." Early missionaries noted that the very real subjection of a woman was counterbalanced by her actual influence, which one priest commented was "out of all proportion to her theoretical position in society." At the levels where power lay, the alluring concubine could become the intriguer-consort and perhaps eventually the despotic mother-in-law. Behind the screen of coy politeness, many early travelers found that Korean women could be abusive, even violent. But all agreed that the *chesa* role of men in ancestor veneration, especially in the case of eldest sons, was a counterpoint to the power of the *mansin*, and especially to her power over other women. In the world of occult politics, the *mansin*, in return, could use the spirits to enhance the role of a wife's ancestors in the travails and fortunes of a family.

The hereditary *mudang* followed, and follows, a sort of gypsy occupation, predicting the future, decreeing where a house should be built and in which direction it should face, and so on. But the charismatic *mansin*, or *naerim mudang*, who will be looked at more closely in the next chapter, is a flying horse of a different color. She has a vocation, announced in girlhood by the anorexic *sin-byŏng* sickness. She is Fatima and Bernadette and Agnes of God and the Dragon Lady. But the ordinary housewife, by her control of the budgeting of her husband's earnings, her sole ownership of whatever pin-money she makes from market gardening, embroidery, thrift association (*kye*) membership, and even usury, is certainly not without resources.

4

A LIFE WITH THE SPIRITS

O SU-NA RISES EARLY IN SUBURBAN YŎNG-DONG. A heavy mist hangs over the Han-gang as she takes the bus across the bridge to the downtown area where she works as a clerk in the huge Dae-u Building facing Seoul station. Work does not begin there until nine o'clock, but she wants to go first to the Cho-gye-sa, the main Sŏn (Zen) temple in Seoul, whose abbot usually represents the Buddhist clergy at any large ecumenical ceremony in the capital of the world's most ecumenical country.

Miss O, in her early twenties, is not mystical or particularly intellectual. She had good high school grades but was rejected first by a university in Seoul, then by a lesser one in the provinces. Only a minority of those who pass university entrance exams are actually accepted, and being the only child of a widow with neither money nor influence, she had known it would be difficult.

She chose the headquarters of Dae-u (called Daewoo in America), one of the country's largest *chaebol* (conglomerates), as a place of employment because jobs there are secure, salaries are paid on time, and her mother thought her chances of meeting the right young man would be better in such a big enterprise. Finally, after living with a young man who grew tired of her, then with a manager who claimed to be divorced but wasn't, she has now, she thinks, met the man whose wife she would like to be.

She goes to the *chul* not to meditate—that would take longer than the time she has available and is something she has never managed to accomplish. She goes to pray. For her, Buddhism is not just a concept of self, or a philosophy, or an ethic, but a true religion, a belief. Su-na is going to pray to the Lord Buddha, as a Christian might pray to the disembodied Godhead, that he should bless her love for the young accountant despite the fact that he is a Christian. If the Lord Buddha will help her, she silently promises, she will make the sacrifice of not spending her lunch break with the accountant, even though the young man will not understand her absence—indeed, will probably misinterpret it.

After work that evening, having carried out her temple promise, she makes a second spiritual investment. She goes to an obscure house in an alley on the east side of the city, near the P'yŏng-hwa market, where she has made arrangements by telephone to consult with a *mudang.* There are three things a *mudang* can usefully do for Su-na. She can consult with the accountant's grandfather, his immediate dead ancestor, to persuade the conservative wraith that the young Buddhist clerk will make a good wife and mother for his grandson. She can try to project herself into the accountant's mind and make him both desire Su-na and reject the competing advances of a svelte computer operator who is more physically attractive than the plump, "country-faced" Miss O. Indeed, the *mudang* not only sets a date which is propitious for this exercise, but as a bonus she recommends a particular herbal recipe, obtainable in the *mudang*'s brother's *han-yak* nearby—which, if swallowed at a particular time on a particular day, will make Miss O virtually irresistible, at least for a while. And finally, if O Su-na believes her courtship is sufficiently advanced to justify the expense, the *mudang* will conduct a *kut* at which she will bring Su-na together with her dead father to ask him, since he had no sons, if he would accept propitiation from a son-in-law. She has no reason to think that, because her intended husband is a Christian, he might have objections to taking part in shamanist rites.

O Su-na is not unusual in having so many devout insurance policies on the infinite. Nor is her iconoclastic approach to fate a reflection of her modest intellectual powers. Company presidents, generals, professors, and politicians tend to share her universalism, although men may be more discreet about their shamanism, and prominent men prefer to consult their *mudang* by telephone. The manager who was Su-na's lover until his wife found out believed that the future of the country lay, as in Singapore, in a closer observance of Confucianism. Both to please him and to inform herself, she read and discussed some of the old Confucian classics, which saw ancestor veneration as a useful form of filial discipline.

When the young accountant had mentioned that he always went to a Methodist church on Sunday mornings, she had dropped a rather large hint by saying that she had never witnessed Christian rites except on TV when the Pope had been shown blessing a vast throng on Yŏ-ui-do Island. She would have been equally flexible if her accountant had belonged to one of the syncretistic cults—without having any less confidence that Siddharta Gautama was God, or that you could only avoid the mischief of the spirits, ancestral or otherwise, through the mediation of a *mudang*.

Are Koreans, then, obsessed with religion? Just the opposite! Religion sits feather-lightly on the Korean conscience, but superstition is buried deeply in his or her nomadic Siberian soul. The ceremony associated with an infant's survival is more shamanist and superstitious than devotional; a wedding is a bizarre blend of shamanism and Buddhism; a funeral is brief and Buddhist, but later ceremonies for the "peace of the soul" are almost entirely shamanistic. The relationship between shamanism, Confucianism, and Buddhism may be more established than between shamanism, Christianity, and the cults; but the date for a High Mass wedding in Myŏng-dong Cathedral would more likely be chosen by astrology than by convenience or weather.

To some extent, the Confucian ethic of government and life, which underlies the nation's style, poses a challenge to religion, just as the twentieth century challenges both. Yet there is a very real atmosphere of learning and discipline in the country's myriad monasteries and their scattered mountainside hermitages, where monks and nuns with shaven heads and Buddhist garb lead lives of triumphant abnegation.

Religion in Korea is inextricably interwoven with history. Persecution and martyrdom helped the early Korean Church to gain recognition and credibility. The Church's conflict with the Japanese occupation, and its consequent role in the resistance, gave it nationalist credentials that saved it from its exotic, Mediterranean taint. Despite the advent of Islam and the syncretistic cults, faddish or otherwise, a nation which is nominally over seventy percent Buddhist—or Buddhist-Confucian—and over fifteen percent Christian, remains about ninety percent shamanist. No study of the Koreans can be complete without consideration of the survival and triumph of the witch, with her spiritualist séances (as we would describe them) and her power over even such improbable devotees as the Marxist dynast Kim Il-sŏng. Juntas may come and go, but Kim Kum-hwa, the tragic embodiment of the *mudang* par excellence, will continue to go literally to hell and back in a way that no practicing politician would ever want to do for "his" people—or could do if he tried.

Confucius borrowed ancestral rites. The Buddhists borrowed the lunar new year festival of lanterns as a way of marking Sakyamuni's presumed birthday. Likewise the Christians—who borrowed the yule log ceremony in pagan Britain, and even switched Christ's birthday from March to December to accommodate it—have aligned their own harvest festival on Chusŏk, the traditional one (even though the -sŏk refers to Sakyamuni). It is on the grave of the dead that all the religions and non-religions come together. At a funeral wake, priests chant, prayer pennants fly, paper flowers adorn the tumulus, and of course *jŏng-jong* flows. The site of the tumulus itself will have been chosen by a shamanist geomancer—a tradition borrowed from China to tell people where to live, do business, and be buried.

True Buddhist funerals, of course, involve cremation, and the only interment is of ashes in a wall. Serious Buddhists would expect the dead to be already reborn by the time the white bus with the black horizontal lines—the modern hearse—courses the busy city streets, or the gaily colored, multistoried, streamered casket bumps across the paddies in the countryside, followed by paid mourners wearing hempen gowns and sandals, and by family mourners wearing raffia mourning bands on their sleeves, like the black armbands of a British funeral. Traditionally, the dead should be memorialized for seven generations. This involves substantial expense, and postwar governments, influenced by the ideas of Galbraith, Marx, or Schumacher, have ordered that it be cut to three.

Needless to say, there is nothing resembling a state religion in South Korea. Buddhism is primus inter pares as these things go, and there is a Confucian underpinning to the society. But Confucianism, by any serious definition, is not a religion; and Buddha (if Siddhārtha Gautama had only known that his interpretations of the Vedanta and the Upanishads would one day be called *Buddhism*) did not speak of belief, or of God either, however much the lovesick Miss O and millions of others may have deified the Hindu prince.

Taoism, the teachings of Lao-tzu, persists here also. The Korean *tae-guk-ki* flag is Taoist. Christianity is as many-faceted here as in Europe, almost as disparate and heretical as in America, and the syncretistic cults can surely only proliferate in the present national atmosphere of uncertainty. Islam, introduced by Turkish chaplains during the Korean War, and replenished by Korean converts who have worked in the Gulf, is perhaps the fastest growing minority faith, with nearly thirty thousand adherents, three mosques, and a half-dozen cultural centers.

Shamanism, however, remains the most Korean phenomenon of all, however much it can often be described as pure superstition. The new Christian cults and syncretisms, like those of the American South, have a strong shamanist orientation. A Japanese is birthed and married in Shinto (today, often in Christian garments), and buried in Buddhism; but the Korean people's hatches, matches, and dispatches are all basically shamanist, whatever the wedding mass or Buddhist sepulcher.

The greatest influence on Korean art is not just Buddhist but *Sŏn*—Zen—the branch of the flexible Mahayana (Major Vehicle) Buddhism, which is the principal Buddhist influence in the West. (Hinayana—Minor Vehicle—Buddhism is inherently religious, and flourishes mostly in Theravadhist Sri Lanka and Southeast Asia. In Bangkok, bar hostesses burn incense sticks to Buddha to ensure a good business evening.) Korea's *Sŏn* and other Buddhist temples, with their shamanist deities carved in the entryway, are as flexible as Islam in West Africa, with its acceptance of tribal votive saints and amulets. Buddhism's impact stems partly from the fact that it is so undemanding.

The acceptance of Buddhism as a state religion in the old

principality of Gaya, and subsequently in Ko-gu-ryŏ, Paekche (which absorbed Gaya), and Silla, has been mentioned earlier, as was Ko-gu-ryŏ's and especially Paekche's role in spreading the word to Japan. Buddhist teaching is believed to have made its first impression on the peninsular mind when King Kim Su-ru of Gaya (42–119) married a Tamil princess and named his domain after Buddha's place of enlightenment under the *bodhi* tree. Historians differ regarding the region where the canon was first introduced by an Indian monk, but it seems more likely to have been Gaya than Paekche. (Although Gaya became part of Paekche, and historically disappeared, its name persists in that of the oldest Korean musical instrument, the stringed *kayagŭm*, and in Mount Gaya, home of Hae-in-sa.)

It was King Sŏng-myŏng of Paekche who sent monks, notably A-chik-ki and Wang-in, to the court of King Kimmei of shamanist Japan. The objective was to gain Nippon as an ally against Silla, but the watershed result for Japanese culture was enormous. Koreans built the great Hōryū Temple at Nara, decorated by Tam-jing, a monk from Ko-gu-ryŏ. A tree called the Paekche tree (*kudaragi*, in Japanese), planted near the temple by Paekche scholars, still lives in the grounds. It was Paekche which had earlier brought Confucianism and the skill of reading to Japan, although it had been Ko-gu-ryŏ which had first accepted these skills in Korea, in the first century, and which was the first Korean kingdom to establish a Confucian academy three hundred years later.

Buddhism flourished under Unified Silla, especially through the "pan-Buddhist" teaching of the famous abbot, Wŏn-hyo, and in Ko-ryŏ, as well. The monastery became the focal point of education, art, and literature. Success bred corruption, so Buddhist "power" gave way to Confucian "power," with its detrimental effects for women, but giving a clear constructive framework to government and society. Wŏn-hyo, who married Princess Yo-sŏk (referred to by some historians as Prin-

111

cess Kwa), sister of King Mu-yŏl, propagated a less rigid approach to monastic life, including marriage. He fathered the writer Sŏl Ch'ong. The more spiritual Ŭi-sang (625–702) fostered the *Hwa-om* (Flowering Splendor) school of Buddhism. His seaside temple, facing Japan at Nagsan, is said to be the oldest monastery in Asia.

It was the seventh century that saw the great "Korean enlightenment" of Japan, with the now relatively settled civilizations of Paekche and Ko-gu-ryŏ sending the island nation a constant brain drain of monks and other scholars, philosophers, doctors of medicine or pharmacy, professional court historians, sculptors, artisans, painters, musicians and other artists, even agronomists. Korean Buddhism is especially associated with the ancient Japanese religious capital of Nara—not only the artistic Nam-jing but the more scholarly monk Hyi-ja, who became the preceptor of Prince Shōtoku, one of the architects of a true nation-state in Japan. Confucianism also crossed the Dong-hae, with Koreans bringing to Japan the five-note atonal scale of Confucian music as played at the courts of China and at those in the three Korean kingdoms.

The growth of Buddhism in the peninsula also increased Korea's contacts with China, the intellectual mother lode of the era, and this in turn brought the Korean elite of monks and other traveling scholars into contact with the outside world, as the latter took the silk road through the mountains to Cathay. From Arab travelers there, Koreans learned more astronomy and mathematical skills, bringing devices such as the first astrolabes to Kyŏngju to amuse the king. In the eighth century, the Ch'ŏm-sŏng-dae observatory was built there, and it remains to impress visitors today. Other direct or indirect imports from Cathay included cotton seeds, new spices and drugs, gunpowder, and the Gregorian calendar of the Mediterranean world, along with new ideas about medicine, architecture, and metallurgy. Koreans then carried much of this intellectual trove to Japan.

Buddhism, like Christianity later, gained by losing caste and becoming associated with the "common people." During the later Lyi era, monks, as noted, bore the same caste indistinction as slaves and grave diggers; but like *ki-saeng*, who suffered the same *in-yon*, they were all the more impressive for that. The monasteries were centers of opposition to the Japanese and Chinese incursions and, like the churches, to the Japanese occupation in this century. Japan, on the other hand, imposed Shinto as its state religion (an anachronism, since it was of Korean origin, and only later related to Japanese ancestors). It did not discourage Buddhism as much as Christianity, because Buddhism could not be equally condemned as exotic. Indeed, the Japanese helped some of the incelibate Korean Buddhist *sang-ha* (orders) to establish themselves.

Today, nearly twenty thousand monks and female bonzes, living in about two thousand four hundred monasteries with about five thousand *am* (satellite hermitages), are grouped in eighteen *sang-ha*. Christmas, being essentially copied from the West, is inevitably a more exuberant commercial festival, but Buddha's birthday has become, in recent decades, the single most important national holiday of the South Korean year.

Koreans like Miss O Su-na, who require their dead father's approval to wed—and who believe Buddha, despite attaining extinction, is a God—also believe in the reincarnation cycle (in Korean, *song chu kui kang*—creation, existence, destruction, and nothingness). This implies that Miss O's father, who died a decade ago, must not only be a mischievous or demanding spirit who can be contacted in the spirit world by a *naerim mudang*, but also, perhaps, a beggar boy in today's Calcutta slums, or a wealthy businessman's schoolgirl daughter in Helsinki, or a mature zebra in Tanzania.

Her probable future husband from the white-collar Dae-u

skyscraper will need his Methodist pastor's permission to bring his "pagan" bride to the altar of Christ, but may thoughtfully omit to inform the cleric when he later bows before the smoked pig's-head centerpiece of a shamanist altar and offers himself to his late father-in-law to play the role of his surrogate son (as well as his own father's) for all eternity.

Koreans' acceptance of *in-yon* (cause-effect), which we in the West usually describe by the Indian word *karma*, informs the nation's stoicism; it also explains the usually nonviolent nature of the country's stylized, even ballet-like political furies. Buddhism is pacifist by definition. It does not oppose political struggle or the martial arts, but it was surely from Buddha's interpretation of the Vedanta that a West Asian called Jesus plucked the idea of turning the other cheek.

Confucianism, like Shinto, is considerably simpler. Its founder echoed a trend toward reactionary conservatism present in virtually all societies, and mourned a supposedly golden era in China's past. It was the prestige of T'aejo Lyi, the general-king, that imposed Confucianism on Chosŏn (which some say means "Korean Zen!"). In modern times, Confucianism, with an estimated eight hundred thousand adherents and about twelve thousand officiants, has been exploited—not always with evil intent—to support industriousness in the workplace, law and order, and respect for government; but it has suffered from being associated with the military.

Well over a million Koreans are Catholics, headed by a cardinal-archbishop. The country has produced one hundred three saints, ninety-three of them native. The religion first entered Korea during the Hideyoshi invasion of 1592. One of his generals, Konishi, whose troops were all Jesuit-trained, was anxious to show that their exotic faith did not hinder their Nippon loyalty to Hideyoshi (who probably saw them as eminently expendable battle fodder). Like Jesus in his time, the Japanese Christians, with their revolutionary notions of equality in the eyes of God, posed a threat to the social order. Konishi brought two chaplains to the peninsula, a Japanese and a Father Gregario de Cespedes, who made no religious converts. Father Gregario, however, brought his private sack of red pepper to relieve the blandness of the food. The Jesuits had had little success with the stuff back in Kyushu; but the Koreans, once acquainted, never looked back.

Korea's first native Catholic was a convert who returned from China in 1608 and who introduced the exotic teaching, which received the name of *sŏ-hak*, Western learning. It was slow to take hold, however, and the next actual record of a Korean baptism was not until 1783, when Yi Sŭng-hun was christened in Beijing. In the repressive atmosphere of those ultra-Confucian times, the faith finally took root, and drew reaction: the first anti-Catholic edicts date from 1791.

By the end of the eighteenth century, it is estimated that there was the astonishing number of four thousand Catholics in Korea. A diocese was established in 1831. Its Korean clergy had often been ordained secretly, which must have added to the religion's allure. The first of the mass executions took place in 1839. Korea's most famous martyr was probably a twenty-four-year-old priest, Father Kim Tae-gŏn ("Andrew Kim"), whose neck was severed in 1846.

By the mid-nineteenth century, the faithful had grown only to eleven thousand, presumably mostly through childbirth; but a few years later, in 1866, the figure had soared to twenty-three thousand. King Kojong, who had originally tolerated the French Catholic and Russian Orthodox priests, ordered the execution of the Bishop of Seoul, Monsignor Siméon-François Berneux, and three other divines. This time, there were no crucifixions: the quartet was decapitated by sword on Chŏl-tu-san (Chop-head Hill), which was then on the outskirts of Seoul and is now the site of the Church of the Martyrs. Starting the next day, and continuing over the next three years, five more priests and about eight thousand Korean believers were similarly beheaded or, if of the lower classes, burned at the stake, strangled, or simply beaten to death.

One Frenchman, Father Ridel, escaped the pogrom to China, whence he organized a largely unsuccessful gunboat raid of French troops in the Seoul area. His intemperate action cost the lives of thousands more of the Church's Korean converts. Nothing succeeds like excess: when the Pope visited Korea a few years ago, he canonized the one hundred three martyr-saints.

In the last century or so, Christianity's less demanding Anglican, Protestant, fundamentalist, and syncretistic branches have pushed the figure of those who proclaim themselves Christians to about six million—eighteen times the Christian proportion of the population of Japan. Christianity's rocky road to success was paved with martyrdoms of different sorts, just as its beginnings in Palestine grew out of opposition to the establishment and the colonial hierarchy. (In contrast, Christianity collapsed in France because it was opposed to the Revolution.) Often, to be on the right side is as much a question of chance as of wisdom or virtue, and Christianity was certainly strengthened by being persecuted, at least in its Catholic form, by the later Lyi dynasty, and repressed by the Japanese imperialists.

The Anglicans and Protestants arrived late on the scene, but concentrated on a more vulgarized, less elitist approach to education. Consequently, their congregations grew faster. Today, non-Catholic (including fundamentalist) Christians, and syncretists, number about four or five million. The initial Scottish and German pastors have been succeeded by twenty thousand contemporary indigenous clergy.

The missions founded colleges. Ewha Women's University is Asia's largest female institution of higher learning. Yonsei University, the heart of the democratic "revolution" of the 1980s, is a Presbyterian institution. Private Korean schools followed the foreign example—Po-sŏng (now Korea University), Yang-jŏng, and Hwi-mun for boys, Suk-myŏng and Chin-myŏng for girls.

In recent times, fundamentalist Christianity, which tends to devalue Jesus and emphasize the Old Testament—even the Book of Revelation, regarded as heretical by most Christians—has grown in importance, profiting from its similarity to charismatic shamanism.

The first mosque, in Seoul's Latin Quarter section, I-t'ae-won, was dedicated in 1976, in the presence of forty leaders from the Islamic world. Mosques have since been built in Busan and Kwangju, and Islamic centers established in half a dozen other towns, largely thanks to Arabian and North African philanthropy.

The first syncretistic cult, Ch'ŏn-do-gyo, dates from the mid-nineteenth century and is said to have, still, nearly a million adherents. It was a leader in the early *dong-hak* (Eastern learning) movement for popular education. The fact that the Lyi court had to use Chinese and later Japanese help in crushing this grass-roots movement increased its popularity. The execution in 1864 of its founder, Ch'oe Che-u, a member of the petty gentry, added to its significance.

Won-bul-gyo differs from Ch'ŏn-do-gyo in being less influenced by Christian concerns for human rights in the political sense, but it is similarly opposed to *sŏ-hak* (Western learning—that is, Catholicism). *Bul* means Buddha, and it is intended to be a syncretism of Buddhism. It was founded in 1916, shortly after the Japanese takeover.

Nationalistic but not strictly speaking syncretistic is T'ae-jong-gyo, which worships Tan-gun, the mythical father of the nation. Aided by nineteenth- and twentieth-century nationalism, this organization, roughly similar to British Druids or Amerindian shamanists, still has followers, especially in the southern provinces.

Fundamentalist Christian churches, with their cathartic shouting and loud singing, stomping and hollering and "speaking in tongues," have inevitably made their inroads in this profoundly shamanistic society, and new syncretisms can be expected to grow. One of the more fancifully heretical is the Tong-il (Unification) Church, whose North Korean-born leader, Mun Sŏn-myŏng, believes he is the Messiah whose disciples ("moonies") will be "raptured" during the "war of the worlds," and who will all wake up speaking Korean on January 1 of the year 2000. According to Scott and Jon Lee Anderson (*Inside the League*), the portly North Korean self-proclaimed divine originally exercised the right of *jus primae noctis* on his earlier maidenly proselytes.

Buddhism pays lip service to shamanism, the country's popular religion, by its carvings and shamanist spirits at the entrances to Buddhist monasteries. It would be comparable to having Capuchins enter their sanctuary, rosary in hand, past castings of Jupiter and Zeus, or even Snow White and the Seven Dwarfs. The mountain god and the Korean tiger are among the popular myth-figures which greet a Buddhist as he passes into the temple at Hae-in or Nagsan. But the commitment to a religious and shamanistic form of Buddhism in Korea goes much further than that. The whole spirit of Korean Buddhism is different; alone in East Asia, it resembles the fantasies of Southeast Asia.

If there is another striking difference between the reposeful Buddhist retreats of Japan and those of the peninsula, it is the bewildering array of colors. Korea's temples are as polychrome as a Korean woman's *han-bok* dress, making a sharp contrast with the Zen discretion of the islands. The love of color surely speaks of the origins of Koreans as gypsies of the steppes.

Dr. Jon Covell seems to have reached the same conclusion. She explains:

> The bright colors (cinnabar red, lapis blue, malachite green, etc.) of Korean temples and palaces followed those of T'ang architecture, which had itself adopted such hues from central Asia. Today, the bright color combination (*tan-ch'ong*) is preserved in the palaces and temples but not used for ordinary buildings. Japan dropped most of its once bright (colors) in medieval times, under Zen influence.

Grete Diemente Sibley writes in a guidebook essay:

> Korean temple art is as bewildering as it is beautiful. Demons crouch under the heavy burden of roofbeams, sword-wielding guardians put off anyone with ill intent, and serene Buddhas hold meditative poses under the staring eyes of a hundred scowling faces. Figures and legends are depicted in an array of colors and distorted imagery foreign to the Western eye.

A Buddhist temple will always have a minimum of two gate guardians or "gods." In China, these are called Heng and Ha. In Korea, they are the *kum-gang-sin-ch'ang*. In most cases, pilgrims will be greeted by the four heavenly kings, who are said to have helped Sakyamuni himself (in Korean, Sŏk-ka-mo-ni), the future Gautama Buddha, escape from his father's house.

The guardian of the North, Ta-mun-ch'ŏn-wang, holds a pagoda in his hand. The guardian of the South, Jon-jang-ch'ŏn-wang, brandishes a sword. The guardian of the East, Chi-guk-ch'ŏn-wang, carries a lute, while his contemporary for the West, Kwang-mok-ch'ŏn-wang, flourishes a dragon in one hand and a jewel in the other.

Buddha figures (*bul*) are numerous. The Amita-bul is, in Sibley's expression, the primordial Buddha, often extending his left hand, palm outward, in the mudra of "fulfilling the vow," if standing. If sitting, he has an upturned palm. Some Amita Buddhas have other gestures.

Sŏk-ka-mo-ni-bul is Sakyamuni himself. Like Amita Buddhas, Sŏk-ka Buddhas are usually attended by two bodhisattvas, forming a trinity. Bodhisattvas are essentially beings who have deferred nirvana (extinction) in order to be reincarnated and help the living. *Bodhi* means "wisdom" and *sattva* means "the determined one."

The *Mirŭk-bul* or Maitreya Buddha is the Buddha of the Future, and corresponds, in the religious approach to Buddhism, to the Messiah. The *Mirŭk* is usually seated with his right elbow on his right thigh and the rest of that leg stretched across him. His right hand is to his face. The most celebrated version, the huge Ŭnjin-mirŭk, is a standing figure, and there have been theories that this is not a *mirŭk* at all but a *kwanseŭm-posal*, the bodhisattva of mercy.

Usually depicted as female, this latter figure has another monstrous representation over the sea at Nagsan. These enormous representations have a grotesque quality to the Western mind, but they are in the tradition of North Korea and Japan (Kamakura, for instance) and elsewhere: the reclining Buddha in Bangkok, almost as long as a city block, is perhaps even more bizarre. Kwanseum means "hearer of cries," and Sibley says one of the many representations in which she exists includes a "thousand-eyed, thousand-armed form" which can be traced to the tantric Buddhism of Tibet and northern India.

Yaksayŏrae is the healing Buddha and appeals to the sick,

the unfortunate, and those who feel beset by ignorance, while Virojana (or Varokana) is a sort of evangelical Buddha, venerated by *Hwa-om* Buddhism, and often displayed with attendants in a trinity.

Tongjin-posal is the bodhisattva who guards the lotus sutra, one of the keys to Zen, which teaches that truth is communicated by intuition and silence, rather than by words. Jinjang-posal is the bodhisattva of the netherworld—clearly a shamanist concept.

Ch'il-song, who is both Taoist and shamanist in origin, is a manifestation of the Great Bear constellation, which is visible all year, and is revered by infertile women seeking children. San-sin, the shamanist mountain spirit, whose portrait—accompanied by his faithful tiger—appears in many temples, is also associated with fecundity, and is said to have a good track record in ensuring male progeny. Tok-sŏng-in (lone and holy) reminds Buddhists that they should not seek enlightenment outside of themselves.

There are ten bodhisattvas in all, many more "historical figures," and still more attendant demons and servants. The carvings on altars are often arranged in trinities. These may consist of a Buddha and two bodhisattvas, a Buddha and two historical figures, a bodhisattva and two historical figures, or three bodhisattvas. Crowned figures are bodhisattvas or shamanist figures. Buddhas are uncrowned, and are characterized by black, frizzy (Dravidian) hair, long earlobes (a sign of intelligence in the East), and at least one brain-bump on the cranium, as well as several other traditional marks.

What is evident in all this is that the shamanism of central Asia, with its concepts of paradise and hell, has marked East Asia just as these ideas have informed the religions of West Asia (which we in the West call the Middle East). For a majority of Buddhists, nirvana has become paradise; hell has replaced an unsatisfactory rebirth, and the occult spirits of shamanism have become akin to bodhisattvas, some of which are even believed by many Koreans to have been associated with Sakyamuni himself.

None of these quaint heresies need distract the casual visitor, who should find enough intellectual challenge on the aesthetic plane alone. The Bulguk-sa (Buddhaland temple) in Kyŏngju, with its Zen-like *yang* (male) pagoda and its exquisite, curlicued *ŭm* (female) pagoda, is one of the greatest wonders of the medieval world, as is the nearby Sŏkkuram (Sakyamuni's hermitage), which is a grotto designed as a private chapel for royalty, and dominated by a huge granite Buddha. It was begun in the year 750 and is the work of the architect Kim Dae-song. After falling into disrepair in the later Lyi dynasty, it was restored by the Japanese, and later (in 1960) by UNESCO. Equally beautiful on a smaller scale, and sited in low, forested mountains which are shrouded in mist at dawn, is the Hae-in-sa (Sea Echo temple), the center of Korean *Sŏn* (Zen), home of the Tripitaka Koreana. At the time of this writing, its abbot has been in constant meditation for just over twenty years.

For the visitor unfamiliar with East Asian custom, it should be noted that visiting a Buddhist temple is not quite the same thing as visiting Chartres or San Marco or Canterbury. Do not stand, which would seem as gauche as to wear shoes indoors. Just kneel, sit back on your heels, contemplate, and enjoy.

Shamanism predominates in Korea's life with the spirits, and shamanism is a feminine imperium. It would seem to have blended the tradition of the charismatic witch in the ecstatic Siberian tradition with the concubine tradition of imperial China. As Dr. Alan Covell has phrased it, Korean shamanism has a "sexual core." What is perhaps most curious is its survival in Marxist North Korea.

Kim Il-sŏng has encouraged the belief that he is a modern version of the shaman-kings of old, responsible not only for the success of the latest five-year plan, but also for the rain, the harvest, and so on. Yet he sometimes acknowledges the need for other shamans—*mudang*—to pacify supernatural demands.

It was reported in the Korean press a few years ago that in 1958, President Kim had asked a P'yŏng-yang witch to perform a *kut* for his younger son, who had, it was said, drowned in a pond at the age of ten, in 1948. The *mansin* performed a *chinogwi saenam to-ryŏng kŏri*, making the descent into hell to place the child in paradise and separate his querulous spirit from his family forever.

Later research contended that the ceremony may actually have been for Kim's younger brother, and perhaps for his first wife, as well. A doctor in Seoul related to Jon Covell that his father had been called to the Kim residence before the Korean War, to find Kim's wife dying on the floor from a gunshot wound. The President had ordered the doctor to "let her be." Murder? Suicide? This source had also said that Kim's younger brother had drowned in the pond at the family residence, and that there were rumors that the two brothers had been fighting at the time. Did the younger brother fall, or was he pushed? Did Il-sŏng deliberately fail to rescue him?

Unexpected, violent deaths and deaths by drowning are considered, in this maritime country's religious folklore, to create the most restless and mischievous spirits, forever interfering negatively and jealously in the lives of their surviving kin.

The key feature of such a *chinogwi kut* is the descent into hell by the witch, who will have assumed the role of Pari Kongju (Rejected Princess), the most difficult exercise in the profession of a shamaness. A twist of paper with some rice, covered by a cloth, represents the dead person. A primitive candle of waxed cloth is placed above it and lit. The story of Pari Kong-ju is chanted by the *mansin*. In some versions, Pari Kong-ju is the eighth child of an emperor who could father no sons, and her father (in some versions, both parents) treated her badly because she was not a boy, even confining her to a tomb or cave. Then, the father (or, in the alternate version, both parents) fell ill and died. The princess forthwith descended into the underworld and labored nine years there, finally bringing back an elixir which restored her father (or both parents) to life.

In yet another version, she was the seventh child and seventh daughter, and the eighth was a boy who died. In this version, Pari Kong-ju—considered today to be the first *mudang* and the patron saint of them all—scoured hell to rescue her little brother and bring him back to life. While away in hell for nine years, she married and bore seven children—all boys, of course. When she returned to life with the little brother whom she had revived, she brought some of the magic water that had accomplished this feat—which was just as well, as her parents had died in the meantime and were in need of the same medication.

After chanting the Pari Kong-ju legend, the *mansin* lifts the cloth from the rice, intentionally toppling the pile. Alan Covell writes that any tracks in the rice that resemble birds' prints or butterflies' wings "mean that the soul is ready to fly from hell of its own free will." Sinuous, snakelike imprints imply that the "soul is not ready for release." No tracks at all indicate a confused soul requiring the help of Pari Kong-ju, who must descend into Hades.

Those who have witnessed such a "descent into hell" report that the exercise is terrifying to watch, and can result in the witch's heart ceasing to beat. After the deceased has been dead for three years, rescue from hell is said to become particularly difficult; yet Kim Il-sŏng was reportedly concerned with a son's death which had taken place ten years before. The death of his first wife and his brother had occurred even earlier.

The principal guardians of hell are the *ag-wi*, or hungry ghosts, whose throats have been constricted to the diameter of a pin. To deal with them, the witch ceases to be the princess and becomes an *ag-wi*, greedily swallowing food and wine from the *kut* tables and, because of the throat constriction, vomiting everything into a bucket carried by an assistant.

The rescue dance that follows displays elements of Taoism and "religious" Buddhism. The *mansin* gyrates, brandishing knives with which she cuts through the (Taoist) Gate of Man, the Gate of Heaven, the Gate of Demons, and the Gate of Earth. These four gates lead to nine chambers, through each of which she dances three times.

A separate knife is used to cut each of the four gates, and is then tossed back to an assistant until needed again on the second and third operations. The *mansin* wears the red and yellow *han-bok* said to have been favored by the princess whom she has momentarily become. To reach hell, she dances her way through hemp, splitting the material with her hips. Next, she comes back to life by splitting huge ribbons of muslin. As she passes the last gate, an assistant burns the paper effigy, which floats free in the air—the rescued soul, on its way to what some Buddhist sects refer to as the "Western paradise."

Whatever reasons determine the *mudang*'s vocation, her role is clear: she is there to protect her clients from the spirit world. To be a prophet, she must depend on insider tips from the spirits. She is a doctor, an apothecary, and an alchemist; and, as Peter Hyun points out in a delightful book, *Koreana*, she's also an actress, a dancer, and a singer.

By the end of the Lyi dynasty, in the early years of this century, there were an estimated two thousand *mudang*. In 1930, according to Hyun, the Japanese counted over twelve thousand. Travails strengthen any religion, and by 1966 the figure had grown to about sixty-three thousand. President Pak despised and repressed the art, as President Rhee had done, but under Ch'ŏn Du-hwan the witches were back in the guidebooks as a proud element of Koreana. One *mudang*, Kim Kum-hwa, was even sent overseas to represent the national culture.

Although some deities and votive spirits make more frequent appearances in *kut* than others, there seems to be no absolute limit to the number of them. Each mountain or tall hill has its *san-sin*, each market garden, each body of water—especially medicinal springs (*ke-su*)—its deity. And the *san-sin* is conscious of history. When he is portrayed, he may wear a Confucian hat and brandish a Taoist fan. He and other votaries can fly when they need to. Jon Covell compares the mountain spirit to Santa Claus with his reindeer—a shamanist myth of our own, where the choice of mount surely points toward Siberia as its origin.

In the peninsula's north, including the northern part of South Korea, the *mansin* receives the call in childhood or early womanhood through *sin-byŏng*, the possession sickness, an annunciation. The closer one gets to Siberia, the more charismatic the witch becomes. The *talgollae* of the southern provinces and the *simbang* of Jeju Island are hereditary, not charismatic, and some are men.

Halla Pai Huhm, the encyclopedist of the *mudang*, says the rare male officiants, called *mu-gyŏk, paksu,* or *pŏpsa*, also experience *sin-byŏng*. Elsewhere, she tells us, the names change. The female *mudang* is *osimi*, the male *t'osaebi*. Those who feel called must go to study with a *mansin*, where the girl novice is called the *mansin*'s spirit daughter. Only a few novices, however, manage to go the whole way; most remain *kidae*, playing instruments, singing, and otherwise assisting the *mansin* like lifelong altar girls. Musicians, including occasional males, are also called *chŏnak* and *aksu chaebi*.

If Halla Pai Huhm is the witches' encyclopedist, their Boswell has been Laurel Kendall, the American museum curator for whom *mansin* have become a lifelong fascination. Kendall has noticed how much of a canon Korean witchcraft has created. Different spirits and different ancestors are summoned by different music, different dances, different clothes. The same sort of lighthearted adversary relationship seems to develop as that which characterizes a West African wake. The difference is that, through a *mudang*, the dead and the supernatural speak. They invariably say that the gluttony and the alcohol are insufficient, and the women chant back: "So make us rich; we will give you more!"

While men must perform the ritual of honors for the ancestors, it is women who are charged with placating the household and other spirits. The wife, Kendall notes, leaves rice cakes and a cup of *jŏng-jong* or *makkŏlli* on the main beam of the rafters, with some pine needles. Elsewhere, there is a jar of rice for the Birth Grandmother, a sort of midwife spirit. Candles burn. Bows of obeisance are made.

There are minor spirits everywhere—over jars of *kimch'i* or soy, even in the toilet. Unless propitiated, the spirits ensure that misfortune arrives. The dead come back (despite rebirth), and the touch of these wraiths brings illness. Says Kendall: "Ghosts, wood imps and baleful humors pour through the walls and strike the family." As in Africa, such problems call for a consultation with a medium.

To prejudge the future, the main divination tools are grains of rice and old coins. When minor rites fail, there is a *kut*, possibly even a major *kut*, which may last three days. It takes place all around and in the house, which is invaded by the insistent beat of the *chang-gu* hourglass drum. There are constant demands from the spirits: for money, which the *mansin* keeps; for food and wine, which is splashed on the walls. The *mansin* may even become the Knife-riding General, dancing on bare blades. The housewives themselves also dance. The woman sponsoring the *kut* may dance to exhaustion.

Further down the occult orders are the *chŏm-changi* diviners and the male *pŏp-sa*. They cannot, however, match the charismatic *mansin*. They cannot perform *chosang-gŏri*, in which the shamaness is possessed by the dead, sometimes in awesome ways—for example, by *yŏng-san*, ghosts who die unmarried and with no children, perhaps violently and away from home; drowned fishermen, for instance. There are plenty of those every year in the typhoon season. They are not entitled to *chesa* food, so they are perpetually hungry and are more difficult to deal with than the ordinary *cho-sang* ghosts.

Kendall advises that those who visit the *kuksa-dang* on the hilly northern periphery of Seoul should bring coins and thousand-*wŏn* notes. Always drink whatever is offered, she says, leave a coin on the saucer, and eat the pickle or other food that follows. Women visitors, she warns, may be asked to dance and even to put on costume.

This writer has witnessed *kut* and has seen a family awed when Kim Kum-hwa spoke in the exact voice of a dead father-husband. Kendall, however, has observed and chronicled some very elaborate rites, beginning at the moment when the *mansin* first strikes the drum and everybody leaves the house, making sure to stand clear of the gable.

In one of her narratives, Kendall describes the awakening of the house spirits. Unclean spirits are driven out like roaches. Mountain and other spirits are invited to enter. The *taegam*, or housekeeper spirit, possesses the *mansin*, whose task is to cure a sick elder, Grandfather Chŏn. There is drumming and dancing as the *mansin* who has become the *tae-gam* takes a dried fish offered to her by Grandmother Chŏn, breaks off its head, and flings it into the field, splashing wine after it, for the ghosts and the "noxious spirits" to consume. Then she flings down the rest of the fish. The neck points toward the gate, so evil spirits remain in the compound. More wine is tossed. The fish is thrown down again. Now it points toward the field. The goblins have gone. The *mansin* and her two *kidae* take the *kut* "within the walls," and a *pu-jŏng* (purification) rite is conducted. Grandmother Chŏn lights candles, sets out money, bows to the floor. The *mansin* sings—then rests and smokes.

When the rite resumes, recent ancestors, followed by various spirits, are invoked. The *mansin* removes her red robe, revealing a green one beneath as she "becomes" another spirit; then she puts on a yellow robe to become the Great Spirit Grandmother (*samsin halmŏni*), the one identified as being responsible for the old man's illness. She picks up a trident and stabs into a tub of rice cake, displaying greed. She grabs a Chŏn daughter and makes her bow. She berates Grandmother Chŏn. Then she promises to make her husband well, in return for gifts.

The *mudang* next becomes the old man's parents, then his first wife, who is embittered by an early death, but who is bought off. A woman neighbor of the Chŏns is then possessed, also. She too berates Grandmother Chŏn. She walks on all fours to indicate that she wants a whole pig, then awkwardly on two, to show that she wants two legs of beef. The antics raise laughter.

More money, food, and wine are extorted by the spirits. More of the congregants, like Holy Rollers, are seized by ectoplasms. The *mansin* balances a cooked pig on the prongs of the trident, which does not fall—signifying that the offering is accepted. The ailing grandfather is awakened and made to kneel on the porch, where he is pelted with millet to drive ghosts away from him. The *mansin* circles his head with a kitchen knife, sits on his shoulders, wards off spirits with stabs at the air. She offers him a choice of divination flags. The one he chooses turns out to represent the Seven Stars, to which he has a special devotion—the exorcism has been successful. It is three A.M. and the rite has been going on for twenty hours. This précis of Kendall's lengthy account only gives the flavor.

In the morning the *mansin*, in a green robe, becomes Ch'ang-bu, the clown god of dead actors, singers, and acrobats, and who is a guardian against accidents. She presses a mirror into a tub of rice and "reads" the pattern of those grains that stick to the glass. One of the neighborhood women is possessed by T'ŏju Taegam, who is legendarily greedy and bibulous. A daughter-in-law of the Chŏns follows with a *jŏng-jong* kettle and gives some of the wine to the invisible door guard spirit, *sumum taegam*. Wine and rice cake are scattered around. Granddad Chŏn is again pelted with millet, and the treacherous air around his head is stabbed. Food scraps are carried into the field, luring misfortune with them. A dead chicken is given a quasi-human burial.

The *mudang* and her assistants divide up the money and food, according to the strenuousness of their individual contributions to the rite. Grandmother Chŏn invites them to eat, but they decline and hurry off to catch the bus for Seoul.

Kendall synopsizes what has taken place:

> The dead are dangerous simply because they are dead and do not mingle well with the living.... The *mansin* finally shifted the lingering vestiges of [the grandfather's] illness to the body of a white chicken that she cast out and had buried like a corpse.
>
> But one is also struck by Grandfather Chŏn's minimal participation in events performed ostensibly on his behalf. The *kut* was a women's party. Grandmother Chŏn made the initial arrangements and led the bantering with the gods and ancestors. The gods also made heavy demands on the daughter-in-law since the son's household would also draw luck and blessings from the *kut*....

Some benefits . . . also reached the neighbors and friends who spent small amounts of cash on divinations, lucky wine and sweets from the Birth Grandmother's tray, and who danced *mugam* and savored the *kut*'s inebriated gaiety. Not passive spectators, these women formed a concerned chorus. They importuned the gods and commented on the unfolding drama. They found almost everything funny that did not make them weep. They approached the gods and ancestors much as they approach life—with a sharp tongue, a sense of humor, and a good cry.

Unlike Christianity, Islam, or most other religions, shamanism evades the humdrum. In a talk to the Smithsonian Institution's Wilson Center, Kendall said: "What gives the *kut* the power is its measure, however slight, of spontaneity or unpredictability.

"No one knows just what the spirits will say when they arrive, what antics they will pull, or what it will take, finally, to satisfy them. . . . Without this element of inspired spontaneity, the shaman's claim to divine power would not be compelling."

Even contemporaries—and not just one's parents—can become shamanistic spirits. General MacArthur's foolhardy but successful landing at Inch'ŏn was described in an earlier chapter: to a *mudang*, the controversial figure's unnatural luck suggests supernatural intervention. Thus, it is hardly surprising that one *mudang* in the Inch'ŏn area has made Megada, despite the decidedly Japanese harmony to the Korean pronunciation of his Scottish name, into a god to whom she owes a special allegiance. When she trances, it is the ectoplasm of MacArthur which possesses her; when she chants triumphantly, it is the general who has entered her; when she collapses in satiation after invoking the flamboyant soldier to perform some feat for her clients, it is Douglas who marches back to barracks—pardon, heaven.

Says Alan Covell: "Korean female shamans are often very sensual. . . . The ecstasy felt in the trance and during the dance can substitute for physical or sexual satisfaction in ordinary family life."

Elsewhere, Covell, who seems to have been the only young Western male to have been possessed by this garish subject, notes that "some of the dances by the female shamans are sensuous and somewhat ribald. When tempting the wandering spirit [the deceased] into the spirit house which resembles a coffin, they rub the spirit house on the lower parts of their bodies in a sort of tempting manner."

Covell bites the bullet and asks: "Has Korean shamanism survived because it fills a psychological need that is basically sexual in connotation?" He notes that nearly all the spirits are male, and the few male *mudang* wear transvestite clothes to attract them. He further notes that *sin-byŏng* is cured by an ecstatic surrender to the male spirits, and that many witches look younger than their years, as though they had a well-requited sexual life.

During a *naerim kut*, the ecstatic moment is described as *sin baram* or "spirit wind," with *wind* having a sexual association, as in Hindu myths. Each *mansin*, after her initiation, offers water on her altar to her "god-husband" every morning. To quote Covell again: "A disengagement from normal sex life is frequent as the mystical union with the divine has taken its place. . . . The West has parallels, such as St. Theresa, represented by . . . Bernini in a pose of 'ecstacy' with her spiritual bridegroom, Jesus Christ. St. Theresa in her writings refers to being a 'bride of Christ' and a somewhat similar term is used even today when a nun takes her vows." There are, of course, many other examples of sexual overlays to Christian religious possession besides Theresa; Joan of Arc, Fatima, Bernadette, and, not least of course, the Virgin Mary.

Alan Covell is a zealous historian of Korean religious art, which is everywhere peppered with shaman iconography. The "core theme," as he calls him, is the *san-sin*, the mountain spirit. Every *mudang* has a portrayal of him in her *dang*, or shrine. He represents Tan-gun, who was born under the shade of a birch tree on T'ae-baek-san mountain and who ruled for ninety-nine years before returning to the snowy fastnesses at his death. Icons picture him as a kindly old Chinese-Korean with white hair, usually smiling, sometimes accompanied by his wife, and usually attended by a pet tiger.

Next in importance in the pantheon, according to Covell, is Yong-wang, the Dragon King. He is the benign maritime equivalent of the *san-sin*. In depiction, he usually has two beautiful (human) daughters, whom the first kings of Ko-gu-ryŏ and Silla are supposed to have married. Fishermen pray to Yong-wang for calm weather and big catches. At a Hyundai launching in the Ulsan shipyards, he is invoked at the *kosa* ceremony. At Inch'ŏn harbor, there is an annual Yong-wang festival.

Yong-wang is, in short, a positive figure, a rainmaker. Alan Covell's description makes him sound like a god designed by a committee—"the head of a camel, the horns of a deer, the eyes of a rabbit, the ears of a cow, the neck of a snake, the belly of a frog, the scales of a carp and the paws of a tiger." There are said to be eighty-one ridges on his back, and Covell asserts that all major cities in Korea and Japan are built so that they have a "dragon ridge" to the east. Japan's royal family reputedly descends from the Dragon King, and his depiction appears in every Korean Buddhist temple. Just as Tan-gun became the mountain spirit, so King Mun-mu said he would become Yong-wang after death, and protect his country from Japan.

On the first full moon of the lunar year, Seoul has a dragon festival, called *taeborum*. Women wade into the Han-gang to float rafts bearing candles and written prayers. A similar rite is staged in Jeju Town, which is home to the famous Dragon Rock. A *mudang* offers incantations, lamentations, and entreaties to the Dragon King daily, before dawn, on the rocks of Hae-un-dae beach, near Busan.

Other personae portrayed in the witches' *dang* are numerous: there is Tok-song, the "lonely saint"—thought to be Pindola, the disciple whom Sakyamuni reproached for his frivolous miracles. (On one occasion, Pindola flew through the air, tripping on a mountain and causing a woman to miscarry. Buddha, it's said, ordered him to remain on earth until the coming of the Maitreya in five and a half billion years.)

Depiction of the Ch'il-song (Seven Stars) is less anthropomorphic. There are shrines to this element of Siberian mythology everywhere, because Ursa Major, which had a role in Taoism, is said to be good for childbirth, a healthy infancy, virility, long life, and prosperity. Praying for a hundred nights in succession at a Ch'il-song shrine on In-wang hill, just north of Seoul, is said to ensure a birth. The constellation is supposed to represent the male erection. Similarly, Korea on the map is said to be the male element and the Japanese islands the female element. (This symbolism seems only recognizable if the viewer twists the globe and places himself, as it were, in northern Mongolia.) In Buddhist shrines, the Great Bear is sometimes represented as seven bodhisattvas—notably at Bongwon-sa, headquarters of the noncelibate Taego monastic order.

Sam-sin (Three Spirits), sometimes called Sam-bul (Three Buddhas), brings numerology into the occult equation. Nine, three, seven, five, and one are the best numbers, in that order.

All are male numbers. *Mudang*, like Buddhist priests, always bow three times. The Trinity concept is of course germane to Christianity. In shamanism, it is said to represent two female stars and one male star—the womb and the male organ, therefore procreation. Superstitious Buddhists say it represents the Buddhas of the past, present, and future.

Equally certain to be found in any *mudang* gallery are the generals of the five directions (north, south, east, west, and center), by any or all of whom the *mansin* may be possessed. They are distinguishable by the colors of their garments: yellow (center), blue (east), red (south), white (west), and black or deep purple (north). Some *mudang* have their favorite generals.

Among the *mal chang-gun*, the horse-riding generals, the most powerful rides the red-soil horse; but grays were ridden by Korean royalty, notably Lyi Song-gye, founder of the dynasty. The wall of the Flying Horse Tomb in Kyŏngju is graced with a gray, inevitably bringing to mind Mahmoud, the gray who bore Muhammad to heaven. If the rider is depicted leading—not riding—the gray, Covell says, he is not a general but a messenger from hell.

The Chon-sin or Hananim (heavenly spirit) is found in both Buddhist monasteries and the *dangs*. In the temples, the spirit may be a Buddha with a so-called bodhisattva of sunlight and a bodhisattva of moonlight. In shamanist settings, he is accompanied by sun and moon children.

The hodgepodge of faces decorating the walls of most witches' shrines usually also include Cho-yong, the guardian against disease; Chi-u, the tusked guard against strangers who is often carved on roof-tile ends; Taegam, the greedy, bibulous, sometimes female housekeeper or overseer who resides behind the chimney flue or in the kitchen with the spices, and usually hovers over the soy jar; and finally, the conception deity, or Chesŏk-bul, of the home, who is mostly concerned with procreation. Covell believes the latter may be the mythical Buddhist monk who seduced the mythical Birth Grandmother.

Anthropologists dispute the complete origins of Korean shamanism. Dr. Kendall believes they lie largely in China, but that Siberia usually receives the credit because of Korea's need to "prove a northern origin." Certainly the Siberian *saman*, who crossed the Bering Strait to become the shaman of Amerindian lore, has also had his or her influence on the *mudang*.

The phenomenon is universal; only the aspects vary from culture to culture. As in Europe—which presumably got it from central Asia, via the Huns and the Visigoths—the restless dead torment the living. Says Alan Covell: "Seoul's rites are a combination of Korean shamanism's northern inheritance (via Siberia and Manchuria) and Tao-shamanism's hell-sequence which migrated into Korea from northern China."

The Asian shaman tradition is returning to America: Ch'oi Hui-a, the first American *mudang*, was a spirit daughter of Kim Kum-hwa (who was "called" at age eleven, had already reached her twenties when forced to leave her native North Korea during the war, and who danced on the Washington mall in 1982).

The largest burial tumuli are those of the old shaman-chieftains, both in Siberia and the peninsula. The "flying horse" theme on these graves seems to be Siberian in origin. According to Covell, an uplifted tail indicates an Arabian horse, as opposed to the usual Mongol ponies. The Altai, however, considered reindeer the most magical of animals and wore reindeer antlers on helmets for longevity, virility, and fecundity. The Chinese, in contrast, preferred to fly to heaven on a three-legged bird.

Both the shaman-kings of Silla in Kyŏngju and the shaman-chieftains of Siberia also saw the silver birch as a ladder to heaven for anyone currently out of reindeer or horses. This ladder-tree appears on the Sillan crowns. Some see the birch as a tree of life, with a leaf for each mortal, and superstitious

Buddhists lay a gilded leaf in front of a Buddha for each close relative who dies.

Alan Covell has written of the essentiality of music in shamanism. The *chang-gu* is a toylike drum which is hit from one side with a stick and from the other with the palm. There is a primitive brass cymbal called a *ching*. Other percussion instruments include the "princess bell" and the floating calabash. There are also groups of bells, with a brass handle or a cloth strap, which may originally have been horse bells. These are used to summon the spirits. Weapons such as the *chang,* or trident, the crescent halberd called the *kom*, and the chopper called the *kal*, are also used to provide accompaniment to music.

Fans are used—a different one for each spirit—especially by the clairvoyant *chŏm-jaen-gi* or *chŏm-changi*. *Mansin* are actresses, and the different spirits that possess them require different costumes. They usually wear all of them at once, and strip off the outer garments as the ritual proceeds.

Alan Covell has remarkable pictures of *mudang* flirting sensuously with knives. Why is there no bleeding? He offers hypotheses—that the trance slows the heartbeat, reducing circulation, or that it is simply mind over matter in altered states of consciousness. There's a twelve-year-old *mansin*, he says, who, being so light, can actually *leap* on knives. Perhaps balancing a whole pig on a pole is just as difficult.

Clothes of the dead also play an important role in shaman ritual. Says Covell:

> The soul of the dead is summoned back by the presence of his or her clothes placed beside the altar. The spirit-medium raises these clothes up and swings them around in a dance, then wraps them around her body as she feels the soul taking possession of her. At this point, the spirit-medium is able to speak with the voice of the deceased.

137

The family and friends or relatives then converse with the dead, lamenting with loud voices. Finally, the angelic spirits take the dead soul away.

Later, he relates, the *mansin* may be possessed by the messenger of the king of hell:

This messenger, Iljik Saja, is strong and willful. He will attempt to destroy the main altar and also to reach the white paper (with the name of the dead person) on the central altar, so that symbolically he can carry the dead soul directly to hell.

The relatives are expected to guard the altars and protect them from Iljik Saja, for the shamaness, when possessed by him, is extraordinarily strong.

Halla Pai Huhm lists the extreme variety of memorial *kut* and virtually every other ritual, including the *hon-nyŏng kut* for marrying the dead. She describes the great range of food offerings, from "boiled whole pig" to "dried Alaskan pollack," displayed on the tables, which may number from three to ten, depending on the region and on the spirit invoked. She presents a compendium of the different classes of charismatic witch, the costumes, musical instruments, decorations, tools, even the symptoms of the *sin-byŏng* annunciation sickness. She describes and names the different singing styles and choruses.

She gives a detailed description of knife-dancing. The "knife" is the *chakto*, a sort of machete. It is used in the *chakto gŏri* and the *changsu* (army general) *gŏri*. The *mudang* wears trousers, a blue top, and a red overcoat. A pitcher of water is placed on a mat in the yard, with a container of uncooked rice on top. The *mansin* sings *mansubaji*, picks up two *chakto* tied together with cloths, and invokes the *changsu* spirit. When he possesses her, she puts the *chakto* on the pitcher, dances and steps onto the blades, facing in each compass direction in turn and dancing to *t'ang-ak* music. She carries a rice-cake steamer, which she gives to the sponsor of the *kut*. Finally, she steps down from the knives.

Halla Pai Huhm also gives one of the most complete descriptions of the funeral *chinogwi kut* in Ch'un-ch'ŏng and Ch'ŏlla provinces, where the "movements" (*gŏri*) are more numerous than in the Seoul region. The impressive *gŏri*, in which the ghost narrates through the throat of the shaman, is the twelfth or *wŏn yŏngsil gŏri*.

This writer has observed similar ceremonies. In the nineteenth rite, *saja samsong,* the *mansin* uses her body to tear a hempen cloth to separate the wraith from the family, who put money on the cloth to placate the messengers from Hades. In the twentieth rite, the *mudang* becomes Pari Kong-ju, wearing royal garments to take the deceased to paradise.

The twenty-second ritual is *kilgarugi* ("parting roads"). Cotton cloth represents the road from this world to the next: hempen cloth is the entrance to the other world. Ribbons of each type of cloth are cut into twelve-foot lengths for a man, nine-foot lengths for a departed female, seven-foot ones for an unmarried person of either sex. Four people hold the four ends. The *mansin*, to the tune of the *chang-gu* and the *chegŭm* playing *t'ang-ak* music, splits the ribbons with her hips. When cutting the cotton cloth, the *mansin* carries a *chegŭm* in either hand and has hemp wound around her; when cutting the hemp, she holds swords in both hands. Four more rituals follow before the congregants can share the food with the last of the demons being chased away.

Dr. Lee Du-hyun of Seoul National University must also have recorded almost every known *mudang* rite. A professor of Korean literature who has specialized in popular forms, he is an acknowledged expert on trance possession. He has provided a memorable account of a *sumangogu kut* for drowned fishermen, which lasted three days and in which the souls of the dead were transferred into a "spirit basket."

Dr. Lee describes how, on the second day, one mother becomes particularly possessed and begins shaking the son's basket violently.

The *mudang* cries: "You came!" and appeals to the dead youth to speak. "Are you leaving forever without saying a word?" The family cries: "*Yŏboseyo*, Ch'an-su! Why don't you speak?" The mother shakes the basket more violently. The *mudang* says the young man has gone to the other world.

Another becomes possessed and, speaking with her dead son's voice, cries: "Father was unjust with me!" She smites her husband with the spirit basket, and he says: "I'm sorry. I was stern with you so that you should become a good man." The dead youth bemoans the sinking. His mother picks up her son's guitar and finds she can play it. She dances.

This dancing is called *mugam*—trance possession by a *mudang*'s client. Lee says the hereditary *tan-gol mudang* of Jeju Island, for instance, rarely go beyond what he calls "pseudo-possession," but that their clients are often more inspired.

According to Lee, "possession" and "ecstatic cults" characteristically develop among "the weak and oppressed, and particularly young women in male-dominant societies." He has also concluded that "daughters-in-law lighten their pent-up feelings of oppression and solace themselves with the *kut*."

Lee has made a study of *sin-byŏng*, and cites some pertinent descriptions by others. Kim Tae-gŏn described it as "persistent illness for no apparent reason, appetite loss, unwillingness to eat meat and fish, craving for cold water, weakness or pain in the limbs, hallucination and crazed wanderings." Lee says that the symptoms, which are relieved by the trance which makes the girl a shaman, also "mark the would-be shaman in Siberia, the Americas, Africa and Australia."

He cites Kim Kwang-yel, a psychiatrist, as dividing *sin-byŏng* into two phases. In the first, the future *mudang* exhibits "hysterical or psychosomatic symptoms such as anorexia, weaknesses, insomnia, indigestion and/or functional paralysis of the extremities." In the next phase, termed "depersonalization," the "symptoms are aggravated" and accompanied by "hallucinatory experiences, dreams of revelation or prophecy, confusion, with or without psychomotor excitement." Dr. Kim interprets this as an attempt to resolve "longstanding inner conflicts."

Rhi Bu-yong, whom Dr. Lee says is a psychiatrist "of Jungian orientation," claims that shamans are "recovered neurotics or psychotics." K. I. Kim concurs and maintains that Korean shamanism is an institutionalized system of sublimation, with positive and negative effects. The *mudang* is a "severe neurotic or psychotic" who serves society as a lunatic surrogate. Dr. Kim Dŭk-ran, a clinical psychiatrist who teaches at Kang-nŭng University on the east coast, has told this writer that she is of a similar opinion. She attributes the *mudang* "calling" to early tragedies, sometimes including rape.

Interestingly, it is a scientist in the Soviet Union, where shamanism is theoretically forbidden, who disagrees. S. M. Shirokogoroff contends that shamans have a normal personality. Two of his colleagues are of the same opinion: *sin-byŏng* is not neurosis, only "uneasiness."

The late Youngsook Kim-Harvey, a Korean-born American researcher, defines the relationship of a shaman and her possessing spirit as "transactional and mutually binding, as in a marriage." She describes *mudang* as being highly intelligent, imaginative, with an above-average capacity for creative improvisation, highly articulate and persuasive, willful, self-centered, self-reliant, "goal-oriented," intuitive, calculating, manipulative, self-righteous, dramatic, and artistic.

At the bottom of the occult hierarchy are the fortune-tellers. Virtually everyone, including pious Catholics, frequents them. An American researcher, Barbara Young, found that 85 out of 106 women, and 22 out of 41 men, had consulted seers. The wealthy arranged house calls or contacted their clairvoyants by telephone.

Female clairvoyants are highly intuitive and draw on the occult as much as other *mudang*. They see their work as a vocation imposed by occult forces. Many people seek an annual horoscope. Some go to more than one seer, to see if two or more agree. Not only the Chinese zodiac but also ancestor roles are taken into account.

Twelve-year zodiacal horoscopes about character and destiny are similar to those we in the West have inherited from Egypt and read in our local papers. There is a similar attachment of importance to the exact time of birth, so as to calculate the four *saju*—year, lunar month, day, hour—and the eight characters, which in turn are subdivided. There are sixty possible permutations, depending on cycles. (If you want to do it yourself, you will have to learn Korean or Chinese and buy an almanac!)

Divination through the spirits requires a ritual similar to a *kut*. This involves music and feasting, and costs money. Rice grains, like the tea leaves of Europe, will be read. Alternatively, the seer may throw coins, bamboo sticks, or small metal rods. Some clairvoyants are "physiognomists" who look not only at the face but the palms, fingertips, feet, and bone structure.

The seer consults the *I-Ching*—the Chinese Book of Changes. In *sae-chŏm*, caged birds are used. The customer buys one and releases it. The first of several white papers at which it pecks is opened and read.

Numerology is as important in Korea as in the Arab world, and enters into name-giving. The three Chinese characters of a person's name are selected not only for sonorousness but also for their number of brush strokes and for whether they are suitable for divination.

The *mudang* entered the twentieth century powerfully, under the patronage of the formidable Empress Min, who made her *mansin,* Chil-yon-gun, a princess, and to whose son she gave a high post. The Westernized presidents Syngman Rhee and Pak Chung-hi, as noted, tried to suppress shamanism. In the North, it fell under the ax of Marxist anticlericalism, but exceptions were growingly made because of the shamanist nature of Kim Il-sŏng himself. In both Koreas, during repression, it moved to the countryside and acquired a dissenter's halo. Now, the Mudang Association's *kut* center on Mount Samgak, on the northern fringes of Seoul, operates on a dawn-to-dusk basis. Currently, the South Korean constitution respects "all ancient cultural traditions without prejudice."

Shamanism informs the new faiths. Christianity, especially Korean Protestantism, has incorporated much of shamanism. In the Korean Bible, "God" is translated by the same word, *Hanamin,* that witches use for the "Great Spirit." Investigations have shown that most Koreans believe that dead "souls" can be contacted after death.

A 1983 *Korea Times* survey revealed that 80.6 percent of Korean Protestant pastors believed that mental illness was the "work of devils." Sixty-five percent endorsed faith-healing, preferably in a family environment. What could be more shamanist! Researchers who questioned fundamentalists about persons who become excited at "revivalist" meetings found that 84.6 percent thought the exalted were "possessed by devils." Many Korean churches teach—as Jean Calvin did—that misfortune is the reward of "sin."

Grace Halsell tells us that there are forty million fundamentalist and televangelical Christians in America (equal in number to American Catholics), and that these believe that the Last Trump will come, in a decade's time, at a nuclear Armageddon, when only they will be saved. It is an age of occult superstition, of shamanism. One can only imagine the fortune waiting to be made if, behind every Korean grocery in Washington, D.C., there was a *dang* shrine with a *mudang* who could speak to a customer in the voice of his or her dead father. The *mudang* has a longer track record than the medium in Europe or the shrink in America—but she similarly needs a suggestible customer. Marx said that religion was the opiate of the masses. Korean *mudang,* like fundamentalist Christians and Muslims, may well be proving him right; but they have clearly overtaken his own appeal to the senses.

All Korean priests and pastors are male, which may help explain why the *mudang,* whose appeal is mostly to women, has survived the challenge of Christianity in the country's current phase of Westernization. Nevertheless, the *mudang* profession, like the stage in Shakespeare's time, is still seen as slightly disreputable; there are sniggers of disbelief when a *kosa* is held to inaugurate a new hotel extension in Seoul or the Friendship Bell Pavilion at San Padro's Angel Park, overlooking Los Angeles harbor.

Moreover, being born in a hospital or living in an apartment without rafters challenges the need for some time-honored rituals. The *taegam* overseer spirit can no longer live, in modern homes, behind the *ondol* chimney flue. Does a toilet spirit exist when the toilet is no longer in a separate building from the home? As Alan Covell points out, shamanism is also challenged by the fact that women are no longer confined to the "compound."

Modern work schedules cannot make more than minimal allowances for "inauspicious days"—which if strictly observed would leave only the last two days of each ten-day sequence as auspicious. (For a wedding, however, an auspicious day would probably still be chosen by a qualified seer.) Hygiene education and modern medicine have replaced malevolent spirits with bacteria as the cause of disease. Yet the fact that some people have immunity while others don't (some heavy smokers live to old age, while some nonsmokers die) still leaves an argument for the spirits. AIDS may well bring new followers to shamanism, if a purposeful confidence is the only cure.

THE KOREANS

1.

2.

A LIFE BY THE SEA

1. Repairing nets at Hae-un-dae [Russell Warren Howe]
2. Schoolchildren walk home on the beach at Daech'ŏn [Russell Warren Howe]
3. Inns by the sea at Daech'ŏn [Russell Warren Howe]
4. Re-enacting a traditional farmers' dance [KOIS]
5. Tightrope skipping at a rural festival [KOIS]

THE KOREANS

1. Monks shaving at Hae-in-sa [Russell Warren Howe]
2. The temple of Hae-in-sa [Russell Warren Howe]
3. Buddha and bodhisattvas at Hae-in-sa [Russell Warren Howe]
4. Rice farming near Hae-in-sa [Russell Warren Howe]
5. An inn at Ham-dŏk on Jeju Island [Russell Warren Howe]
6 & 7. Jeju sea diving women preparing for a competition [Russell Warren Howe]
8. The "Falling Flowers" cliff at Nak-hwa-am. It was here that many Korean court women took their lives a thousand years ago to avoid capture by a Chinese army [Russell Warren Howe]

5.

6.

7.

8.

5

A LIFE WITH THE SEA

The islanders believe that pregnancy, childbirth and the growth of a child are governed by the goddess of life, *sam-sin*. Thus, if a woman is barren for a long time after her marriage, a prayer is given to *sam-sin* by *tan-gol* or an older woman who may be her mother or mother-in-law. At dawn in a corner of the inner room, the women's quarters, which *sam-sin* is believed to inhabit, a bowl of rice and a cup of pure water are offered on a small wooden table and a spell for pregnancy is chanted. The ritual is the same for a married couple that has no male child but many girls. During the pregnancy, the prayer to *sam-sin* is also offered for a safe childbirth and for the good fortune and health of the child after birth. All the rituals concerned with pregnancy and childbirth are enacted mainly on the initiative of the woman's natal family. Her parents, especially, are anxious first about her safety in childbirth and then for the birth of a male child which will stabilize the new mother's status in her husband's family.

The birth takes place at home and delivery is assisted by the woman's mother or mother-in-law, as there

A LIFE WITH THE SEA

is no doctor or professional midwife on Kagŏdo. Once delivery is completed, the umbilical cord and afterbirth are burned in the courtyard. A bowl of rice and *miyŏk* soup are offered to *sam-sin* to express thanks for the safe childbirth. The main gate of the house is stretched with a left-twisted strawrope to protect the newborn baby from harmful spirits for at least three weeks, during which time the new mother may not go outside of the house, and strangers or unclean persons are prohibited from entering. For two or three weeks in the postpartum period, the maternal grandmother helps by taking care of the new mother and child as well as by doing domestic work.

On the one hundredth day after birth, a small feast is held to give formal recognition of the child's membership in the community as well as in the family. Close relatives and neighbors, usually only adults, are invited to the feast and entertained with rice, *miyŏk* soup, white cake and wine. At this time, the baby's maternal grandparents bring with them such gifts as clothing and a carrying blanket for the baby.

———Han Sang-bok, *Korean Fishermen*

A PENINSULA IS NOT AN ISLAND, BUT ALMOST, and Korea is an islanded peninsula. A country that is about six hundred miles, as the crane flies, from north to south, but has about 5,500 miles of coastline, plus about the same amount again on its 3,305 isles and skerries, is a child of the sea. A nation that depends on seafood for eighty percent of its animal protein is a maritime nation by definition, even if only five percent of the population are responsible for fishing and gathering it—

just as the United States is the world's greatest agricultural nation, although ninety percent of its population are urban dwellers.

In many ways, Korea's islands—over a hundred of which are inhabited—are museums of the culture in a way that instant communities like Seoul and Kwangju and Taejŏn could never be. Jeju, the largest island, not only has the country's biggest witches' festival and the most famous guild of *haenyŏ* diving women, but also one of the finest *ki-saeng* houses in the country. Chin-do is not only a major fishing center but is also where *chindo* dogs are bred to compete one day in the class of domesticated wolves, no longer dominated exclusively by the German shepherd and the Eskimo husky. The adventures of the longline fishermen of Ul-rŭng-do, in the storm-tossed wild of the East Sea, are no more demanding than the nightly torment of the squid trawlermen of Sŏng-san.

The heavily tidal, fjorded west coast faces seas that rarely go below forty fathoms on the stretch to China. To the country's east, the mountains slip steeply into the Pacific, and beachside hamlets are close to very deep water. In the west, the fishermen of Ch'ŏlla trawl the seabed or chase cuttlefish and octopi with blazing lights. To the east, they trawl the surface for a wide variety of fish. The life is hard and the drinking heavy, with the old salts soaking acacia blossom in their *so-ju* or *jŏng-jong* to enhance the high.

Nowhere is Korea's restless preoccupation with witchery so evident as along the coasts, and the *Tano Che* or festival of Kang-nŭng (*tano* is the fifth day of the fifth lunar month) attracts visitors from all over the country. Because of this popularity, it has perhaps inevitably become debased in recent times by an infestation of lesser fortune-telling *mudang* and *ssirum* wrestling contests that remind one of a country fair in Somerset or Touraine.

A LIFE WITH THE SEA

The nine hundred islands which emerge from the breakers along the Hwang-hae coast are the tops of old mountains, from the days when Paleolithic Korean man could walk due west into China. More than twice as many islands are scattered off the jagged country's southern coast, including 1,841 in the southwest of Ch'ŏlla province. They lie on the path of the migratory fish on their way to the Dong Hae. However, strong winds and fast, treacherous currents have always made the area dangerous for the *ttemma,* the oared skiffs long used for trawling the gray-sanded floor of this shallow sea. Even though almost all *ttemma* have outboard motors today, and larger *chung-sŏn* boats are more and more in use, many fishing vessels are lost each year, especially in the summer typhoons.

The quotation at the beginning of this chapter comes from a study of Kagŏdo Island by Han Sang-bok, a professor of anthropology at Seoul National University. Kagŏdo is the most southwesterly point of habitation in Korea, a thirty-hour trip from Mog-p'o, including an overnight stop. Little has changed there in the twenty years since Dr. Han did his research. About four hundred families live in three villages, built on small coves with natural breakwaters. The skerries, rocks, and other navigation hazards halt the ferry at night, and this makes the trip to the large mainland town of Mog-p'o a time-consuming and rare occurrence. The island is administered from Hŭksan-do, which is the *myŏn* (county seat) to Kagŏdo's *ri* (hamlet), and which also has a *p'a-si,* a mobile fish market.

The *chung-sŏn* boatmen of Kagŏdo follow the glistening banks of anchovy, attracting a swarm with a thousand-watt bulb powered by a noisy dynamo. The skipper opens the throttle and overtakes the swarm. The fish follow the light and swim into the trawl as the boat slows suddenly, then stops altogether to allow the net to be hauled in and its contents emptied into the hold. Thousands of the little silver fish dance a brittle fandango of panic in the harsh glare of the monstrous bulb, and the trawl is overboarded once more, with the pole men extending it. The grizzled salts squint into the sleeting wind, brush the mucus from their nostrils with the back of a calloused hand, wipe the palms dry on their trousers, and light a cigarette, while waiting for the skipper to spot a new swarm.

When the boat is loaded to capacity, it returns to whichever of the three villages—Tae-p'ung-ni, Hang-ni or the "capital," Tae-ri—from which it set out, sounding its horn as the hamlet heaves into sight to summon the wives to collect their shares of the unloading. The boat owner, who gets sixty percent of the catch, brings the crew to his house and serves a light meal—rice, fish, pickles, and rice wine. Then, if there are still enough hours of darkness left, the boat goes out again.

The share-out among the crew is mathematically complicated, with the lion's share going to the skipper, the engine mechanic, and the dynamo operator. The average crewman gets about one and a quarter percent of the catch. Over a season, this amounts to between two hundred and six hundred *tok* of anchovy. (The *tok* is a pot which holds about three pints of water, and in which the anchovies are usually pickled in brine. Since there is no freezing plant on Kagŏdo, all fish must be dried, salted, or shipped quickly to Mog-p'o in a cooling container rented from a *kaek-chu* (wholesaler) there.)

Virtually all the islanders are tied to one *kaek-chu* or another, and many *kaek-chu* now own fleets of trucks and trawlers. They are the key businessmen in the fishermen's lives. When a trawler crew goes to Mog-p'o to see its *kaek-chu,* he boards and lodges them for a couple of days.

The best larger fish in these waters is the *cho-gi,* or yellow corvina, which arrive early in the year to spawn and stay for a month or two. Hundreds of *chungsŏn* of about twenty tons sail into the seas near Kagŏdo with drift or gill nets. The *chogi p'asi,* or mobile fish market, arrives from Hŭksan-do, and *kaekchu* send out *posŏn* from the mainland to buy fish at the *p'asi*. A *posŏn* is a tiny freighter—a floating hold which can take ten tons of fish, packed in with sheaves of ice.

The rocky island grows some vegetables, including sweet potatoes, but no rice—only barley, from which the women make *makkŏlli*. During the *p'asi,* while the men are selling their catches, the women sell vegetables and *makkŏlli* to the *chungsŏn* crews and other "townies"; but mostly it is the strangers who steal the show. Says Dr. Han:

> *P'asi* is a kind of drama in which wealthy boat owners, wage-earning crew fishermen and merchants from the outside are the leading actors, and the madame and prostitutes accompanying the merchants are the supporting actors. And the native islanders are nothing but the spectators who look at the theatrical performance from a distance.

Seaweed farming is another important element of the island economy. Plots are allotted by household, so newlyweds establish separate residences. Another difference from the mainland is that it is the last-born son who remains, with his wife and children, in the parents' home, although the oldest son is still responsible for *chesa*—ancestor veneration. Because there are only eighteen surnames on Kagŏdo, exogamy is not possible. Han says that because of the shortage of marriage partners, parents try to arrange marriages while their offspring are still small. This has led to *ch'ima jari* family pacts whereby sisters or cousins from one family marry brothers or close kin from another, with two families thus forming both an alliance and a conspiracy to keep out marital competition.

To a Scotsman, there is an eery resemblance to life in the Hebrides. There is a paid *i-jang*—village headman—who holds office for two years, and it is he who deals with the "outside world" of mainland officialdom. The police come from the mainland, but their main task is to watch out for North Korean frogmen or "subversives." They rarely intervene in local matters such as barroom brawls because—as in the Hebrides—mainland forces of order are not acceptable to the islanders.

What applies to legal offenses also applies to traditional ones. Filial piety, fraternity, and chastity are communal concerns, says Dr. Han, who explains that punishment is by *tŏksŏng-mori* or *hwaji-gae,* imposed by the elders. A young man who fails in his filial duties is wrapped in a *tŏksŏk* (straw mat) and beaten with cudgels. There are no severe injuries: the principal purpose is humiliation, and the youth will be needed back on deck the following day. He is required to make a public apology. The *hwaji-gae* is for incest or adultery. The man or woman's outstretched hands are tied to a wooden bar across the back, to which is attached a drum, which is beaten as the offender is paraded, shamefaced, through the village for half a day. There is of course no court on the island itself, and even quite serious conflicts between villages or between islands, involving large sums of damages, are settled out of court.

In elections, political candidates do not visit these tiny ocean communities, and the people either vote as the elders advise, or abstain. Only military service gives the young men a glimpse of what Korea itself is really like. For the visitor to Kagŏdo, the island offers a portrait of the country a generation ago, with only electricity and motor-driven boats thrown in.

Marriage and death are matters of enormous ceremony on these islands. The principal determining factor in a marriage is *kung-hap*—the horoscope. If the two *kung-hap* are congenial, the potential groom's family sends *sa-sŏng* to the parents of the potential bride. *Sa-sŏng* is a letter of betrothal containing their son's horoscope, accompanied by a full set of clothes for the girl.

On a date selected by some local servant of the occult, the

chung-bang, or best man, is sent to the bride's house with more gifts, which must include red and blue silk. He is entertained with food and drink. Between then and the wedding day, also selected by divination, kin and friends send gifts, mostly of food, to both families. On the wedding day, the *chung-bang* is sent to the bride's house to announce the groom's arrival. Villagers waylay the groom and pretend to try to prevent his passage. When he finally reaches the bride's house, the *chung-bang* announces the fact dramatically by dashing a pot on the ground. The groom then walks across a fire on the ground while the gathering guests pelt him with soybeans. All these activities are meant to ensure that he does not bear evil spirits on his body or clothing when he enters the home of his future in-laws.

Inside, the groom hands his bride's family a carved wooden goose. The bride makes her appearance and pours wine for her future husband. He drinks and returns the gesture. They bow. The ceremony is repeated—two bows, and three cups of wine each. A wedding feast with music follows, and continues until midnight. The next day, there is a feast at the home of the groom's family. The bride arrives in a palanquin and pours wine for all her new kin. On the third day, the young couple return to the bride's home and stay with her parents for a few days, before leaving to establish their own separate household.

When an islander dies, a small table with rice, fish, and a pair of straw shoes is set up in the courtyard for the messenger from heaven. An elder calls "Return!" three times, and throws the dead person's clothes over the roof, to test whether his spirit has really departed. Friends then watch the corpse for two days, drinking and gambling at cards, while mourning clothes are made of sackcloth, hemp, and straw, and food is cooked for the mourners. An elaborate bier is built, and a coffin made. The corpse is washed, dressed in white, and bound with hempen rope tied with seven knots.

Most work in the village, including fishing and seaweed gathering, stops at this time, as relatives and friends pitch in with work, food, or money—which will all be reciprocated at an appropriate time. The mourning family keeps note of what each has contributed, so important is the theme of reciprocity in Korean life.

Early on the burial day, men go out to dig the grave. Except for a deceased's widow, only men carry or follow a coffin. The geomancer who has selected the grave site performs a ceremony to ensure that the departed is accepted by the earth god. After the burial, another ceremony is conducted for the safe journey of the spirit to the afterworld. The ceremony is simpler for children, in a special burial ground called a *kolchang*. A pregnant woman is buried twice—once for herself, once for the unborn child.

Mourning ceremonies take place at the family altar every two weeks for two years, then once a year. For dead parents, this annual rite gathers the entire family. A host of spirits, including of course ancestral ones, are propitiated. On Korea's islands, one is reminded of certain traditions in Africa: the living believe that the dead are always close—not so much malevolent as quirky and petty if not constantly remembered and propitiated. Similar sensitivity must be shown to the *sŏngju* who lives in the main beam of the house and protects its male head, and to the *chowang* who inhabits the kitchen and watches over his wife. Most Korean death rites are similar.

There are also village ceremonies, conducted on various lunar-calendar dates. The most important of these is the *dang-je* at the village *dang* or shrine. Officiants for this, selected by the elders, must "purify themselves in mind and body," Han says, and live in seclusion until the ritual date. Their houses are "tied with ceremonial ropes to signal that villagers and outsiders may not approach them."

On Kagŏdo, the *dang-je* coincides with the end of the lunar year; afterward, on the third day of the first lunar month, ten or fifteen youths collect on the volcanic beach, forming a band with traditional musical instruments. Children and others follow them as they play their way through the hamlet, stopping at every house, where the band leader prays for the health and prosperity of the family. It takes twelve days to complete the tour, with the players entertained to food and *makkŏlli*. Then begin the first seaweed and shellfish harvests of the nascent year.

These islands are, in short, virtually as shamanist as they were hundreds of years ago. The Japanese occupation and the more recent "economic miracle" in Korea have developed the fishing and other marine economy; but the islanders remain close to their spirits and to their dead. Says Han:

> Although many elements of Buddhism, Taoism and Confucianism have filtered into the islanders' belief system, in Kagŏdo no Buddhist, Taoist or Confucian temple has ever existed as an independent religious institution. There has been virtually no Christian penetration. The only belief and ritual system which involves the entire village is that of the *dang,* where *dang-je* is carried out at least once a year.

Another Seoul National professor who assisted this writer, Ch'ŏn Kyŏng-su, has similarly studied the hardscrabble life of yet another fishing island, Hasami. As in the Scottish islands, the people are crofters—farmer-fishermen—using oxen to till the highland slopes, where they raise virtually all the vegetables and spices of Korean cooking. The women also grow laver seaweed—called *kim*—on bamboo systems in the shallows. With their children, they gather shellfish and net the little *nag-ji* octopi. Laundry covers the rocks of the pebble beach. On warm days, naked children swim, and sometimes their fathers swim with them, when they are not otherwise busy repairing nets—a family activity.

The fishermen of Hasami fish either with the *chunat* method—placing up to a hundred hooks on a nylon leader which may be as much as a hundred meters long—or by the *sammai*, or "triple net." Both are methods introduced by the Japanese, and the *sammai*, which takes even very small fish, is illegal. It can be floated, weighted to the bottom, hand trolled, or laid out on rocks which are covered at high tide.

The most reliable source of income is seaweed, both kelp and laver, bred on bamboo mats in the sea by a system invented by the late Dr. Kathleen Mary Drew Baker of Britain's University of Manchester, who had no idea that her theoretical research had any commercial application. However, the method has come to Korea in recent times from Japan, where there is a monument to her ("Kasserine-san") at Sumiyoshi.

Seaweed is a winter crop but, despite the bitter cold of the water then, it is mostly women's work—women being traditionally gatherers and men hunters (in this case, of fish). However, at the height of the season, the whole family, including small children, work on the laver harvest.

In the Korean tradition, men do *pakkat-yil* (outside work) and women *an-yil* (inside work). All around the jagged coastline, one finds women working alone in the fields while the men fish. A woman on a boat is considered bad luck. The fishing villages are also more generation-conscious. Persons only five or ten years older merit special terms of respect; by the same token, one's father or uncle cannot be one's friend. Old people suffer the least constraints. Elderly women gather at someone's house to drink and sing, or tell bawdy jokes. The older men prefer the wine shop, where they drink, smoke, sing, and gamble for small stakes. They can bring their own snacks if they wish, and may oblige the proprietor to stay open until the early hours. No one drinks alone; cups are passed from mouth to mouth—a practice called *chantoligi*—like the *porón* in a Spanish café or the calabash in Africa. Boys begin to drink at fifteen. When parents are away, a teenage boy or girl may throw an all-night party. These days, they play rock records. The boys drink and smoke. Everybody dances. Sexual activity is prevented by the absence of privacy. Neighbors and parents respect the *ki-bun* of the young and pretend to be unaware of their goings-on.

The poverty of the community lends great importance to the *kye*. The commonest is the *chŏ-ch'uk* (thrift club), referred to earlier in this book, where women withdraw their portion by turns. Another form is the *honsang-kye* (marriage-funeral *kye*). Ch'ŏn's accounts of *kye* meetings are hilarious. *Robert's Rules of Order* do not apply. There is shouting, interrupting, heckling. Gentle insults are traded. The women's groups are the most raucous.

Kye can be formed for almost any reason for which one might ask a bank for a loan. Members are invariably of the same sex and age group. Ch'ŏn cites a case of a man who wanted to buy some land for 350,000 wŏn. He and six friends put in fifty thousand wŏn a month for seven months, with the organizer drawing the first 350,000-wŏn dividend. He tells of cases where members are unable to keep up payments; rather than face the shame, they leave their natal village and move to a city, where they eventually die far from their ancestors' spirits.

The new times have brought new laws, not all of which make as much sense when viewed from so far from Seoul. The old universal principle that a law which will not be obeyed is bad law seems to apply. Where reafforestation laws applied, even the gathering of fallen twigs was forbidden; but inspectors announced their visits in advance and were either paid off by the villagers, or taken to drink while firewood was hidden. The official was viewed not as a corrupt extortionist, as he might be in the West, but as cooperative. As in the West, "justice is for the rich," and few civil or criminal matters on Kagŏdo ever go to court.

The European practice of royal marriages between cousins, such as that of Britain's Elizabeth II, would be considered incestuous and unlawful in Korea—under both national law and Confucian principle. Marriage to someone with a different family name and from a different village—what anthropologists call patrilineal and patrilocal exogamy—is the tradition; but this creates problems on the islands, where at least the taboo on marriage within the village is sometimes broken, once it is agreed that there is no known blood relationship between the parties.

Because of the difficulty of finding suitable partners, matchmaking, often by aunts or other relatives, is much in evidence. Ch'ŏn reports that on Hasami, this sometimes even involves a brief betrothal period, when the couple sleep together before finally deciding to wed.

In this and other ways, island villages like Hasami are more "modern" than distant outposts such as Kagŏdo. On Hasami, engagement parties are even held in a photographer's shop. The bride's acceptance of a gold ring completes the first part of the wedding ceremony. After this, she is referred to as the groom's wife, although the wedding will not be completed for many weeks. More gifts are exchanged.

On the day set for completion, bride and groom sit on either side of a screen in the bride's house. A woman of the family serves the groom food; then through her, he passes some of it to his bride. Says Ch'ŏn: "After the bride eats the food, the marriage ceremony is complete."

The bride is then carried to her husband's house in a palanquin, followed by kinsmen carrying the futon-style bed, a gift from her parents. The groom brings up the rear. Because there are no horses or mules on Hasami, a friend trails a stick between the groom's legs to represent his mount. In a reversal of what Han describes on Kagŏdo, men of the groom's village symbolically try to stop the palanquin, are bought off with cartons of cigarettes, then take over carrying the bride. In another reversal, a shaman lights a fire on the ground at the entrance to the groom's compound, and it is the bride and the bed carriers who must pass over it to ensure that no bad spirits ride on them as they enter. The shamaness pelts everyone and everything with beans, cotton seeds, and salt. Light bulbs are dashed to the ground to make explosive noises. There are other rituals, including throwing a small *bang-sŏk* mattress onto the roof of the house to show that newlyweds are in residence. After that, there is the usual exchange of feasting visits between the two families.

Of course, none of this has any legal significance. For a marriage to exist in the eyes of the government, a form must be filed with the local municipal authority. The husband can do this on his own, using his *to-jang* chop. No consenting gesture is needed from the bride. (This offers obvious prospects for abuse. A few years ago, a Miss Korea collecting her *ho-juk dung-bon* in order to marry discovered that she already had a husband; some unknown admirer whom she had never seen had "married" the beauty queen.) The town hall operation has all the romance of buying a gun license in America or a dog license in Britain. In places like Hasami, it is essentially an afterthought, often left until just before the birth of the first child which—like the official marriage itself—will have to be recorded in the *ho-juk dung-bon*.

Hasami has also moved on from chastity and monogamy, but in a Korean context. Some men who can afford it acquire "second" or "little" wives, even though polygamy is not a part of the culture. The shamanist ceremony for the second wedding is not matched by any formal filing at the *ri* or *myŏn* office. It amounts to respectabilizing concubinage, and avoiding the doomsday-book consequences of divorce, with the husband held to have equal responsibilities to both spouses. Similarly, since widows under Confucianism suffer an interdiction against remarriage (because this would confuse the ancestral spirits), Hasami also has a concept of "surrogate husbands" *(taebogu)* who are married to widows in a shamanist ceremony which is different from that of normal weddings.

Ch'ŏn also found two cases of *sa-hon*, or ghost marriage, on Hasami. They were similar to a *hon-nyŏng kut*. Performed by a shaman, with straw figures representing the principals, they joined young men and women who had died before they could choose marriage partners. The two families would henceforth treat each other as would the families of living spouses.

South Korea's most remote island is Ul-rŭng, one hundred seventy miles from the high-speed ferryboat dock at Pohang on the Eastern Sea. The bumpy six-hour ride puts the tiny ocean province halfway to Japan; although the old-fashioned boat from Mog-p'o to Hasami takes many more hours, Ul-rŭng has a longer tradition of isolation. Now, a few hardy tourists arrive and sleep in the few *yŏ-gwan* around To-dong harbor. A tiny neighboring island, Chuk-do, raises beef, sheltering the cows in protective trenches with thatched roofs during the windy winters; but most of the food is fresh seafood which has never had to see a refrigerator.

Ul-rŭng's hills, green with rain, are embroidered with corn, melons, *in-sam*, camelia and palownia trees—anything that will grow on a slope. The palownia is said to be the only tree where a phoenix will nest. *Haenyŏ* with leaded belts dive in the cold, clear water for the wriggling cartoon creatures called sea cucumbers but known locally as *hae-tam*, "*in-sam* of the sea," because of the virility they are supposed to endow on those who eat them. The women also hunt for abalone and other crustaceans, net shrimp, and trap crab and crayfish. But the principal reason why nineteen thousand people live on this twenty-eight-square-mile (seventy-two square kilometers) ocean speck is squid.

Ninety percent of the ninety thousand tons of fish which Ul-rŭng trawls each year consists of cuttlefish, which are stretched out to cure in endless lines along the cliff-shaded shingle. That's about eighty thousand tons of squid, all roughly equal in size—the cones measure about the same length as battery-raised chickens. Assuming that, dried, they weigh about four or five ounces each, that's about six hundred million cuttlefish, or more than a dozen per year for every single member of the South Korean population. Needless to say, the deep waters around Ul-rŭng are also thick with mainland boats at the height of the squid season—September and October.

Ask any Korean to name one island, and he or she is likely to say Jeju. His parents probably went there on their honeymoon, before he was born. It was the only time they ever held hands in public, and the last time they ate their meals together. For Jeju's year-round inhabitants, it is a place where women often do the *pakkat-yil* (outside) work, while the men stay at home and tend the house. The people speak a strange Korean, with elements of Japanese and Chinese in it.

The bureaucrats in Seoul call the island the "Hawaii of the Orient." They talk of getting Bechtel or some other construction giant to build a great free-trade area which will replace Hong Kong when the island of the *tai pan*s goes Marxist. (Other countries have the same idea.) *Newsweek* has called it the "island of the gods." The *Wall Street Journal* has compared it to Bali.

Bali, it is not. Snow graces the peaks of Halla-san, South Korea's tallest mountain. The sand beaches are quite beautiful, but there are only about half a dozen of any size in its ninety square miles. And although one of the country's most attractive *ki-saeng* houses lies up the hill just outside Jeju Town, the male visitor, despite the reputation for beauty of the island women, should not expect much in the way of fleshly frolics.

Jeju has its folklore village, its five miles of caves (actually, lava tubes), and other obvious tourist attractions. But mostly it is a world of its own, with fields sequestered behind lava-stone windbreaker walls, broken by gates of two or three poles. The position of the poles indicates whether the master is at home and, if not, whether he is away temporarily or for an extended absence. Visible from the bus that runs around the coast, or across the island's saddle in the Halla foothills, are huge tumuli graves that stand out on the sloping pastures.

Newsweek notwithstanding, the people of Jeju do not originate from the heavens, like Tan-gun. They descend from three spirits called Yang, Pu, and Ko, who came out of holes in the ground now covered by Jeju Town itself. These three somehow won the affections of three princesses, who originated the tradition of female toilers and male despoilers by showing the spirit trio the land which they had been farming.

If you don't believe that Jejuans are the descendants of farmer-princesses and horny goblins, you may prefer the historical theory that their forebears came from mainland China, joined in the thirteenth century by a few migrants from Korea's Unified Silla kingdom. Indeed, the very name reflects the disinterest shown until recent centuries: *je* means "yonder" and *-ju* meant "distant." Mariners also called Yonder-Place by several other names: Tam-la, Tan-bŭl-la, Tan-na, and Do-i.

In the late thirteenth century, Mongolia expanded its occupation of the peninsula to the island. The Mongols stayed for a century (from 1276 to 1375), and their features mark the faces of Jeju folk today. This is not surprising: thirty-three thousand Mongol soldiers and sailors passed through Jeju on their way to invade Japan's Kyushu Island, and they must surely have kept the few hundred Jejuan women busy. Until recently, during the windy, kite-flying winter, the mountain people of Jeju still wore leather hats, fur stockings, and other Mongol pelt clothing.

The occupiers brought in the short-legged Mongol ponies, which still run wild, but can be captured and broken by anyone with the inclination. They also imported a light dusting of Buddhism, and the island has a few delightful monasteries, mostly surrounded by orchards of temperate-zone fruit, such as tangerines. But the real religion of the islanders is symbolized by the *tol-harubang* or grandfather stones—phallic dwarfs who slightly resemble the huge statues of Easter Island. Jeju holds an annual witches' festival which, although today rather vulgarized and unmystical, remains a tribute to the island's pervasive occult tradition.

After the Mongols left, and the shipwrecked Europeans mentioned earlier made their unannounced appearances, few foreigners were seen on Jeju until the first Japanese honeymooners and American ground-radar crews began to arrive.

It was thirty years ago that the "test" group of tourists disembarked from the rickety ferry and put up at bathless inns. The streets of Jeju Town were then unpaved, unlit. Today, up in the hills above Hallim, where Irish priests raise Scottish sheep brought from New Zealand, things still look pretty much as they always did; thatched roofs are abundant. But the breezy lady of the Yellow Sea has begun to take a turn for the tarty, and those in thirst for the past should go there before her last shreds of innocence are stripped away. At Jung-mun, near Sŏgwip'o, the island's second port, a fine beach is now the backyard of a splendid Hyatt hotel of impressive octagonal architecture, and condominia are surging up in all directions.

Along the southern coast of what is in fact Korea's warmest district lie farms growing pineapples and bananas under plastic. Little rivers tumble in waterfalls from cliffs into Prussian-blue waters, where the white net buoys of the *hae-nyŏ* bob and tango on the restless chop. In the hotel, honeymooners from Seoul and Tokyo, Busan and Osaka listen gravely to ersatz Americana—a Filipino pianist-singer couple importing the worst of the West.

Little *sik-dang* offer traditional bouillabaisses called *mae-un-t'ang*, rich with shellfish of a dozen kinds, which the islanders usually wash down with *so-ju* at fifty cents a pint. At Jeju's eastern extremity, Sŏngsan-p'o, you can hike up to a fascinating volcanic crater almost entirely surrounded by sea, and look down on a squid fleet festooned with arrays of a score or more of thousand-watt bulbs to lure the lemming-like cephalopods. Back in the village, they and the midget *nag-ji* octopi can be eaten alive with a sauce of sesame and soy and red pepper. They may be, as Buddhism teaches us, nonsentient, but they have a great sense of survival. As mentioned in an earlier chapter, a few inches of amputated paw, separated from the rest of the limb, will make a decided wriggle to escape as the chopsticks fall. While one such piece is caught and duly masticated, its sacrifice will have enabled its twin to reach the edge of the plate, whence it is ambling urgently on its few remaining suckers toward the place where it can leap for its life. How long these bits of flesh go on dancing in the alimentary canal remains a mystery. "Are you killing something living?" I overheard an American woman ask her husband once as he chopsticked the wriggling delicacies down his throat. "I don't think so," he replied. "I think my peptic juices will do that shortly."

Islands, more than mainland places, look toward their capitals, and Jeju is no exception. Jeju Town ("Cheju City" at the Korean tourism office in Seoul) grew up in the shadow of the Yong-du or dragon's head. If Yang, Pu, and Ko came out of the ground, the dragon came down from Halla-san to his natural habitat, the sea, and was there petrified in situ. The wave-lashed lava formation strongly resembles a dragon's head, pocked and lined like a wizened salt, but defiant.

A LIFE WITH THE SEA

Jeju remains best-known for its *hae-nyŏ*—although, surprisingly, they are of relatively recent vintage. When the first hunters and gatherers arrived on the island from China about thirty thousand years B.C. (the Ice Age withdrew from the sea-warmed island before it withdrew from the Siberian peninsula), there is no evidence that their womenfolk gathered anything but shellfish along the rocky shore. But the shamanistic beliefs which have sustained the hardy independence of the *hae-nyŏ* may well go back that far. The volcano kept people away: Halla last erupted in 1007 A.D., however, and is quite extinct today, although signs of its many explosions in the past are strewn over most of the island's beaches.

Cho Hae-joang, an anthropologist, has left an interesting account (in *Korean Women*) of *hae-nyŏ* life on U, a small island just off Jeju. U-do, as the speck is officially described, has eleven tiny hamlets within its one square mile, and is a microcosm of maritime Korea and the *hae-nyŏ* culture.

Says Miss Cho: "Diving yields cash income and is an exclusively female activity." The tiny hamlet she studied had ninety-two active women divers. Their harvest of abalone, crayfish, trochu, octopi, and seaweed reflected the fact that almost all women aged fifteen or over dived "from four to eight hours a day, on an average of fifteen days a month."

She goes on: "They dive during their menstrual periods and even when they are pregnant. A woman may dive up to the very date of her delivery, and resume diving one or two weeks afterward." In the West, women often hesitate to swim during menses because of fear of infection, and many cultures have a tradition that menstruation is "unclean"; but Korea's Buddhist base precludes such notions. Practicality and material need become the guidelines.

Some members of the divers' guild also belong to the fishing cooperative—through which they sell some of their catch, and from which they can borrow money. Guild members meet on the shingle beach while they change their clothes, which they will do unselfconsciously in front of anyone. They talk business—seaweed and ocean conditions—before they plunge to work.

Girls begin learning to dive at seven, by which time they are already accomplished swimmers. They become apprentice divers at fifteen, on completing compulsory education. At about eighteen, they become full guild members and, normal health permitting, stay on the job until the lungs start to falter in their sixties. Middle-school girls can usually do enough diving to earn their own tuition fees, learning from their mothers such basic skills as how to cut weed from rocks without killing the plant.

At fifteen, the mother gives her daughter a professional white buoy, a snorkeling mask, a wet suit with hood, swimming fins, and what Cho calls an "abalone knife." Abalone—*chŏn-bok*—is the bonus catch.

The young woman "learns to plot her diving strategy by the moon's movement, and she knows where to look for game," says Cho. Soon, she accompanies the more experienced women either to the mainland, where they often dive on contract for villages which regard Jejuan divers as the only ones worthy of the calling, or to small skerries bereft of humankind where shellfish are abundant in certain seasons.

Most divers, says Cho, have saved enough money by the age of twenty-five to get married and start a family. As with marathon runners, divers are at their prime from twenty-five to forty-five, but many women still dive into old age because they miss the company of the others if they don't, and because *hae-nyŏ* complain that their bodies ache when they stay on dry land too long. A good diver can go down more than sixty feet, and the writer watched a contest on Jeju in which the winner stayed down for three minutes and twenty seconds.

Frequently, a long dive of this nature is followed by a shriek to expel the carbon dioxide on surfacing, but on this occasion the woman did not even pant but simply waved like a winning boxer to her proud, watching family.

Some *hae-nyŏ* also do farming and market-gardening, but many of these employ men to do the plowing and threshing.

Chesa—Confucian rites for ancestors—is the most important male activity in a community like U. The ceremonies take place at midnight, followed by a feast which the men have cooked. Older men are served first, then other men, then boys, then the women and small children. A woman attends *chesa* only for close relatives, but men go to each others' rites; even in such a small hamlet, this means several parties each month.

The men, who do most of the child care, are reputedly more patient than their rugged wives. During the day, when the women are diving, the men gather in the wine houses with their children; they gossip and drink. Because women are so self-sufficient, widows rarely remarry; but, as in the West, men are seen as less likely to survive as widowers, and families usually find a bride for any reasonably young widower within a week or so of his wife's funeral. Older widowers move in with their eldest son. Widows can either go to live with a favorite son or remain alone; most reportedly prefer the latter solution.

Because the male role is subsidiary, husbands frequently just leave home and set up with someone else. Actual divorce is rare. Concubinage—the "second wife"—is accepted. Most second wives are divorcees or widows with few children. Here also, a man has the same responsibility toward his "second wife" as toward his first. In fact, both wives usually support their mutual husband, and there is an adage among men that "two wives mean two purses."

Says Cho: "Polygyny stems from the men's insecure status in the matrifocal family. Psychologically, it helps men cope with marital conflict and their wives' dominance. Structurally, it provides a way out of marital problems without divorce."

The role reversals are remarkable. Men on U eat only half as much as the women. They are more sensitive and self-centered than their wives, says Cho. They read more. She quotes a young husband as telling her: "Women are too busy to be reflective." There are obvious comparisons with the American black ghetto, where a woman often heads the family. The women of U, Cho says, "rarely defer to men. Whenever a woman wants to speak, she does so. Women . . . even use strong language."

She adds: "The nuclear family system belies filial piety. Grown children do not support aged parents. Mothers-in-law have little power over their daughters-in-law. A young woman at the peak of [diving] productivity has the strongest voice among the women." Another, less Confucian Korea.

6

A LIFE IN ALCHEMY

THE KOREANS ARE A NATION OF HYPOCHONDRIACS. The slightest irregularity, the tiniest spot on the skin is regarded seriously, especially by women. The priest and the *mudang* concern themselves with the soul, but the physician and, more often, the apothecary are taxed with care of its envelope. Just as in Britain there are villages too small to justify a grocery but which have a pub, because the pub is an extension of the home, so in Korea there are hamlets without a general store but with a *yak*, a pharmacy. It may be a *yak-guk*, a pharmacy in the modern sense, or a *han-yak*, a traditional apothecary's shop, but often it is both. Inevitably, there are syncretistic cures—blends of Asian and Western medicine. It is not a drug store—although it has the same self-perpetuating quality of selling cigarettes. It is quintessentially an apothecary's establishment, to which people go not only for purchases but for advice. Just as the British call their apothecaries chemists, so too the Korean *yak-jong-sang* is an alchemist. He (most are men) is often in league with the *mudang*, who will suggest prescriptions of her own which he will fill.

Traditional apothecaries, dealing exclusively in a complex pharmacopeia, most of it a millenium old, are often engaging characters. Their prestige is immense. Although academic science has little faith in some of the curious cures, many others have passed the test of the laboratory, in some degree or other. It is a world of herbs, tree bark, roots, snakes (only one of Korea's serpentine creatures is poisonous), deer's antlers, everything from dog soup to ginger tea to viper wine. A library of legend surrounds acupuncture (*ch'im*), skin pressure (*chi ap*), and massage, the rituals of hot-spring baths, and a menu of energizers, brain stimulants, and aphrodisiacs. As is widely known in the West today, Korea's most highly promoted brain, limb, and sexual energizer is *in-sam*, which we call by the Chinese name *ginseng*. The variegated industry that has sprung up around ginseng is one of the most sophisticated forms of Korean farming and processing, but it is still supplemented by the "hunting" of wild *in-sam*, which is believed to be the most efficacious. In a nation exuberantly devoted to private enterprise, this sector has been reserved to the state, to prevent adulteration and fraud, ensure quality control, and keep prices within reach of all male citizens with libido — or perhaps wondering where their libido went.

Although China and South Korea do not recognize each other diplomatically, and officially have no trade, Korea sells over twenty-five million dollars a year of *in-sam* and *in-sam* products to the People's Republic. It is a notion that would no doubt have boggled such round-eyes as Lenin, but perhaps not Marx, who noted that "tradition weighs heavily in the mind of the living." *In-sam* is now available in many more forms than soup, tea, root shavings, and high-strength capsules — notably wine, chewing gum, and even cigarettes.

Korea's fascination with alchemy is understandable, in a way. Was not the nation born as a result of an apothecary's prescription given by the legendary Hwan-ung? His mugwort and garlic did more than a modern sex-change operation: a she-bear became a woman and gave birth, not to cubs, but to a Mongolian people. Naturistic solutions to physical problems were given a sturdy boost.

Korea's preeminence in medicine was established in 414 A.D., when a doctor from Silla named Kim Pa-chin went to Japan and restored a sick monarch, Inkyo, to duty. By then, there was already a renowned handful of Korean physicians—all essentially apothecaries. Some of the pharmacopeia and methods they used were their own, but much, along with acupuncture, had originated in China. A Han Chinese physician known as Chih Tsung came to the court of Ko-gu-ryŏ in 561, and his knowledge soon carried to the other kingdoms.

A primer of Korean pharmacopeia dated 751 A.D., printed on woodblocks, still exists. Using Chinese ideograms, one hundred fifty Korean medical manuals were produced, from the eighth century onward. A copy of the most remarkable one, the *Ŭibang uch'wi*, was looted by General Kato Kiyomasa during the Hideyoshi invasion of the 1590s. Eventually, Korea's invention of movable type, so long before anyone else, boosted still further the propagation of this knowledge.

What is significant is how traditional *han-yak* remedies have withstood the test of time, especially when compared, say, to Western medical practices prior to the twentieth century. Anyone who remembers the "chemist" shops which still existed all over Britain in the thirties and forties, with pestles and mortars and jars of natural resources, must inevitably question the trend toward seeking every solution in a synthetic drug. Among the skyscrapers of Seoul, both ancient and modern pharmacies live fairly tolerantly side by side.

The traditional apothecary's shop can be spotted by its spectacular window display, with its vials of roots, dried insects, deer antlers, and snakes. A consommé from white snakes is considered a rejuvenant; powdered deer antlers—like rhinoceros horn in Africa—is recommended for virility, so both items are in frequent demand.

The biggest profusion of *han-yak* shops in Seoul is in the Chong-no 4-ga and 5-ga districts, near Dong-daemun (East Gate), but the most famous "herb street" in the country is Yak-chung kol-mok in Dae-gu, in central Korea. Raw herbs can also be bought in most open markets, such as the big Nam-daemun (South Gate) bazaar in central Seoul. Some markets also feature practitioners of Chinese-style acupuncture and Korean-style finger pressure.

Apart from rejuvenants and aphrodisiacs (one of which, dog-meat soup, is now theoretically illegal in Seoul, and so has become expensive), the most frequently demanded items include iris root (to quicken the brain), chrysanthemum root (for headaches), viper wine (for neuralgia and migraines), snakeberry leaves (for irregular menses), and a medley of physical energizers, such as *in-sam*, ginger tea (*saeng-kang cha*), pine nut porridge (*chat chuk*), and a bland popular beverage called *ke-chuk*—rice flour, salt, and water with some sesame seeds thrown in for flavor. All these have to be heated slowly over a fire of coal-dust briquettes. Tangerines, strawberries, and persimmons are also good for people who feel tired. Like our angostura bitters, which serve the same purpose, they can be alcoholized to make them more interesting, in this case by mixing their juice with *so-ju*.

The neophyte hypochondriac is well advised to forgo the open market for the *han-yak*, where he is more likely to find a manager or assistant who speaks English and who, when he sits back to seek inspiration, stares at a ceiling covered with hanging paper bags scrawled in Chinese. The resultant prescription may include anything from herbs and bark chips to dessicated insects, snakes, horns, or meat. On the ground and the shelves, everything not in glass will be stored in pots, since metal is said to deplete the potency of all vegetable and animal matter.

The best *yak* offer a medical consultation, or will refer patients to a traditional doctor in the neighborhood. He will examine the visitor for pulse, respiration, and skin coloration. Korean traditional medicine recognizes ninety-nine different types of pulse, as the speed and regularity apparently vary in different parts of the body, like a river in the course of its journey.

According to Dr. Kim Kyung-ship, Western medicine rejects the significance of this. Dr. Kim owns one of nearly three hundred *han-yak* clinics in the East Gate area. He is more expensive than most modern Korean physicians, and his work is not covered by insurance; but he is one of a group of apothecarial elders who are helping a West German research team decide which traditional remedies science should adopt. Dr. Kim boasts that none of his remedies have any side effects.

Pak Chae-yon of the Won-jae clinic agrees. His eighty-year-old establishment was opened by his grandfather, and he says most of his regular patients have nervous, digestive, or circulatory problems, with a daily smattering of "fatigue" and "bad back" cases. His *che*, or prescription, usually composed of twenty *chub* (packages), normally costs between forty and sixty dollars, but fees of one hundred dollars or more are not unusual.

Herb mixtures should be boiled in a covered, nonmetallic pot for at least two hours, strained, and then drunk two or three times a day, according to instructions. The prescription will also recommend the type of water (lake, river, fast-flowing stream, etc.) and the temperature, which may be anything from cold to scalding. Sometimes the water should be boiled slowly, sometimes fast. Most medicines are taken with meals, and the patient will be told whether to sip or gulp. The majority of practitioners recommend against taking them with white meat, beans or peas, or radish.

Whatever the main ingredient in their various prescriptions, both Kim and Pak say, these usually contain one or more of an array of panacea. These include licorice, which is considered a good "mixer," and also helps to reduce fever and pain; ginger, especially for indigestion, constipation, and nausea; jujube (Chinese dates), peony, kudzu vine, peppermint, and yellow vatch.

The early part of the diagnosis should determine if the illness or condition is on the surface (often meaning psychosomatic) or internal. Once all the symptoms are collected, the apothecary will probably consult the famous manual of Hojun. Most prescriptions from this work combine herbs and other materials representing the four elements—earth, water, air, and fire. They specify which part of the herb should be used—flower, stalk, or root. It seems safe to assume that the very arcane complexity of all this helps convince the patient, and thus aids in effecting a cure inspired by faith.

As with modern medicine, professional advice is not necessary in all cases. Virtually every Korean knows that the best preventative for skin disorders is bamboo. In a country where the slightest pimple is treated like a wound, there are even bamboo clothes to sleep in, and a bamboo bedroll, known as a bamboo woman, on which to rest insect-bitten ankles. Many housewives know enough skin pressure to cure childish sprains. Pressure is not always applied to the area of the anatomy that has been affected. Hemorrhoids, according to one pamphlet, are cured by chest pressure, appendicitis by pressure on the thighs.

Even Westerners who loath to try anything unfamiliar seem to frequent Korean saunas and massage facilities. In the sauna, steam baths are usually followed by a dip in cold and very hot baths, calisthenics, more sauna and baths, and a "total shampoo." This is usually performed in front of a mirror and involves washing the body and hair and, for men, shaving. Everything, from toothbrushes of varying stiffnesses, disposable razors, and conditioners, is provided. A final shower and lotioning prepares you for the rest room, where you can be massaged or watch television, or both. By then, you are feeling self-righteously healthy, and may not wish to imitate the habit of the Korean and Japanese business community of never relaxing without alcohol; most of your neighbors, however, will be knocking back undiluted scotch.

Stone Age acupuncture needles of granite and bone attest to the vintage of this treatment, which dates from about 2500 B.C. Western medicine today accepts that acupuncture can serve as anesthesia and as a cure for some conditions. Blood is rarely drawn, except at the extremities. The least that Western doctors generally say of the practice is that it does no harm.

Because some acupuncture cures for common maladies, such as indigestion and motion sickness in children, are so well known, many families use do-it-yourself gadgets like automatic pencils to insert the needles, or simply use matchsticks instead.

Acupuncture's underlying theory about the human anatomy has been largely rejected by modern medical science. However, this fact does not lessen the proven effectiveness of the system. Lee Tong-kol, a Korean journalist who has written on the subject, says:

> The human body was thought to consist of fourteen physiological or functional systems, each associated with a major visceral organ, and a pathway, or meridian. Through each meridian flowed a vital life force, *ki* (*chi* in Chinese), which was thought to circulate according to a certain rhythm.
>
> Disturbances in the flow of the *ki* resulted from disruptions in the natural forces within the individual. If not corrected, such disturbances would eventually lead to disease, either in the organ associated with the me-

ridian in which the blockage of the *ki* occurred or at some point along that pathway.

Acupuncture and other stimulative health arts were developed in order to eliminate blockages of energy and to correct excesses and imbalances in the flow of the vital life force. More than 365 insertion points have been located on the meridians for treatment through manipulative therapy.

Modern Korean acupuncturists concentrate on the hand, seen as a microcosm of the body in terms of meridians and stimulation points along them, so that puncture of these is echoed in the affected organism. The palm is thought to mirror the front of the body, the reverse of the hand the back. One advantage of hand acupuncture is that treatment can be effected without removing one's clothes.

If claims about curing cancer by acupuncture must be treated with reserve—although not necessarily with disbelief—there are huge numbers of documented cures for pneumonia, peritonitis, appendicitis, and tuberculosis—and even for impotence and sterility.

Acupuncture's acceptance is spreading throughout the world. Dr. David Schweitzer of Vienna claims acupuncture of the hand is a sure remedy for cholera. It is used in the Soviet Union for asthma, having been introduced there by Dr. Yatsu Mitsuo of Japan. Dr. Yatsu, a dental surgeon himself, uses it mainly as anesthesia in dentistry. In the U.S., acupuncture has begun to compete with conventional medical practice in the treatment of asthma, chronic pain, and even for breaking the smoking habit.

Korea's leading acupuncturist is probably Dr. Yu Tae-u, who is also the leading exponent of finger pressure (*su-ji-chim*, or hand-finger-needle).

The fact that Western and Oriental medicine start from

different theories, one preoccupied with the blood circulation and the other with life forces, is probably irrelevant. If one assumes that all is an emanation of self, one illusion is worth another. Certainly, the notion that only Western medicine is valid would be as ethnocentric as to think that only homeopathic or holistic systems work. Whatever cures, works. The reason why depends on the illusions with which we begin. Millions of Americans believe the world was made in seven days and that this millenium will end with Armageddon; so there seems no reason to be surprised that it may be possible to cure life-threatening diseases by pricking one's thumb, which surely requires less of a leap of faith than Revelation or Ezekiel. Nevertheless, we are an oral society, preoccupied with the mouth, so not surprisingly no aspect of Korean pharmacopeia has caught on so much in the West as *in-sam*.

It is, let's say, a breezy, sunny day in the forested mountains and hills that stretch down from the Diamond sierra running almost to Manchuria. A group of five men have arrived at a sort of base camp area, where they have built a rough structure of thatch under which to pass the night. They have brought a *mudang* with them to bless their endeavors, and the witch goes to work at once.

The team of men, who must always be of an odd number, for good fortune, set out foods for the spirits—fruit, rice cakes, and the like—while the *mudang* establishes a periphery with candles and chants and dances to purify it. Her main invocation is to the mountain god himself, who possesses her. Now, she is wearing his costume and telling the *in-sam* hunters what they must do on the morrow. In the form of the god, she makes demands and is wined, fed, and paid—then again, then again. As she dances, one of the men strikes her *chang-gu* drum, to get her heart beating faster.

The ectoplasm of the god departs. The *mudang* takes off the deity's horsehair hat. The ritual has ended, conveniently, in time for her to descend the mountain path to her village before nightfall. The boy she has brought as a carrier puts her paraphernalia into suitcases, and they set off. The men eat some of the rest of the purified food which the *sam-sin*, when he possessed the woman, was unable to finish, but they avoid the alcohol. They retire to sleep early.

In the morning, they rise before dawn and wash thoroughly in a nearby stream. Then they set off, with the youngest of them in the lead, as a lure for the mountain spirit. (A youth looks more like a woman than a mature man does.) The leader brings up the rear. At the point which they sense has been designated by the god, they divide into groups of three and two, and search the area along parallel tracks, with each little group beating on trees from time to time to let the other know where it is.

When wild *in-sam* is discovered, a cry goes up and the others join the enraptured finders. Everything found at that place will belong to the individual who was, supposedly, lured to the spot by the plant itself, at the behest of the god, but everyone will help him "lift" it. There is no actual digging, just a gentle scraping of the soil with the fingers, trying not to break the hairlike tendrils. The root that emerges looks something like a torso with limbs. Sometimes the torso has protrusions, but for the most part it is masculinely flat-chested. The legs seem to be wearing overlong trousers tied beneath the feet, like some clown in a circus sack race. The root invariably has two shorter limbs resembling arms and a fifth and finer member which can only be its penis. *In-sam*, in short, is almost as "anthropomorphic" as those Korean pictures of the spirit of the mountain, which show him looking like a sprightly local great-grandfather with two young wives, or as Christian renderings of the godhead looking like William Ewart Gladstone with an unkempt beard.

What the hunters find is a fraction of a huge industry. Most

A LIFE IN ALCHEMY

in-sam is now farmed, rather than hunted, and is strictly controlled. All over the country, one encounters orchards of the plant, with each row of plants (about the size of potato or pea plants) sheltered by a long, doll's-house-wide thatched roof. The farmers say it is a demanding plant, taking so much nitrogen from the soil that crop rotation is necessary, with *in-sam* only being reseeded on the same lot ten or twenty years later.

Caravans from China entered Korea in search of ginseng in the third century B.C., according to some historians. It is mentioned in Chinese pharmacopeia at least as early as the first century B.C. It was an article of tribute to the T'ang emperors there in the seventh to tenth centuries. Marco Polo brought it back to the courts of Europe. Rulers preceded government in making it a sovereign monopoly, and licensing its gatherers.

A regular *in-sam* trade with Europe was established by Dutch captains in the seventeenth century, and the French Academy of Sciences held a seminar on the subject in 1697. When a Jesuit, Father Jartoux, penetrated Manchuria and what is now North Korea in the eighteenth century, he sent back to France a report on *in-sam*. This was read by another Jesuit, Father Lafitau of Montreal, who discovered an inferior version of the plant locally, in Canada. Inferior species have also turned up elsewhere in North America, in Siberia, and in other places where there is a hardwood canopy to offer shade.

There was a "ginseng rush" in Canada for a while, much like the "tulipomania" in Turkey earlier. Fortunes were gambled, won and lost, with Boston exporting the stuff in considerable quantities to the Chinese—one ship alone carried fifty-five tons of the coveted root. Virginia joined in, exporting over three hundred twenty tons in 1862.

In Asia, wars were fought over ginseng. In modern times, when a sub-rosa trade first arose between Communist China and South Korea, organized through their respective consulates-general in Hong Kong, Beijing's first demand was not

183

microchips or color TV, but ginseng. When fishermen from Taiwan, which is too warm to grow the root successfully, started a similarly illicit trade with Beijing even earlier in the middle of the Formosa Strait, they exchanged the wristwatches and transistor radios of Taipei and Kaohsiung for China's relatively poor-quality ginseng.

A non-habit-forming stimulant, *in-sam*, whose Latin name, *Panax schinseng*, means "the panacea with the five-bladed leaf," is something of a worldwide economic phenomenon today. Consumption figures imply that about eight hundred thousand Germans take it regularly in capsule form. The rest of the West tells a similar story, with Switzerland marketing a highly popular mixture of *in-sam*, vitamins, and minerals, called *Pharmaton*. It is included in rations in the Japanese armed forces, as it was for officers in the Vietcong. Growing ginseng has brought new hope to the dirt farmers of Appalachia, who export one hundred ten tons each year to Hong Kong.

Five hundred Soviet *in-sam* hunters are licensed to seek the wild plant in the hills to the north of Vladivostok. In 1972, a Soviet forestry employee found a huge root that took him three hours to scrabble free without damage. Its five limbs were all over a meter long, and the concentric rings showed it to be over two hundred years old. There are (possibly apocryphal) stories of roots twice or four times as old as that. Yet the cream of the crop, for some reason, still comes from the Korean peninsula.

Very big, top-quality roots which sell for more than one thousand dollars each are found every year in South Korea, but the bulk of production comes from the eighty thousand farmers, who grow a wide variety of qualities. A program run by Professor I. I. Brekhmann of Vladivostok is attempting to grow high-quality *in-sam* in Siberia, and the plant is now a fully recognized "drug" in the Soviet Union; but, in Korea, the high-quality plant grows almost effortlessly, and the poorer grade of *in-sam*, equivalent to that of Siberia, Appalachia, and China, is used for secondary *in-sam* products, such as skin lotion, hair conditioners, eye cream, makeup, shampoo, soap, and jam. It is even mixed (where else but in Korea?) with whisky and cognac.

Traditionally, *in-sam* is held to be strong in *yang* (male, positive) energy. Modern science has analyzed it to be a healthy, legal, nonprescription stimulant containing glycerine, B vitamins, enzymes, protopanaxdiol, panaxafriol, and other substances. It stimulates the central nervous system, reduces stress while increasing mental acuity, relieves fatigue, including sexual fatigue, and low metabolism, and reduces hypertension and anemia. Like acupuncture and skin pressure, it is said to cure or help cure cancer, but this claim probably arose because Korean hospitals give it to cancer patients to diminish radiation sickness after chemotherapy. A British medical team has attributed its stimulant effect to certain glycosides not yet found elsewhere.

Professor E. J. Shellard of London University says ginseng has "anti-infective and anti-fatigue properties and there is accumulating evidence of its anti-stress activity. . . . It delays mental and physical fatigue." Stephen Fulder of the British National Institute for Medical Research says it "can improve the general health and vitality of old people by delaying the onset of degenerative conditions associated with old age, such as impotence, arthritis and arteriosclerosis." Its reputation as a sexual stimulant has led to the conviction that it is an aphrodisiac, but its exact role with the testes and ovaries remains unexplained.

Soviet reports claim that ginseng's anti-fatigue, anti-stress, and anti-infective properties have proven their usefulness in the cosmonaut program, and that it stimulates such workers as typists, proofreaders, and cryptographers to greater accuracy. Chinese reports echo the usual claims regarding its curative effects on debility and anemia, and also note successes in treating insomnia, neurasthenia, gastritis, low and high blood pressure, and arteriosclerosis.

These Beijing reports also make even more ambitious claims for dysentery, cancer, malaria (due to its anti-anemic properties), and diabetes (because ginseng reduces blood sugar and produces glycogen). It has been proven to be a histamine liberator, promoting cell and tissue growth. Seoul's College of Oriental Medicine, which trains and grants diplomas to the most serious new practitioners of *han-yak* today, reports cures of tuberculosis, burns, cirrhosis of the liver, and even baldness. Much of this appears interrelated: something which affects the testes could be expected to grow hair on some patients; something anti-infective would be likely to help cure burns more rapidly, and so on. The implications are that *in-sam* does different things for different metabolisms—quite simply, for different people.

Traditional medicine flourished in Asia along with other developments in science—astronomy in Korea, for instance—at a time when Western medicine was largely left to barbers and the like. One English king died from eating "curative" lampreys (eels), and George Washington was bled with leeches.

When the West began more exhaustive exploration of the anatomy and more daring experiments with surgery, and as research on synthetic drugs opened up new paths, there was an almost inevitable clash between the intuitive and the experimental, although both rely on trial and error. The role of Dr. Horace Allen, the medical missionary who treated the Korean royal family at the turn of the century, helped establish the reputation of Western medicine, which clearly has a more ambitious pharmacopeia. However, within the context of Western culture, Norman Cousins has shown the enormous role of the patient's mind, and particularly of humor, in fighting ill health. Both disciplines, Western and Oriental, have their limitations, and there is clearly room for both. If naturalist cures appeal to some because of their simplicity, too great a faith in Western medicine may derive from the almost occult nature of its complexity. Put simply, *han-yak*, acupuncture, and *su-ji-chim* would not have survived for millennia if they didn't work. The ancient Koreans, like all cultures of those testing times, put their unsuccessful quacks to death.

THE KOREANS

1. Buddhist monk [KOIS]
2. Pope John Paul II and Cardinal-Archbishop Kim meet the Christian faithful [KOIS]
3. Kim Kum-hwa, the shamanist witch, listens for the voices of the dead [Lee Du-Hyun]
4. The feast of the lanterns: Buddha's birthday [KOIS]
5. The pagoda at Nagsan-sa, which dates from the 8th Century and contains the ashes of some of Korea's most distinguished monks [Russell Warren Howe]
6. The grotto at Kyejo-am on Solag-san [Russell Warren Howe]
7. The Woljong-sa temple nestled at the foot of Mt. Odae-san. The octagonal pagoda in the courtyard was constructed in the 1st Century [KOIS]

4.

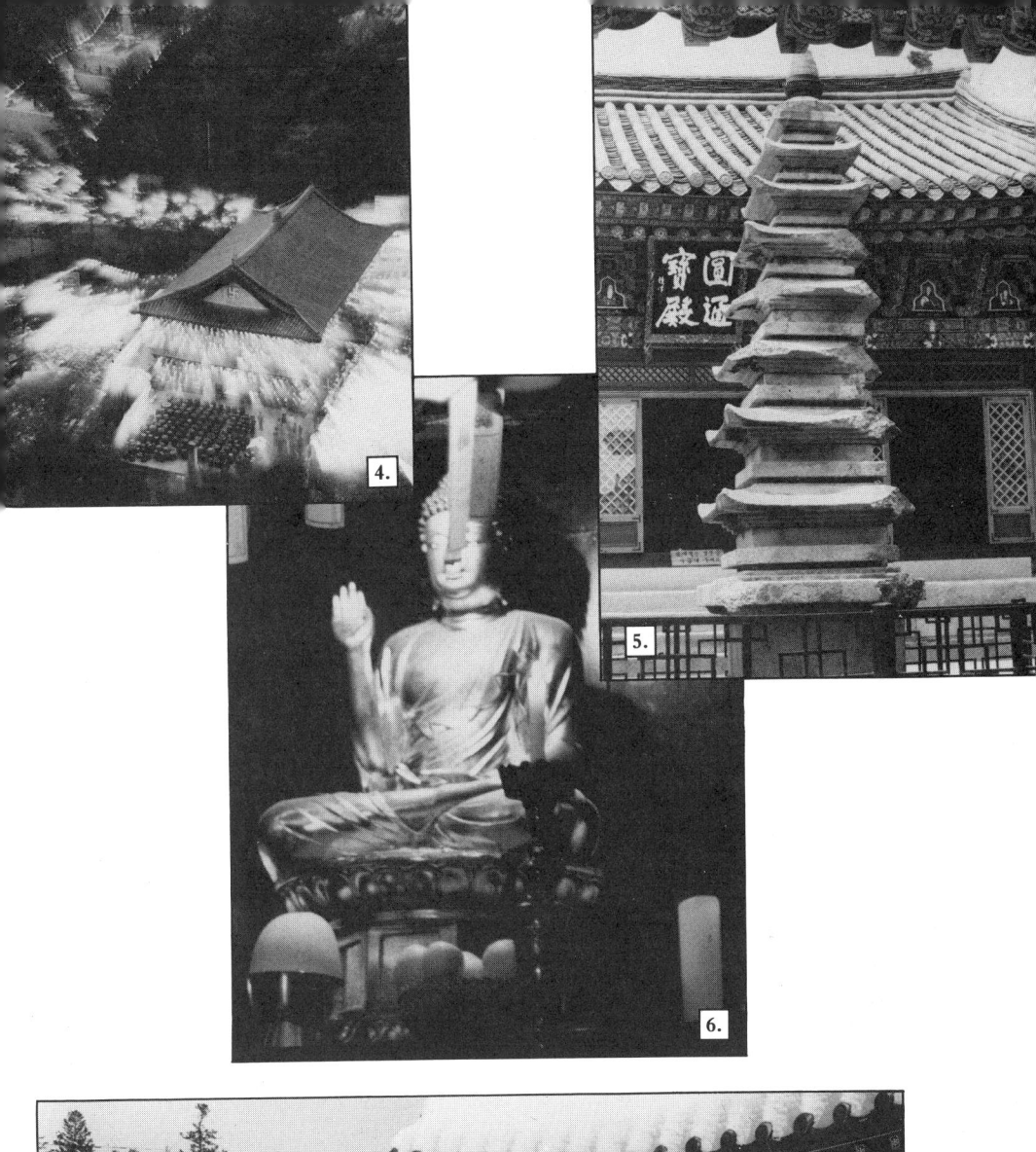

圓通寶殿

5.

6.

7.

THE KOREANS

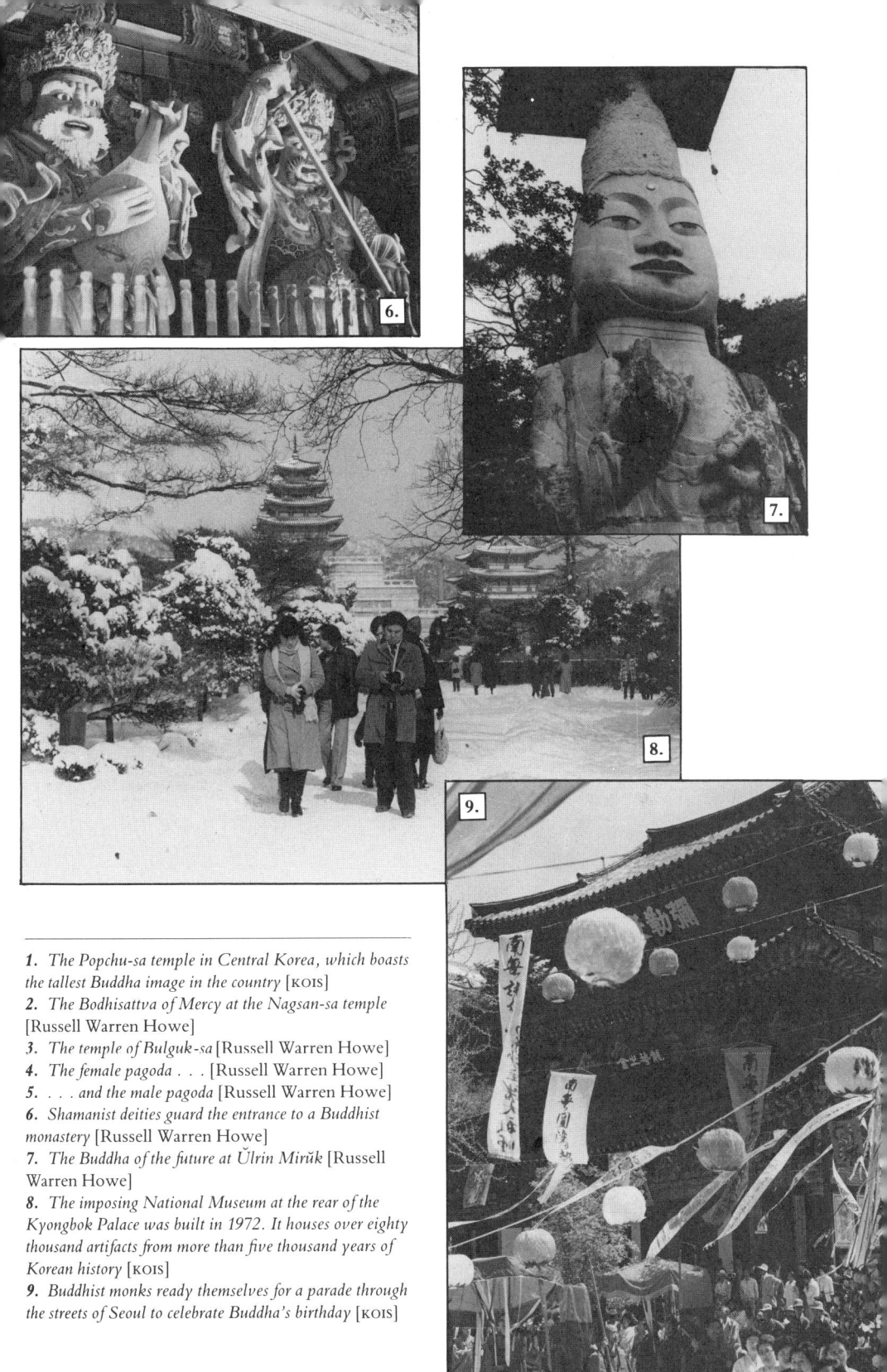

1. The Popchu-sa temple in Central Korea, which boasts the tallest Buddha image in the country [KOIS]
2. The Bodhisattva of Mercy at the Nagsan-sa temple [Russell Warren Howe]
3. The temple of Bulguk-sa [Russell Warren Howe]
4. The female pagoda . . . [Russell Warren Howe]
5. . . . and the male pagoda [Russell Warren Howe]
6. Shamanist deities guard the entrance to a Buddhist monastery [Russell Warren Howe]
7. The Buddha of the future at Ŭlrin Miruk [Russell Warren Howe]
8. The imposing National Museum at the rear of the Kyongbok Palace was built in 1972. It houses over eighty thousand artifacts from more than five thousand years of Korean history [KOIS]
9. Buddhist monks ready themselves for a parade through the streets of Seoul to celebrate Buddha's birthday [KOIS]

7

A LIFE IN ART

A NATION CAN BE DEFINED BY MANY THINGS, and buildings are certainly among them. The matchbox structures which America copied from Milan reflect not only the role of Italian-American construction companies in New York at the turn of the century, but also a utilitarian approach to life in the New World. The difference between the traditional American home and the traditional homes of Europe is particularly interesting since most Americans are European in origin, and their forebears more so. Similarly, the differences between homes in the Northeast and the South and the West tell us more than just that the West is more Spanish and the South more British than the Northeast.

A nation may be equally well defined by its houses of meditation. Koreans, Japanese, and Thai, like the French, the Germans, or the British, and unlike Arabs, Americans, or Indians, are nations of roof builders. And in Korea, the ornate roofs of the monasteries extend to the dwellings of those who can afford such indulgences, to the love pavilions, the *ki-saeng* houses, and the resplendent gates of Seoul. Even the gates of modern bourgeois courtyards—indeed, sometimes those of farm fields—are overhung with intricate gables.

A LIFE IN ART

In an insightful essay, Jon Carter Covell has written that Chinese roofs are "vertical in feeling," created by a nation determined to conquer all, including nature. Japanese roofs, she says, are more Zen—earthbound and asymmetrical. Korea's ceramic rooftiles, she suggests, match the nation's rhythms, rather than challenging them:

> Korean ceramics appear less perfected, warmer and more approachable, so that the viewer touches the potter's hand in spirit. Less than perfectly symmetrical, these long and subtle Korean curves grow on the eyes in a quiet way.

Japanese homes are considerably more disciplined and ascetic in design, appealing to those from a similar culture, such as that of Scotland. Korean homes, Covell notes, were designed to comfort the body as well as the questing spirit.

But if there are differences, there are also similarities. The Koreans, like the islanders of Japan and Britain, love bodies of water—not just seas, but lakes and streams and waterfalls. Perhaps it was the Koreans who passed this passion to the Japanese. They are concerned with space, as are most people who are rural by nature. (Cities, as in Japan, are a tolerated inevitability.) The plan of the traditional Korean home, with its *sarang-bang* for the head of the family opening onto the outside world, its *an-bang* for the women, and its more or less extensive atria, is repeated in spades in the great palaces, with their dormitories for the soldiery on one side and, well away, similar quarters for the concubines and their and the family's servants.

If the *an-bang* or inner room (of the women) was a prison of sorts, it was also the most lavish room in the traditional compound, with woodwork and cabinetry interlaced with mother-of-pearl of abalone shells or ox-horn shavings, and lined

193

with the skins of eels and sharks. Every shamanistic sign for long life, good luck, and so on, was inevitably incorporated. Geometric signs were drawn on the walls, reminding one of the Arab world.

As in Roman villas, the *ondol* heating system was by flues placed under the floor, so traditional building never exceeded one story. The heated floor held the same attraction as the fireplace in Europe (but of course without its decorative touch of drama), and most of one's indoor life was spent on it. It was a living space for eating, talking, sleeping, reading, calligraphy, everything.

Long ago, the Japanese surpassed their forgotten Korean mentors in the beauty of their architecture, but the Koreans may well have been the first, anywhere, to master the art of how to live elegantly in a cold climate. *Ondol* heating dates from the Stone Age, and continues today in most new single-story Korean houses. There seems little doubt that Japan is abandoning the floor as a living space more rapidly than Korea; perhaps it was never quite as important there. The Koreans even declined to follow the Chinese in the use of thrones.

Korean homes are less clean-lined than those of Japan. There are, today, knickknacks and dust-catchers. But the *yo* and the *ibul* and the *pegae* are still stowed away in the closet every morning, since beds and quilts and pillows are not usually needed during the day. The traditional low tables and seat cushions (which Koreans generally prefer to tatami mats) make for less clutter than in Western homes — even if there is more clutter in the peninsula than in Nippon. These days, the *pegae* are not always stuffed with barley husks, dried beans, straw or — to avoid insect infestation — the porcelain chips once favored by the spartan aristocracy. Styrofoam now does just as well. More spacious living in both Korea and Japan will inevitably make for more gadgetry and appliances and a different concept of the home; but for the moment, the Korean interior retains some restful qualities. Screens and scrolls still divide space into instant rooms. There are sliding ricepaper doors, with walkways on which to leave outdoor shoes. Just as France, say, is more advanced than Italy, which still remains the site of Ancient Rome, which civilized France, so there is a feeling in Korea that it was here that the great East Asian love affair with style and grace began.

Considering the country's role as a causeway between imperial China and Japan—later, between imperial Japan and China—it is amazing how much art survived the hideous carnage of the territorial imperative. Korea, with considerable influence from China, passed on to the islands a tradition of ceramics, notably celadon (of which the modern copies, although beautiful, are nowhere near as delicate and translucent-looking as those of the past), along with what later became Zen gardens and brush-drawing. The latter was an art learned from China; as *sumi-e*, it has been carried to even greater heights in the islands, which have also become the home of the most overpowering meditation gardens.

The Koreans, like the Japanese, are miniaturists. One mark of an aristocrat was the smallness of his or her writing. It was, however, left to the Japanese to develop bonsai and, much later, transistors. In counterpoint, the Koreans seem more attached to the natural as nature made it. Their entertainers never loved facial makeup as much as the Japanese and the Chinese. They would understand the American cult of driftwood. An octogenarian friend of the author has a garden at Kangnŭng almost entirely composed of phallic pebbles and other stones with human shapes—a tribute to the legacy of animism which informs all the East Asian peoples, including those of the Soviet Far East. The most delicate form of leather, eelskin, is a Korean specialty; and where else do girls carry purses of peacock and pheasant feathers?

As in Europe, the cross-currents of cultural interchange are hard to unravel. Even more than in Europe, there is sensitivity about who started what. There must be millions of Americans who believe that other Americans invented the piston engine, the motor vehicle, radio, television, and motion pictures, and who discovered nuclear energy and antibiotics. When they learn this isn't so, they are not mollified to know that an American really did invent the bottle cap, popcorn, and the pneumatic tire. Asians are similarly devoted to their own versions of reality. Few Japanese and Chinese know much of Korea's seminal role in the region's culture—and the Koreans, of course, respond by exaggerating it.

Because Koreans discovered the use of paper as housing insulation, they soon became expert makers of all sorts of papers, including that used for art. Some of the finest early calligraphy was made possible by the use of this material. Paper was used on walls in Korea long before it became a Western fashion, and paper is still even used on floors.

The peninsula's great concern with creature comfort is shown in the frequent use of abstract designs to please the eye, and in the art of cabinetmaking, often inlaid with these abstract designs. Some Koreans claim that the swastika, the universal sign in Asia for sanctuary and places of religion (which the German régime of the 1930s bizarrely used backward, with no visible meaning), originated in the peninsula; but it more probably came from the Indian subcontinent.

If one single Korean plastic art dominates all others, it is celadon—blue-green in its original forms, and known as the "kingfisher glaze," and white with a bluish tinge (known to collectors as "Mohammedan blue"), in the work of more recent centuries. Fortunately, much was looted by Japanese forces, otherwise little would have survived the country's wars, especially the most recent of them. Indeed, much of the old work was discovered by the Japanese when they unofficially occupied Korea while defeating Russia in 1905, and began excavations for the government railroad, which was to lead from Busan to Paris. They uncovered many lost tombs of rulers, buried with their bowls and pitchers, to be ready for dinner in paradise.

Treasures dating from almost a thousand years ago make it clear that the most recent work, even when of museum quality, lacks the ephemeral, falsely translucent appearance of the old. What is curious is the ceramists' virtual obsession with nature: rice bowls, wine cups, or whatever, take the form of rabbits, tortoises, geese, cranes, ducks, even the chow dogs with exaggeratedly lionlike heads favored by the Chinese. Long before the Playboy glasses, there were Korean celadon *jŏng-jong* pitchers in the form of lissome serving girls. The blue-green glaze varies in shade, with some favored results known as "rain and wind on the sea" or "blue sky after rain." Designs of birds, trees, and the sea are inlaid with white clay in the way that mother-of-pearl is inlaid into wood.

The intricacies of Korean ceramics are too numerous to examine in detail—the choice of glazes, the importance of using fire made from pine needles to obtain certain effects, and so on. The visitor must explore for himself.

Dolmens, bells, carvings, and tombs of grotesque size, exuberances of gold—a profusion of art was sustained by the court, financed by taxes on the peasantry, who won their livelihood from the land belonging to the royalty and the gentry. Painting reflected not only religion and "great men," as in Europe, but daily life as well. Many modern Korean academics now give much more importance to the country's "folk art" than have the country's museum apparatchiks. They have been encouraged by a folk-art approach to painting in Europe under the influence of the Impressionists and their successors. Folk art would seem to echo the fact that, in Korea as in nineteenth- and twentieth-century Europe, religion is not a controlling discipline. Only shamanism holds some sway.

Folk art for the house incorporated the male-female *yang-ŭm* symbols, those of the five geographic directions, the five colors (black, white, red, blue, and yellow), and the five elements: fire, water, metal (*kim*), wood, and earth. There were symbols of the animals of the twelve-year calendar, the ten symbols of longevity, the most propitious birds and fish, the good-luck ideographs. You couldn't go wrong with turtles, dragons, deer, cranes, pine trees, *pullocho* (long-life mushrooms), pomegranates (the national symbol of fertility), tigers, chrysanthemums, the lotus, or ideograms representing *bok* (good fortune), *bat* (happiness), *su* (longevity), *yŏng* (peace), *kang* (health), the orchid (symbol of scholarliness), the lotus (for "truth" in the Buddhist sense), the butterfly (romance), or the plum, which signifies the independence and wisdom that comes with age. These symbols also appear on *han-bok* dresses, linen, furniture, and combs. They are often introduced with a touch of humor.

Korea's oldest pictorial art is unabashedly shamanist; particularly good examples, brushed with solid ink and with mineral pigment, often set in fish glue on birch bark, are to be found in the remarkable Flying Horse Tomb in Tumuli Park at Kyŏngju. Later in history the motifs became shamanist-Buddhist, shamanist-Taoist, or shamanist-Confucian. Artists were artisans, and their names have not been preserved. From birch bark, the painters moved on to layered mulberry-bark paper and shimmering silk. Favorite colors are royal or Prussian blue, cinnabar red, green, and yellow. Only in our own time have oil colors been used.

What gives these pictures an unfinished, "Zen," two-dimensional effect is the absence of shading or chiaroscuro. Some particularly interesting examples are to be found in the

E-mil-e Museum in Seoul, where many of the shamanist pictures, having served a practical purpose at *kut* for generations, have a patina of incense smoke and even candle grease.

The richest period of Buddhist pictorial and sculptural art was in the eighth and ninth centuries, when many of the great temples were constructed. Bulguk-sa and the Sŏk-kur-am grotto at Kyŏngju are the finest examples of the period's art and architecture, although the original wooden sculptures of Bulguk-sa were burned during the Japanese invasion of 1592. Huge bronze bells and pagodas (reliquaries for the remains of high-ranking monks) were characteristic of the era's monasteries.

In the post-Buddhist period, painting, like architecture, borrowed Chinese styles, emphasizing landscapes, plant and animal life, including pets (especially cats), and portraits. More durable backings were used. Calligraphy was the most common art form—still using Chinese characters. Folk art, often distinguished by its humor, became more sought after, as was also the case in Japan, where it was often more boldly erotic.

The Koreans are also a people of the performing arts. Like the Japanese, to whom they passed the five-tone scale, and atonal music generally, they swiftly fell under the charms of European music. The two nations today produce an inordinately large number of young pianists and violinists every year. And if Japan is a nation of *karaoke*—bars providing the accompaniment while the customers sing the entertainment—Korea is the land of the ballad. Throaty tenors and coloratura sopranos are as much a part of the landscape as they were in the England of the first decades of this century, before first radio and then films and television atrophied the self-entertaining instincts.

Korea's love affair with Western music has unfortunately been less selective than Japan's; but it is interesting to find students with an equal zest for Bach and Bachrach. Korean taxi drivers will serenade you with tapes or radio broadcasts of

Mozart, and also with some of the most adenoidal American pop singers you ever heard.

Korea's musical appetite is, in short, gluttonous, if not always discerning. Traditional ballads, mostly sad, will, as noted earlier, remind travelers of the Algarve; but the singing and dancing which go with hiking and picnicking include Japanese-style karaoke marching songs—called *p'ong-chak norae* in Korean—or bawdy barroom lyrics accompanied by clapping and shouts of "*Chot-ha!*" or "*Ŏlssi-guna!*" (Bravo!).

The five-note scale involves different intervals between pitches, so that in Western terms traditional Korean music is atonal. Says Gary Rector in an essay in the Apa guidebook, *Korea*:

> No system of harmony is used, but this lack is more than made up for by melodic ornamentation, including unusual attacks and decays, subtle microtones, startling vibratos, unexpected changes of the timbre of the instruments when changing registers, and highly complex rhythms.

A rhythmic counterpoint is produced by relatively simple instruments of bamboo, metal, calabash, stone, skin, silk, or clay. The silk-stringed, zitherlike *kayagŭm* or *gayagŭm* and the hourglass *chang-gu* or *chang-go* drum are the commonest native instruments, occasionally with a six-string version of the *kayagŭm* called a *kŏmungo*. The shrill traditional *p'iri* oboe and the *taegum* flute are almost equally essential to "orchestral" music. There are metal and stone chimes, gongs and cymbals, and the *yang-gŭm*, a dulcimer of Chinese design which is rather like a cross between a piano and a xylophone.

Confucian court music (*ch'ong-jae*) and religious music (*il-mu*), both arranged for dancing, are of clearly Chinese inspiration, greatly developed during the reign of the scholar-king

A LIFE IN ART

Sejong. The *tang-ak* and *a-ak* orchestrations of the T'ang and Sung dynasties were replaced by *hyang-ak*, with its *hyang-ga* Buddhist psalms of Silla. Although this music survived for a while among the common people and poor scholars, it is rarely heard today except on suffocatingly official occasions.

From all this developed *chŏng-ak* (chamber music), *san-jo* (solo) music, *ch'wi-t'a* military music, *kasa* and *kagok* ballads, and *si-jo* poetry set to music. Because court dances were for the delectation of the king and a few familiars, they have been the hardest to preserve: those that do exist today have survived thanks mostly to the choreography of a royal prince, Ik-chong, a century and a half ago. Ik-chong was himself a dancer.

Even the choreographed dances which one sees on the stage have a spontaneous character which is deliberately suppressed in most cultures. In Korea, somehow, it works. The dancer must have *hŭng*—the sort of inspiration which the Irish refer to when they say: "May the spirit be with you." Dancing, like every art in Korea to be well adjudged, should also have *mŏt*, or taste. With art, this means grace. With dance, it also embraces sensuality.

Korean dancers use the whole torso for expression, much as African dancers use the pelvises and shoulders. The back is held straight, as though suspended from the sky. The most characteristic movement is that of the dancer standing on one foot with the free leg extended, as the shoulders shimmer up and down. It is the dress that portrays the movement—rather than the legs of our ballerinas. (Most major traditional Korean dancing is done by women.) Extended sleeves are as important as in Japan, and become great animated fans. Most of the turns are on the heel, not the toe; the long skirt, concealing the foot, gives the impression that a dancer is bending under a strong wind rather than swiveling on human bones.

Korean dances, unlike those of, say, Thailand or Europe, tell no story, but only, like haiku, express a mood. The exception is the mask dance of medieval satire, still a popular feature of staged entertainments.

The most popular of the court dances is the *hwa-gwan-mu*, or flower-crown dance, named after the dancers' hair adornments. Another favorite is *mu-go*, performed by eight dancers around a large drum which they beat with drumsticks hidden in their ballooning sleeves, called *han-sam*. *Ch'un-aeng-mu*, a light solo dance, was created by Prince Ik-chong himself.

The mask dances, or *t'alch'um*, according to Rector, probably come from central Asia. Like Renaissance English plays, they satirize corruption, greed, lechery, hypocrisy, charlatanism, stupidity—all the faults associated with the governing and religious classes in any society. The caricatural masks emphasize the themes. The villains were as real as those of American literature and life—the greedy landlord, the concupiscent cleric, the nagging wife, the pompous politician. The slightly more sympathetic figures of fun were the bibulous scholars, the cuckolds, the Mrs. Malaprops and Bowdlers of the peninsula, prancing clumsily to their deaths of derision. A typical "hero" is an apparently foolish, actually cunning servant.

Farmers' dances (*nong-ak*) which most tourists see at the Folklore Village near Seoul go back to the fifth century, according to Chinese records of Korea. They vary by region, and there is always room for improvisation. Head twirling (as illustrated by the *hodori* or tiger cub on the Olympic symbol), acrobatics, and even tightrope walking are features of the farmers' dance called *chwado-kut*. These frolics are associated with shamanism and are intended to ensure rain, a good harvest, a clean well, and so on.

P'ansori ballad singing, which originated in Paekche, the southwest kingdom, is perhaps the best-loved form of Korean singing. Between reciting narrative bridges and singing the lyrics, a *p'ansori* singer may be on stage for five or six hours, although it is common today to split the performance up into two or three evenings.

One of the most popular *p'ansori* concerns the "Cinderella" daughter of a rural *ki-saeng* who wins the love of a handsome prince; another has a sort of Cain and Abel moral; yet another recounts at great length how the king of the sea needed a rabbit's liver to cure an illness, and of how a hare was lured into the depths, but escaped with his organs intact. Other *p'ansori* moralize about filial piety and other virtues.

Underlying these often folkloric songs and dances is the Korean interpretation of a Confucian theme—that music, as Confucius himself reportedly first said, "hath powers to soothe the savage breast of men." The Korean twist is often to challenge this soothing intention.

As in Elizabethan England, another cultural era perhaps more devoted to song than music, it was the marriage of prose or poetry with the chanting of the vocal chords that spawned much of the Korean musical tradition. *Si-jo*, like Shakespeare's sonnets, were composed to be sung. Korea, too, had wandering minstrels, who sometimes used a drum or a stringed instrument to accompany themselves. The ballads became synopses of the narratives and novels which, until *han-gŭl* vulgarized them, most Koreans could not read or even afford to buy. Since these were often expressions of social protest, they were entertainment for the people rather than for the rulers.

In many respects, Korea has taken folk art further than other Oriental countries. Artists portrayed everyday subjects rarely considered worth the effort outside of Europe—old men chasing cats away from the food, or being scratched on the back by grandsons; a writing class of little boys with braided hair, one of whom is crying after being chastised by a fierce teacher; *ssirum* wrestlers; men disporting themselves with *kay-agŭm*-playing courtesans. Sin Yun-bok came closest to the free-spiritedness of his Japanese counterparts with his famous scenes of novice monks spying on naked women bathing in a stream, or a fully clothed and hatted *yang-ban* copulating with a fully clothed *ki-saeng* sitting in his lap while another well-dressed dandy contemplatively waits his turn.

In short, shamanist art, the love of singing, the gregarious love of dancing and display, and a folk theater tradition, has set Korean art forms apart, and given them a unique place in Asian culture. These qualities also help modern Koreans in their conquest of Western classical compositions. With the love of spontaneity and even vulgarity in many of their traditional art forms goes a love of ceremonial music. Just as traditional oboe players dress in scarlet silk and ebony hats to play Confucian court arrangements, so their brothers or sisters or sons or daughters put on the penguin suit of our philharmonia, and discipline themselves to the conductor's baton.

It must be a truism that peoples are at their best when they are at their most indigenous. It is certainly then that Koreans are the most revealing of themselves. And if the houses, palaces, and temples with which they dressed the Siberian Riviera landscape echo their personality, how much more is this true of the clothes in which they dress the capsule of their souls?

Korean clothes are basically Mongol in origin, and seem to date from the Manchu period in Ko-gu-ryŏ. Women traditionally wore a colorful sack dress which was essentially a long *ch'ima* skirt with a sleeved bolero top and long ribbons. This *han-bok* is still regularly seen on holidays and other special occasions, and worn by restaurant and department store staff. Under the Mongol influence, both the skirt and blouse were shortened, and the *chŏgori*—the Mongol name that the top then took—was tied across the breasts instead of being belted. Men wore, and still do, in the countryside, a cross-breasted *paji*

Manchu jacket with overlong sleeves, or a *chŏg'i* waistcoat, along with baggy pants bound at the ankles.

The Japanese changed some of the Korean appearance, temporarily, beginning by making the men cut off their Chinese-style topknots, called *sang-to* in Korean. They imported military-looking uniforms with sensible narrow collars for the boys; since they were uniform, they were probably a good idea. Schoolgirls were dressed in sailor suits. These great equalizers were rejected a decade ago, but have recently been readopted for boys.

The loosely tied toga of the monks resembles the *paji* and comes from T'ang China, and the heads of monks are shaven in the Tibetan and South Chinese style. Courtiers' heads were shaven down the middle, either straight or in a circle, in the Mongol manner—a fad later taken up in Japan. Women coiled their hair in plaits on top of their heads, Mongol-style.

As in Nippon, traditional men's clothes were made of large, fairly shapeless pieces, for laundry reasons; the garments were picked apart at the seams for washing, bleached flat on rocks, ironed or beaten, and then sewn together again.

The Mongol influence was inevitably pervasive after King Ch'ŏng-yol became a royal vassal of the Mongol court and married a Mongol princess. His sons, Ch'ŏng-son, Ch'ŏng-suk, and Ch'ŏng-mok, and his grandsons also took Mongol brides, so that each generation's progeny were more Mongol than the one preceding. This bequeathed to Korea not only its national male and female dress, but also what is still disparagingly called the "country face"—as opposed to the finer features of those more influenced in their genetic descent by China.

As in Europe and elsewhere, you could not necessarily wear what you could afford. The gentry, male and female, wore silk, and the men wore semiconical hats of woven horsehair. Today, any man can wear one, provided he is sixty years old, but the practice seems to be dying out in this generation. Cotton and hemp (*sam-bae*) were for the plebeians. Traditionally, everybody's clothes were white and, unlike those of China, they were purposely loose-fitting—there was and is a fastidious distaste for the odor of perspiration.

In 1899, a wealthy Korean patrician, Yun Ch'i-o, returned home with suits cut on Savile Row and Western dresses in the hourglass style of the day for his wife. This outrageous modernism, when it made some converts, was mildly encouraged by the Japanese when they took over the country shortly afterward, since they sought to eradicate all outward signs of nationalism. Today, men wear the three-piece suit which has become the hallmark of modern life in temperate climes, and the young women vie with those of Japan for high fashion— except in hairstyles. It is, however, almost a Confucian conceit among middle-aged or elderly women to wear unfashionable clothes in discreet, often drab colors. When the Reagans visited Beijing, and Korean women watching television saw Nancy meeting Chinese dignitaries in a bright red, figure-fitting Chinese dress, the reactions of hilarity and scorn matched those which an elderly foreign president's wife would earn in Washington if she made a state visit in a miniskirt and a see-through blouse.

Not being a tropical country, Korea has taken to Western dress for much the same reason as Westerners: today's man needs lot of pockets; he is carrying more than the bag of coins of his ancestors. The tie and the shoelace seem likely to go the way of the cravat and spats, worldwide, and sleeves may be abolished in warm countries, but Western male dress, with some innovations, seems broadly accepted. Western female dress appeals because of its infinite variety. It can be run up in a factory, and you can wear different attire every day of the week without being rich; the styles and lengths are limitless. When the great courtesans of Japan's past and the literary *ki-saeng* of

A LIFE IN ART

Korea discoursed on clothes, they spoke of colors and ribbons, of the number of layers in a robe. The *han-bok* remains the formal ceremonial standard, the robe to be married in; reasonably priced copies of Pierre Cardin and Yves Saint-Laurent are for the workplace and the disco. Japan, too, has had its obvious influence on fashion design, in everything from airline, police, and school uniforms to high fashion.

Grace extends beyond ornate roofs, atonal court music, celadon, and clothing to life itself, and even to some forms of aggressivity. Martial arts probably began in China, and Korean *t'aekwŏndo* clearly has links to kung-fu and kung-fu's other child, karate. The persistent theme is mind over muscle. Philosophy and violence lie down together, as lamb and lion. Boxing requires quick reflexes, as does fighting between two dogs; but *t'aekwŏndo* requires concentration. The whole idea is not to be heavier and hit harder, but to win even if you're only half the other fellow's size. The legend of David and Goliath is of a lucky fluke, like hitting a quail at five hundred feet; but the lesson of *t'aekwŏndo* is like the legend of how Salah ad-Din put Richard the Lionheart to shame in a contest to evaluate the sharpness of each other's swords. Richard's two-handed monster cut a rock in two, mostly because of the king's own strength; but "Saladin" merely extended his blade and let a silk scarf cut itself in half as it fell upon it in the breeze.

Thanks to *t'aekwŏndo*, this rather hot-tempered people has an unarmed police like Britain's. No soldier may serve on the sensitive frontier with North Korea who is not at least a green belt. (The American troops up there must be at least six feet tall—shades of Richard's broadsword.)

Koreans, nomadic in origin, are outdoor and sport lovers. One of the candidates for the 1987 presidential election called his inner circle the Alpine Club. To belong, one had to hike with the fifty-nine-year-old leader. On a walk into the granite hills that ring Seoul to the north, one is likely to encounter, along with meetings addressed by evangelists, courting couples, and rock guitarists, a substantial number of rock climbers. Now that the Han-gang has been cleaned up and stocked with fish, its newly paved banks are full of weekend fishermen.

Despite their relatively diminutive size, Koreans defeat Indians and Europeans and Arabs at football (called soccer in the United States). Despite their short legs, they placed second in the 1986 Asian Games, only one point behind China, which has nearly thirty times Korea's population. India, with more than twenty times Korea's numbers, and other populous nations like Indonesia or Bangladesh, were well behind. Not all of this can be explained by the fact that the Koreans had the advantage of running and jumping on their home turf.

Despite their salty diet and their adoration of booze, the Koreans are a highly health-conscious nation. Even though most are poor swimmers, they love the sea. They push their children into calisthenics, aerobics, and, of course, *t'aekwŏndo*. They are number one, globally, in archery, a martial art that women can and do practice well. Like most other East Asian peoples, they respond to the discipline of team sports; but they are quintessentially individualists. Not surprisingly, when Japan won the Olympic marathon for the first time at the famous Berlin Olympics of 1936, the man wearing a kinomaru on his vest, Sŏn Ki-chŏng, was a Korean from the colony. The two main Korean papers front-paged his victory after airbrushing the Japanese sunburst standard from Sŏn's chest, for which sublime impertinence both were suspended from publication.

Like China's, Korea's government has taken prowess in international sport to be as much a key to global prestige as technical advance—such as having the world's largest shipyard. When a Korean president chose a colleague as his candidate for the succession in the 1987 elections, he first gave him the challenging task of organizing the Seoul Olympic

Committee. In Asia, only highly developed Japan had been chosen to play host to the Games before; Korea was the first "developing" nation to be trusted with the horrendous task of orchestrating what is perhaps the greatest (by volume) show on earth.

The highly spectator sport of football, which can be played on pastures and in parking lots, with teams that don't necessarily always add up to eleven (they may even be more numerous), and with goalposts often made of players' jackets or garbage cans, is as much of a lay religion in Korea as in Dominica or Düsseldorf, Dubrovnik, Dubai, or Dakha. A primitive form of the game was invented in the seventh century by Kim Ch'un-ch'u, who later became the twenty-ninth king of Silla. He called it *ch'u-kuk*, the name still used for football today. The modern form, with its more complex rules, was introduced by the crew of a British warship in 1882. Professional teams are a new development of the eighties, with many owned by *chaebol* (conglomerates). The ultimate accolade is that many Korean players are now being "bought" by European clubs.

American football and its antecedent, rugby, have not established themselves in Korea; but baseball was introduced in 1906 by German's Goethe Institut. Although in Korea it is mainly—like its forebear, the British game of rounders—a pastime for children, there are now a few professional teams. A Korean group won the world (amateur) baseball championship in 1982.

Basketball dates back to 1907, and has also brought international trophies to Korea, for both male and female teams. Volleyball was introduced by the YMCA in 1917. As in America, tennis is mainly a sport for the bourgeoisie, and the first public courts opened in Seoul only in 1971. Korean women players won bronze medals at the Montreal Olympics, and gold at the 1978 and 1982 Asian Games. Korean women's teams have also been internationally successful in table tennis. As in

Japan, golf has become the lazy man's sport and is now played by an estimated 1,300,000 Korean men, or about one-sixth of all working-age males. Almost as many people—about a million—are said to have tried skiing, a natural sport for a country of mountain snows.

Every possible form of Asian and European wrestling, most notably *ssirum*, the national version, as well as boxing, has appeal to Koreans. Modern versions of other older sports such as skating, archery, and shooting are also popular. Curiously, swimming has failed to capture the imagination of this maritime people, but some interest was fanned when Koreans won three gold medals at the 1970 Asiad.

Clearly, however, *t'aekwŏndo* is Korea's national sport par excellence, and the one that has sent Korean instructors around the world. A Korean government publication claims one hundred million *t'aekwŏndo* enthusiasts in one hundred countries across the globe; the numbers seem suspiciously rounded but, like predictions of rain, reality will sooner or later catch up with them. (Peter Hyun has asserted that seven thousand Korean instructors in one hundred seven countries train three hundred thousand beginners every year—which sounds more plausible.)

T'aekwŏndo was selected as an exhibition sport for the 1988 Seoul Olympiad. A self-defense system about two thousand years old, it is practiced by almost every healthy Korean male at some point in his existence, and about a quarter of all adult men belong to the country's T'aekwŏndo Association. This is, in short, not a country in which to get into a brawl, for whatever reason, as many a drunken GI in Yongsan has learned.

The wall paintings of the great royal tombs speak of a nation that, at least at the level of the gentry—particularly in Silla's *hwarangdo* "flower of youth" chivalric movement—loved fencing, riding and archery. Even running and jumping are portrayed as popular at a time when these sports had been thought by historians to be the monopoly of Ancient Greece. Horsemen played a form of polo called *kyŏk-ku*. *Ssirum* wrestling was already established, and must have resembled that seen at any Korean fairground today, where every male with a pint of *so-ju* under his belt wants a try at throwing another in the soft sand. Such folk sports were particularly associated with lunar and other festivals.

In the Chosŏn era, Confucianism was repressive of sport to some degree. This perhaps explains the gusto of its modern revival.

Not surprisingly, the Korean legacy of extrovertive art, mask plays, dances and the like, has led to the emergence of a film industry—but one still well behind Japan's, and shackled by the interference of censorship. Because Korean films have been forced to be so "tame," there is a popular taste for the more absurdly gory foreign films, particularly those from Hollywood.

The handful of valid Korean films that have been exported over the years suggest that what Korean actors need most is more rigid direction. For the profession of acting to grow and improve, there is also a need to accept it as respectable, especially among women. Most well-known actresses are in the pre-marriage age group, and grandmother roles, both in film and on television, are invariably played, as in high-school dramatics, by young or fairly young women who wear their hair in a powdered bun and raise their voices a crotchet.

There is a current trend, in cinema, toward new themes, but some of these are melodramatic to the point of often being unintentionally humorous in Western terms—an infatuated Buddhist monk, a pregnant Catholic nun, for instance. One film of this melodramatic type, *Agatha*, won acclaim in Europe, however, and certainly one would expect that erotic subjects would be natural for Koreans. A few Korean films have won prestige awards at international festivals. Judging from these, and the rare good Korean films shown on television, Korea seems, like Japan two generations ago, to be groping toward the major league primarily through historic themes; in these, the author or director can posit a moral without appearing to be contemporaneously self-righteous or naive. Censorship and self-censorship remain problems.

Korean television is frankly poor. The most hackneyed soap operas are the order of the day, with the "historic" soaps being marginally more engaging than the modern ones. The advertising is puerile, heavily copied from New York's.

There is a suffocating diet of game shows and talk shows, which seem to address the lowest common denominator in audiences. On the other hand, there is a clear tradition of comedy and comedians, which is quite rare in Asia. Koreans, however, still get most of their best television from the BBC, the RTF, and PBS.

8

A LIFE IN LEISURE

IN ETHIOPIA, in happier or at least less devastating times, they used to import wines from France. After the Medoc or the Riesling had bobbed its way through the Mediterranean chop, had been simmered to a turn in the Suez Canal, resimmered and shaken like a cocktail in the Red Sea, and finally rattled to extinction on that wondrous railroad that climbs eight thousand feet from Massawa in a matter of miles, it was heavy with *cif* (carriage, insurance, and freight to the export-import cognoscenti) and virtually undrinkable. Yet for about a dollar a bottle, or less than ten percent of the price of the imported stuff, you could order a delightful, unpretentious Ethiopian dry-white that went with just about everything except *injera* and *wot*.

Why does a traveler not simply order local cuisine and its liquid accompaniment, wherever he goes? The only excuse for not doing so must be where the local food is distinguished only by its absence of real distinction. *Dis-moi ce que tu manges et je te dirai qui tu es,* said Brillat-Savarin, a writer of the First Empire. Tell me what you eat, and I will tell you who you are. Just so. This fact has two useful effects. Not only does the diet help to explain the culture, but it also offers an easy way to make that discovery. It is yet another reason why one should eat the cuisine and drink the wine of the country.

If the Korean personality can be seen through the arts and religions and architecture and restraints and courtesies of daily life, it can be detected even more quickly in the restaurants and winehouses and inns where the nation drops its guard and bares its soul. Often the contrast with disciplined daily life is so great that one detects at once why so little entertaining is done at home.

People who work hard tend to play hard, and perhaps no one in the world works as hard as Koreans. Weekends, honeymoons, retirement, "sick leave," and even the new, Western gimmick of "vacations" draw legions to the littoral, to the marine and lacustrial fishing spots, to the warm springs and ski resorts, and to the extensive national parks in a country of mountain forests. There, the reserve breaks down: if the visitor has six words of Korean, it will be enough for him or her to be invited, even if only as a curiosity, to join in the festivities, the singing and dancing, and above all the picnicking which is the great delight of all traditionally nomadic peoples. It is not hard to guess what to expect, or what is expected.

The Koreans undress their personalities on the beach and the mountaintop; and one sees, to nobody's justified amazement, that there is a wide spectrum of traits. For instance, because marriage is taken as seriously as birth and death, honeymoon couples dress formally—jackets and ties, or high heels, on the sands and the mountain path. Yet this apparent formality is belied when a brigade of normally coy schoolgirls grab a single, vulnerable male, preferably an exotic foreigner, as they might snatch up a puppy, and insist on having their picture taken with him.

North Korea's Kim Il-sŏng never understood (unless he understood only too well) that Koreans are a nation of footloose people. That a permit should be necessary for internal travel in North Korea, and that the capital should be closed to all nongovernmental traffic (even private bicycles) is so hard for South Koreans to believe that most of them simply don't believe it. A rural people by nature, they flee the cities with the passionate instinct with which a swimmer comes up for air.

An air-conditioned bus leaves Seoul's Yŏng-dong terminal for Busan, the country's second metropolis three hundred miles away, every five minutes—and almost always on time. Commuter flights between the two agglomerations were recently doubled in frequency to every thirty minutes. It's not unusual to see fifty tourist buses standing in the parking lot of a famous monastery, or two hundred or more at a popular beach—and virtually all the passengers are Koreans.

For these reasons, Korea's hotels and hostelries, especially the traditional *yŏ-gwan* inns, are tailored to Korean life, not to that of the Japanese or Western business visitor or tourist who sometimes contributes to their profits. So, it is in doing what comes naturally, indeed inevitably, that a visitor learns the most about this watershed culture in the forested hills of the Siberian Riviera. The *yŏ-gwan* and the more modest, usually intensely familial *yŏ-in-suk* tell you more than the modern-style hotel—and even many *yŏ-gwan* now have raised beds for those who prefer them to the floor-level *yo* and *ibul*. If the traveler can break through the language barrier (take a student to lunch as interpreter), he or she will also see how regional cuisines translate the regional characters. And, be it said once more, Korea is not a country for teetotalers: like the Japanese—and the Mongols and Siberians from whom Japanese and Koreans both emanate—the people are creators of a vast cellar of alcohols, made from every imaginable grain, fruit, and vegetable.

Not surprisingly, in the cities and particularly in Seoul, there is a frenzied nocturnal life which, as in Japan, stretches

215

well into the night and challenges the early hours at which most Koreans rise. The affluent may still go to the *ki-saeng* houses, especially if they are "on expenses" and therefore entertaining for the greater gain of the company or political party; but the disco and the *sul-jip* wineshop have a larger clientele.

At a fashionable "stand bar," the visitor is initially surprised that drinks cost little more than in the street-corner *jip*, and only about fifty percent more than in the grocery store. The reason is *an-ju*: whereas, in America, a neighborhood restaurant expects to make most of its profit from beer and cocktails, in Korea it is the snacks, such as fruit and dried cuttlefish, which ease the pain of the bar-owner for the low markup on the beer.

An-ju—"something-to-eat-with-drinks"—comprises more than the plate of nuts of the United States, or even the appetizing *tapas* of Spain. The fruit, for instance, comes carved into imaginative shapes, as though the apples and pears were origami of moist, flesh-colored paper.

At the core of nearly all Asian and, indeed, most third-world food is rice, the bread of the tropic zone; but in Korea another essential element is *kimch'i*, made of fermented and salted vegetables, mostly bok toy cabbage, turnips, and white radishes, but also including, in fancier places, cucumber, zucchini, and pumpkin. *Kimch'i* accompanies everything, and the sauce involved can also be put on raw seafood, such as *yŏng-dŏg* (spider crab), other crabs, ark shells, and clams.

When this writer first went to Korea in 1968, he was strongly advised by officials of the Food and Agriculture Organization of the United Nations to avoid *kimch'i* because it was, they said correctly, infested with worms. Since then, the use of human manure, which ensured a permanent cycle for the ringworm, has been forbidden by law, and *kimch'i*, being pickled, is safer than fresh vegetables in the same way that ham and bacon, being smoked, are safer than mutton and beef.

Kimch'i is said to be high in vitamins and nutrients, notably its generous garlic content; but its salt content is high also. Some visitors find it too piquant. The main ingredients are the vegetable itself, salt brine, red pepper, garlic and ginger and, where obtainable, the local equivalent of Viet Nam's *nuoc mam,* usually made from small fish or shellfish.

The making of this sauce, strongly reddened by the pepper, is called *kim-jang,* and everything needed can be purchased in supermarkets or from countless street carts pushed by country women who invade the cities in the fall, when the vegetable harvest is in. *Kimch'i* is put up by housewives then for the rest of the year. This almost ritual aspect of the practice may soon disappear with increased access to refrigeration, which theoretically makes it simple to put up *kimch'i* in smaller quantities all year round, thus making less demands on limited apartment space.

Despite the fact that *kimch'i* is only one of several side dishes served with everything, and the quantity consumed each time is rather small, an average family will, in the course of fifty-two weeks, go through about one hundred cabbages, one hundred giant radishes, eight pounds of red peppers (roughly, the contents of one hundred fifty American supermarket spice bottles), four pounds of garlic onions, and fifty ginger roots. All this *kimch'i* is stored in jars which, in country districts, are buried up to their necks in the ground to prevent freezing. In the month of September, it is said that Seoul alone buys one hundred thousand tons of cabbage, five thousand tons of pepper, and two thousand five hundred tons of garlic, and it is a common sight to see fat, suntanned and sun-lined country women of uncertain age being pulled into town by their husband, son, or varlet in an eight-foot cart filled with pungent crimson peppers, above which the matron's head barely emerges. Red pepper is almost as basic to Korean cuisine as rice. It was, as mentioned earlier, introduced into Nagasaki by Jesuits from Portugal in the sixteenth century, and was brought to the peninsula by a Portuguese priest who accompanied the Hideyoshi invasion of 1592.

The basic requirements for any meal are *pap*—rice, which is small-grained and, by the epicurean standards of southern Asia, overcooked; *kimch'i*; and a little fish (or meat), usually with soy sauce. The most important element is not the protein but the rice. A common greeting in the countryside is *"Pam-mŏ-gŏ-ssŏ-yo?"*—"Have you had rice (today)?"

The main meal is lunch—sometimes, in the countryside, breakfast. In the city, where whatever goes with coffee or soup or barley tea in the morning may be perfunctory, the real breaking of the fast comes at noon. Dinner is not a part of traditional custom, although it has been for two or three generations a custom in the cities, where many men cannot come home for lunch. It is also a feature in the countryside during certain agricultural seasons, when work must continue uninterrupted. But even today, in Seoul, many wives and mothers still bring the main meal of the day to their menfolk at the factory in time for the midday break.

For more complete cooking, a condiment of choice is sesame, usually mixed with soy. As in the American South, various greens are the favorite vegetable. Seafood is the main protein; but, because of its rarity in the past, there is now a fondness for meat, especially beef and pork. A dish Koreans have tried to export is *bulgogi*, marbled beef cut so fine that it is overcooked almost at once, barbecued on a brazier in an aromatic sauce with a garlic, sesame oil, ginger, and pepper base, to which the natural juice of the fatty cut of meat adds relevance. It is advertised in English as a barbecue, but it is almost the Korean equivalent of snails, eaten for the sauce rather than the spongy protein itself. The honor that Koreans accord to this dish is shown by the prefix—*bul* means Buddha. However, whether attempts to make it popular abroad will be any more successful than American attempts to export frankfurters made of beef is questionable.

Curiously, this nation of garlic eaters finds the smell of mutton offensively strong. Korea's best meat dishes are probably those made with pork. The favorite dishes of most Koreans are beef ribs (usually stewed but sometimes grilled after being marinated in sesame, soy, pepper, and garlic), and oxtail soup. A typical treat is *gujul-pan*, eight vegetable, egg, and meat offerings which the diner mixes at random, folding them into a crepe with his chopsticks. As in China, soups come last—usually clear soups, often chilled, but also including abalone, clam, or anchovy chowders.

Korean cuisine is primarily one of the sea and of herbs and condiments. Seafood is often consumed dried and cured. If fresh, it is grilled, fried, or stewed—or, of course, eaten raw. A taste Koreans gladly confess to sharing with the Japanese is for raw fish, a cold-climate luxury, served alone or on sticky rice packed with horseradish sauce. Freshest of all, of course, is the live variety.

In addition to those herbs already mentioned, Koreans also indulge in day lily, bluebells, asters, mugwort, delicate ferns, sow thistle, and many others. Add all sorts of beans, anchovy tofu and other forms of soy, seaweed, scallions, sesame leaves and, above all, another natural endowment which Korea shares with Japan: the various, irregularly shaped "elephant ear" black mushrooms which grow on the bark of trees. As in West Africa, grated dried shrimp is also sprinkled on many dishes. (Actually, what is used is not shrimp but an even tinier crustacean with the Latin name *mysis*. In stores, the dried version is called *sae-u-jŏt*.)

My own favorite Korean dish is *kung-jung chon-gol*, a pungent bouillabaisse of fish and shellfish cooked at the table. Unlike bouillabaisse, it also contains vegetables. The more modest *mae-un-tang* (*tang* is one of the words for soup) is almost as good.

If you are really poor, the cheapest places to eat are the noodle shops, as in Japan. Even in downtown Seoul, for instance in Myŏng-dong, there are several that serve a bowl of noodles, pork, and vegetables for just over a dollar. At a *tong-daeg-jip* you can get the world's cheapest meat—the West African-style fried chicken which has colonized the working-class palate of the United States. In a *yŏ-gwan*, there is usually an extremely cheap *han-jong-sik* ("pot luck"); this is enough to feed a ditch-digger and costs about two dollars.

A jumbo-sized package of potato chips, shrimp crackers, or onion rings costs about twenty-five cents in any grocery. At a stall, a hard-boiled egg, with its little wrapped pinch of salt, costs about eight cents. Eggs may be pitched into anything—including my breakfast coffee, one day, in the hostelry for visitors at the fabled Hae-in monastery.

In Tokyo, the impecunious who want something better than a stall, especially on a rainy or snowy day, go to Chinese restaurants; but in Korea, where they attract mostly Japanese visitors (Koreans usually find Chinese food too sweet), genuine Chinese restaurants are relatively expensive. Japanese-style restaurants, serving raw fish dishes and yakitori (barbecued) meat and seafood, are reasonable, especially compared to prices in Japan.

There is an etiquette to eating, as in the West. Chopsticks, like the knife and fork, should never be laid on the table once eating has begun. The ceramic chopstick rests used in Japan are less in evidence in Korea, so it is normal to lay the sticks on the bowl, as we lay our own dining implements on the plate. It is considered coarse to thrust the chopsticks into the rice like a garden tool: this gesture is a sort of working-class symbol—for instance, in films—much like cutting square sandwiches across the middle instead of from corner to corner.

In the West, spoons are always laid on a saucer to the right, in the supposition that most people are right-handed. In Korea, they lie between the cup and the diner, who puts them behind the cup when he is finished, much as a Westerner puts his knife and fork on the left side of the plate as a signal to the waiter to remove his dish. In Korea, a similar gesture is placing chopsticks on the table, which is a signal that they will not again be put in the mouth.

Just as in the West a plate is served so that the meat is immediately in front of the diner, with the vegetables behind it, so a rice bowl should be placed in front of a customer or guest in Korea—a reminder that it is the centerpiece of the meal. Everything else is distributed in no particular order in the typical *sik-dang*, or in a tasteful design in more expensive places. To call for service, there is no polite tinkling of a bell, as in England, no discreet tapping of spoon on glass or cup, as in France; Koreans, like Americans, tend to holler like sergeants when they want something.

The myriad *panch'an* are comparable to side dishes, but they are offered as first courses while the main dish is being prepared; they serve to stay hunger. Any *panch'an* dish that is finished before the main dish arrives is usually replaced at no charge. Like the *panch'an* and soups, the fruit that closes the meal is included in the price of the plat de résistance. The most common fruits in restaurants are the giant Korean pear, watermelon, or a juice. In homes, *ttŏk* (rice cakes) may be offered.

About ninety percent of Korean men seem to drink the liquor *so-ju* with their meals—unmixed, un-iced. Younger men may prefer beer, which is of course less strong, but more expensive. Most women choose soft drinks, although they are beginning to drink beer and alcohols publicly, especially if a Westerner is present and there is therefore an excuse to do so.

In more rural places, *makkŏlli*, made from rice or other grain, is often preferred. The more bourgeois diner may prefer *jŏng-jong*, which Koreans could easily export as successfully as sake if they tried. The country produces grape wines, but they lack character. Because of the small production, they are highly priced. On top of that, they are taxed, so that they are mostly for the unsuspecting tourist on his first day in town.

After *yak* (apothecaries' shops), *jip* seem to be the second most common retail outlets, about on a par with grocery stores. There are *makkŏlli jip, sul-jip*, "pub" bars, stand bars (the Korean equivalent of the French *bar américain*), and even *p'ojang-mach'a*, tented street stalls for drinkers, like those in Japan. Most groceries sell alcohols. Some coffee shops (*ta bang*) serve only coffee, tea, and soft drinks, but many stock beer, and even scotch.

It is said to cost more to keep a Korean husband in booze than in food, despite the lusty Korean appetite. Much in Korean customary life is as impossible without drinking as it would be impossible to accomplish without food or without wearing clothes. In the countryside, if the liquor runs out at a wedding party, it is customary for the male guests to hang the groom upside down and beat him. At a *kut*, the gods and the ancestors, even the recently dead, get their share of the sauce. Korean Air barely has time to get halfway to cruising altitude on its daily flights to Tokyo before the stewardesses are offering quadruple shots of whisky to all passengers, with teetotal female travelers being urged by male neighbors to "say yes, and hold it for me." (East of Boston and west of San Francisco, all whisky is scotch, just as football is a game played with the foot. Travel is a great reminder of just how provincial America is.)

The bibulousness of the culture harks back to the nomadic

A LIFE IN LEISURE

Mongol and Siberian origins of the people. Cold climates make for more ways of warming the vitals than simply fire. Back in the tenth century, a Sillan king, Kyong-ae, was surprised and captured by an army from Paekche while drinking in Kyŏngju; even then, armies on the move made quite a lot of noise, so the beverages enjoyed by the monarch and his friends must have been of awesome potency.

The twelve-hundred-year-old institution of the *ki-saeng*—which may even go back to the fourth century in a more primitive form—helped drinking along, and there were said to have been twenty thousand *ki-saeng* in Kyŏngju at its peak, or one for about every ten adult males. That's approximately the same proportion as of prostitutes to adult males in Victorian London. As noted earlier, *ki-saeng*, who gave rise to the institution of geisha in Japan, were never prostitutes, although they originally fulfilled an analogous function in a more mannered way.

Like most people, Koreans prefer drinking in company. Indeed, in rural areas, to drink alone is deviant behavior. In a *jip* or a restaurant, each person pours for his neighbor and waits for the latter to reciprocate, as in Japan. This imposes a certain self-discipline, not unlike the Western requirement of putting down ones knife and fork between bites. It also involves a little hypocrisy: one is, as it were, only drinking because one's friend insists.

The drinker offers his cup with both hands. The pourer uses his right hand to hold the pitcher or bottle, grasping his right wrist with his left hand. If a convivial neighbor passes you his own full cup to drink, you are expected to swallow it quickly in a gulp or two, because the poor fellow cannot be refueled himself until you have returned his cup; (or glass—the word is the same in Korean, and Koreans prefer cups to glasses. Little cups are called by the Chinese word *chan*, the big half-pint type by our own word, written *k'ŏp*.) On festive

223

occasions, a glass may be passed from hand to hand with the stem snapped off, so that it can only be emptied, not set down. Just as it is an insult to leave a friend's table without eating as much as your alimentary tract can assimilate, so a Korean drinks to satiation. As in Japan, no social stigma is attached to being pixilated. After all, no disgrace is attached in the West to more offensive habits like blowing one's nose in public or talking so loudly that one's neighbors can overhear.

Koreans, being a physically small people, tend to get drunk rather quickly and economically. Because drinking is as yet a new, fairly rare fashion with women (except among grandmothers in fishing and other villages), nagging wives are even more of a problem to bibulous husbands than they are in the West. Nineteenth-century travelers reported seeing fellows "feeling no pain" while being dragged home from the *jip* by their topknot, held firmly by the little woman.

In Korea, since the drinker knows what he wants to drink, the *an-ju,* or accompanying dish, is chosen accordingly. With the sultry flavor of the milk-coffee-colored *makkŏlli,* the preference goes to *nagji* (octopus), *ojingŏ* (squid, usually cured), *kŭl* (oysters), *tŭbu* (tofu), or scallion omelettes (*p'ajŏn*). With *so-ju,* the Korean equivalent of vodka (but it isn't odorless, and it does have a taste), the preferred *an-ju* is fruit of all descriptions, pig's cheeks (which are delicious), *jog bal* (pig's trotters), *sun-dae* (pork sausage), or barbecued pork.

Beer, the drink of the relatively wealthy or the "with-it" young, is usually consumed with kippered squid or fruit. In the classier places, you can now get draft beer (*saeng-maekju*), and this may come with such exotic imports as peanuts. Hard alcohol (virtually only scotch, plus a little vodka) is usually drunk with pears or apples. Korea's locally made scotch, be it added, is virtually undrinkable. All Western-inspired strong drinks are called *yang-ju* (male juice).

If your expense account is up to it, you might try, at least once, *in-sam-ju* (ginseng wine). This comes with a whole root in the bottle, which you are naturally expected to shave up later and eat—perhaps in soup. Snake wine, *paem-sul*, is reputed to be even more of a rejuvenant; once again, you also get to eat the serpent curled up in the magnum.

Because most drunkenness is associated with *so-ju*, Korean women have a strong prejudice against it, even though, mixed with fruit juice or *in-sam* tea, it is no stronger than beer. Although *makkŏlli* is mostly homemade, usually has dust floating on the surface, and is almost as strong as *so-ju* (about twenty-five percent alcohol, or half the strength of vodka or whisky), it is seen as more respectable because it is traditional and yeomanlike.

The best way to go drinking is, of course, with a Korean, just as no Tokyo bar seems quite right again after going to one with a Japanese. Most Korean men have their *dan-gol-jip*—what the British would call their regular pub—where they feel part of the family.

In Seoul, taxis are so cheap that there seems no point in not patronizing the usually polite drivers with their spotless cabs, rather than helping the overcrowded buses and trains become even more overcrowded. If the taxi driver goes through a tunnel, the driver will pay 100 *wŏn* (about twelve cents) toll, and you should add that to whatever you see on the meter. There's a twenty percent surcharge after midnight. As in Japan, no tips are expected.

If you're going to Inch'ŏn or one of the suburbs, the train is the best bet. For further afield, buses and trains are equally good, and the long-distance buses include toilet facilities and a film. In short, they are cheaper than Greyhound, but a cut above. However, air transport is also modestly priced. A trip from Seoul to Busan (equal in distance to Washington–New York or New York–Boston) costs about thirty dollars.

Car rentals are expensive, especially considering the age and condition of the equipment, but the country is so small that this is certainly one essential way to go. The ferryboats to major offshore destinations are comparable to those that go to Martha's Vineyard or Nantucket—sufficiently comfortable for the distance, but with rather poor food. The trains are extremely comfortable, but once again, the food is poor, and picnic baskets may be a better bet.

For a long vacation, what Korea most lacks is hotels with kitchenettes. Renting an apartment in a condominium by the day may frequently be more convenient than a hotel; but these are to be found only in resorts, not major cities. Foreigners remaining in the country for just a few months are usually unable to rent houses or apartments. Most landlords require key money, recoverable on departure, provided that the landlord is solvent—and then only in Korean *wŏn*, which may or may not be convertible. Modern-style apartments for foreigners without key money are expensive by Korean standards, but cheaper than most American or European equivalents; however, there is a waiting list, and the minimum lease is six months or a year.

Foreign students often prefer a *set-bang*—a room in a private house. Another option is to go to a *hasuk chip*, or guest house, where you get a room and food. In early 1988, a room and washing area in a clean, acceptable institution of this nature, with two copious meals a day, in downtown Seoul, was costing about three hundred sixty dollars a month. *Yŏ-in-suk* are mom-and-pop guest houses for the impecunious, slightly more expensive than a *set-bang*, and usually without food. In the *yŏ-gwan*, traditional inns, one will pay a little more than in a *set-bang* or *yŏ-in-suk*—about the same as a *hasuk chip*, but without food. However, the accommodation is usually more modern, and for an extra charge you may even get a private bathroom with a tub. Occasional meals can be ordered for two or three dollars.

The male visitor to Thailand doesn't go to Bangkok solely for the best food in Southeast Asia. The retired civil servant who goes there four times a year on a bucket-shop airfare obtained through his government association isn't solely in search of acupuncture. In the same way, the reason so many Japanese firms hold their annual seminars for young executives in Seoul isn't only because it's cheaper than Kyoto or Osaka. Korea is a city of bachelors, or for men who are bachelors at heart. It's also a place where prospective bridegrooms come from all over Europe and the Americas, much as prospective brides would go to a coming-out party in Victorian England, or to the "cotillions" of the black American bourgeoisie in the days of Franklin Frazier.

But, like Bangkok, Seoul needs to be explained. It is not a city of sexual license—or no more so than, say, London or San Francisco. Nor are Chiang Mai or Phu Ket in Thailand, although Pattaya comes close.

In short, the lonely male will find companionship in Seoul or Busan or T'aejŏn, but without resorting to tarts and certainly without having to deal with pimps. Prostitution exists in Korea, as it does in Japan, Thailand, Singapore, and other places, but essentially for the desperate; but, more perhaps in Korea than in any of these other countries, there is a culture of midinettes, the "girls of noon" who played such a significant role in the life and literature of late nineteenth-century France. In the same way, today's young Korean women are the first generation or two to have a measure of freedom, brought about, ironically enough, by the right to work long hours for low wages, under conditions that seem arguably worse than those of the *an-bang* of their grandmothers. But the factory or the department store seem attractive to young Korean women because they provide an environment composed almost exclusively of other young women; with a job, one can make a contribution to the home not by helping with the cooking and doing all the laundry, but simply by handing over a pay envelope and getting something back from Mother for a midday noodle soup and a new pair of panty hose.

As with the midinettes of late nineteenth-century French department stores—so named because they had a three-hour break at midday, while their male bosses went home to lunch and siesta—today's Korean equivalents are underpaid and must give up most of what they earn to their families, often for the sake of putting younger brothers through school or university. Korea's midinettes should perhaps be called crepusculettes, girls of dusk or even later, for it is only at the end of the working day (10:30 P.M. in department stores) that they have a chance to hunt for the white knight of their dreams—and this is, unfortunately, a time when princes of darkness may be more in evidence.

In the bars, the visiting male will find, from dusk on, a mix of Korean midinettes and a few glazed-eye professionals—prettier and younger than most of their Western equivalents, but clearly over the hill, morally. The thing to remember, perhaps, is that the midinettes, as in Thailand, will accept a gift but will probably not ask for it; they are basically in search of husbands. For that matter, even the girl who has been sent out by her family to make her living that way is expecting to marry before the age of thirty—although she may have to settle for a Korean with a smaller bank account than her own. Pimps are rare, and justice is pitiless for them. Most can have little hold on their women, because the drug culture which enslaves the prostitute in America, Holland, and other places is almost non-existent here.

Korean literature, perhaps even more than our own, is fascinated by the fallen woman who rises. Vaguely akin to our "Virgin" Mary, Mary Magdalene, Nell Gwyn, or Lady Hamilton is Korea's favorite legendary figure, Non-gae, a fifteenth-century *ki-saeng* who took the fancy of an invading Japanese general and murdered him at the cost of her own life by pulling him over a cliff in an embrace. Far be it for a foreign writer to posit the thought that they may both have been drunk, and have fallen by accident. The fact is that Buddhist cultures see only misfortune or, at worst, self-indulgence and concupiscence, where our cultures see "sin."

Today's *ki-saeng* usually lack the musical and poetry skills of their august predecessors, and may depend for support on the music of others, often with Western instruments. They are the product of the industrial age, of female emancipation with its concomitant demands on female earning power—demands which did not exist before. Suffice it to say that the bar girls of Saigon were not what most Americans imagined, and superficial reporters reported, and that the midinettes of Seoul and Busan and other places are even less so.

Despite the excellence of Korea's public transport, the best way to take advantage of the roads and highways that now crisscross the country is to rent a car and carve a personal swathe through this land of market gardens, *in-sam* orchards, and rice paddies, tilled largely by women in floppy hats or headscarves. (A suntan, in Korea, is regarded as about as attractive as a rash.) Every once in a while, you will come upon roadside tent cafés offering strawberries or whatever else is in season, along with beer or *so-ju*. There are turnouts for picnickers, and temples galore, marked by park signs with the sanctuary symbol of the swastika. Wondrous beaches are lined with restaurants fronted by aquaria of fish, shellfish, octopi, and calamari.

A major beach resort not far from Seoul is Daech'ŏn, on the islanded waters of the Hwang Hae. North Korean waters are only an hour or so's sailing time away, and there is a beach curfew from ten P.M. to five A.M. Local fishermen do not go beyond sight of the coast, and the army is ubiquitous; but this is a fact of life to which one soon becomes accustomed.

Not far south, one enters ancient Paekche, with its handsome, restored capital of Puyŏ. A short walk up a forested hillside leads to Nak-hwa-am, the hermitage and gazebo at the site of the Rock of the Falling Flowers, from which the Paekche court women jumped to their deaths to evade an approaching, seventh-century Chinese horde.

In the same region is the Kwanchok-sa, site of the Ŭlrin Mirŭk, the thousand-year-old Buddha of the Future. At once awe-inspiring and grotesque because of its immensity, its Korean features peer out over the treetops. Also not far away is Mount Gaya Park, with the storied Hae-in (Sea Echo) monastery high up in the woods. Prints of sutras from the woodblocks will be pulled for about two dollars, and there is a comfortable *yŏ-gwan* in the village, made prosperous by the daily busloads of pilgrims. To ease the pressures of a day of meditation for the Japanese Zen travelers, there are five nightclubs and many other hostelries.

A drive down Mount Gaya at dawn, with mists still on the paddies, puts you on the road to the inland sea, now named the Hal-lyŏ Waterway, which is arguably Korea's best long-term resort asset. Not far away is the sprawling, rather pedestrian city of Busan, where the ghost of Admiral Yi slumbers in the now enormous natural harbor. On the city outskirts is Hae-un-dae beach, the most popular in South Korea. The author was last there on a rather cool day when, it seemed, no Korean would swim. But a quintet of little girls followed the exotic foreigner into the water, each holding the shoulders of the girl in front, with the ringleader holding mine. Eventually, the convoy swelled to about a dozen and I was drawing a human daisy-chain across the bay. There is something brashly and yet innocently Korean about such a childish initiative, as though the itchy foot with which all Koreans seem to be born would have made the kingdom an ideal one for the Pied Piper of Hamelin.

Just up the coast, the political generals from modern Kyŏngsang province have turned Kyŏngju into a museum of what was once the capital of Silla. This is home to many sites already mentioned: Bulguk-sa (Buddhaland temple), Sŏkkuram grotto, Bun-hwang-sa, the remarkable little Ch'ŏm-sŏng-dae observatory, the tomb-strewn Tumuli Park, the Anapchi Pond with its love pavilion and its quivering lake of golden orfe. The Pomun Lake resort nearby is rather tasteless.

The road up the east coast, between the mountains and the sea, is perhaps the prettiest corniche highway in Korea, and one hopes that détente with the North will one day lead to the removal of thousands of miles of coiled barbed wire which now mar the endless sands.

The markets that elsewhere sell strawberries or persimmons here offer huge bushels of *mi-yŏk* seaweed for soup. At Kyŏng-p'o-dae, the pleasure pavilion where the *yang-ban* once enjoyed sexual and poetic intercourse with *ki-saeng* and courtesans now looks out on a shallow lagoon and an advancing ocean. At nearby Nagsan Bichi stands what claims to be the oldest Buddhist temple in Asia, and it may well be the most beautifully gardened; twice restored over the centuries, following fires, Nagsan-sa retains the original foundations built when the celebrated monk and mystic Ŭi-sang chose the site in the seventh century.

Nearby, beside its clifftop satellite hermitage, Hong-yŏn-am, the monstrous female bodhisattva of mercy mentioned earlier contemplates the main. Ŭi-sang is said to have meditated here for seven days in order to see a vision of the bodhisattva. When he failed, he reportedly threw himself into the ocean, whereupon Avalokitesvara herself appeared from the cave beneath the bluff and saved his life. Despite the implausible nature of this hoary yarn, the monstrous carving of seven hundred tons of granite was ordered by the Cho-gye sect after the current abbot of Nagsan-sa, Ch'oe Wŏn-chol, was approached by a dead priest in a dream in 1972 and ordered to create it. When it was "inaugurated," the monks of Nagsan-sa began a thousand-day meditation for world peace.

A few minutes and several thousand feet up the hillside, the visitor finds himself in the forested heights of the Sŏlag-san (Mount Snow) national park, with its ski slopes and cloud-scraping hotels. The cavern grotto of Kyejo-am, a satellite hermitage of the pretty Shinhŭng-sa monastery, is the principal spiritual attraction, while the Rocking Rock—a boulder of thirty tons which moves to human touch—intrigues less mystical visitors. From loudspeakers in the foliage, Buddhist prayers drift across the valley. Cable cars lead to a lookout point offering extensive views of the coast and well beyond, into the Diamond Mountains of North Korea.

The colorful coastal towns of Yang-yang and Kangnŭng are not far away, and the visitor in *tano*, the fifth lunar month, may, as mentioned earlier, witness the *Tano Che*, a Kangnŭng *kut* for witches, wrestlers, secondhand booksellers, and much else.

What is refreshing is the love Koreans have for visiting their own country. These nomadic rurals, largely confined to cities by the new industrial revolution and the "Korean miracle," echo the former hermit kingdom's love affair with mobility: foreign travel is still restricted for Koreans, but more wide-bodied jets land at Seoul's Kimp'o airport every day than land at North Korea's equivalent near P'yŏng-yang in a year. Every historic site or beach resort draws divisions of Korean pilgrims and tourists. Schoolchildren arrive by the regiment.

If you miss *Tano Che*, you may cross karma with some other country festival, at which farmers decked out in the white garb of yesteryear will build a thatch hut in an hour, or dress up in pairs to play the role of a horse or a cow. *Haenyŏ* diving women will hold contests. One of the best country fairs of this type is the Halla Festival, in spring, on Jeju Island.

THE KOREANS

1. At Kangnŭng, an hereditary mudang flames a prayer for the success of one of the author's books [Russell Warren Howe]
2. The Dragon King of Jeju—a lava formation from the Halla-san crater—turns his head to guard the island [Russell Warren Howe]
3. The witch Kim Kum-hwa purifies the room. Note the roof streamers, which she will later tear down when she is possessed by the malevolent spirit [Lee Du-Hyun]
4. Kim Kum-hwa comforts the widow for whom she is performing the kut [Lee Du-Hyun]
5. The witch closes the door on the restless wraith. She shakes the bells to keep it away [Lee Du-Hyun]
6. As she chants, money is thrown on the hemp. She will "wade" through the hemp, tearing it in two with her hips [Lee Du-Hyun]
7. She becomes the woman's dead husband and speaks with his voice. The teenage boy at right cries when he hears his father's voice in the witch's throat [Lee Du-Hyun]

A SHAMANIST *KUT* TO COMMUNICATE WITH THE DEAD

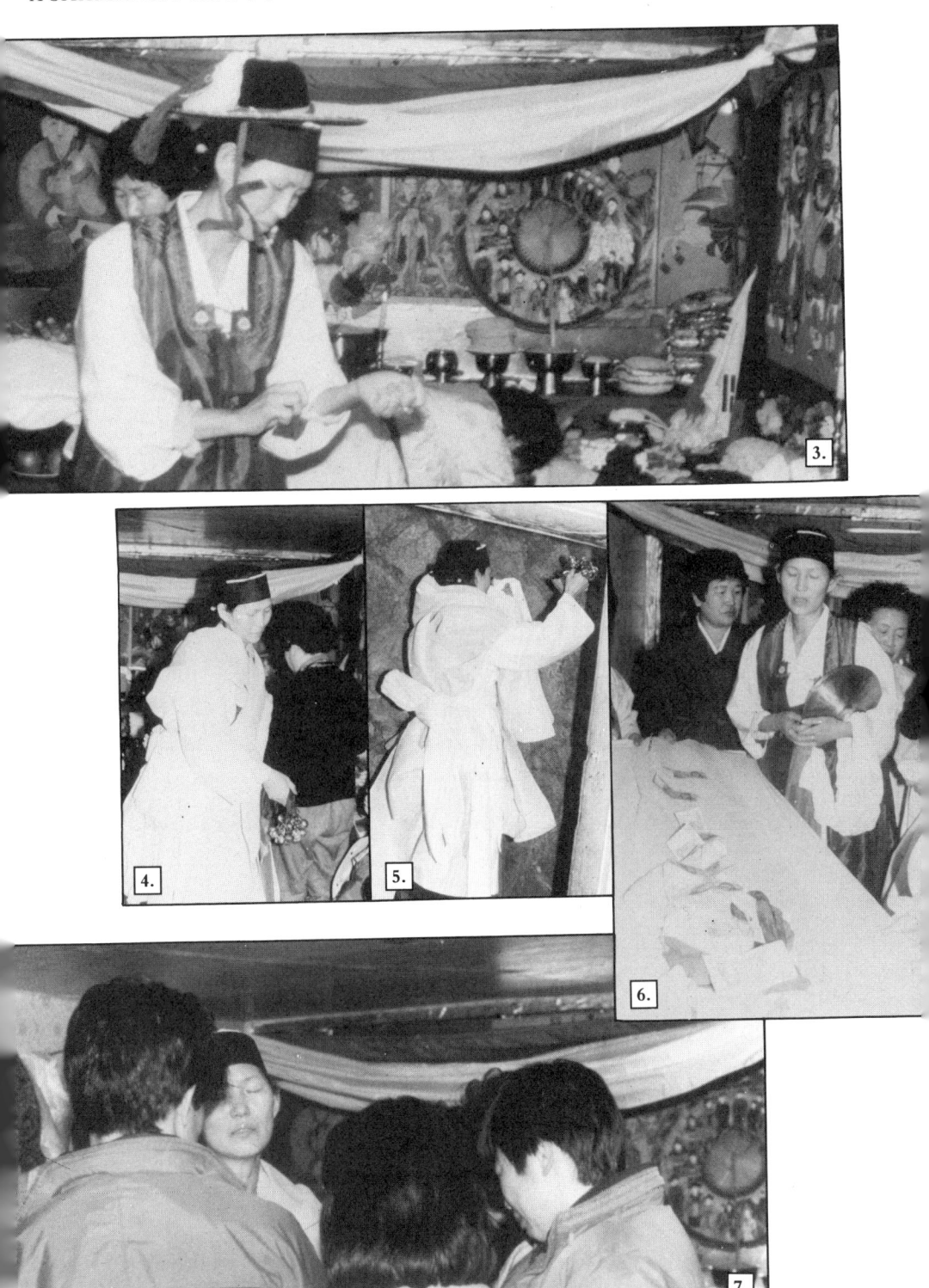

3.

4.

5.

6.

7.

THE KOREANS

1. Behind the "economic miracle" [KOIS]
2. Vertical suburbia [KOIS]
3. University campus scene [KOIS]
4. A mountainside foodstall near Shinhŭng-sa . . . [Russell Warren Howe]
5. . . . and the white sands of Nagsan beach [Russell Warren Howe]

6. *The Asiad and Olympiad sports complex in Seoul* [KOIS]
7. *The high beam* [KOIS]
8. *Football (soccer), a national passion* [KOIS]
9. *T'aekwŏndo training begins early* [KOIS]
10. *Fairground* ssirum *wrestling* [Russell Warren Howe]

9

A LIFE IN *MI-RAE*

A NATION'S GREATNESS depends as much on its future as on its past. The fascinating millennia of Korea's yesterday, however significant and catalytic for the region, does not quite project it into the same rank as China or Ancient Rome. What is principally riveting about Korea cannot be proven, only divined and projected—its *mi-rae*, its rendezvous with the decades to come.

The Koreans are obsessed with the future. They are a nation of overachievers and, like such people everywhere, of emigrants. After all, a nation is not obliged to march in place in order to advance.

Korea's is a culture forged in the crucible of wars, including a particularly devastating one in recent memory. It is a nation on alert. There are ubiquitous security forces, monthly practice air-raid drills, antitank dragon's teeth at the city approaches to Seoul, which is only twenty-six miles from the nearest North Korean short-range missile batteries. About forty-two thousand American servicemen are stationed in the country, with over a quarter of their number in the "invasion corridors" near the border. An American general commands all U.S. *and* Korean forces—at least as of the date of this writing. In the ironically named Demilitarized Zone (DMZ), a mine field one hundred fifty-one miles long, fifty-five Americans and hundreds of South Koreans have been killed in countless "incidents" since the signing of the 1953 armistice with North Korea.

Yet the crucible of wars has not produced drilled automatons. Even before the Korean spring got under way in 1987, political conversations in the little *sik-dang* restaurants and *sul-jip* bars were outspoken, especially after a snort or two of *so-ju*.

To some extent, this reflects the fact that the big cities, and Seoul above all, are centers of urban liberation for people with rural values. The capital is home to a quarter of the population, nearly three-quarters of all the country's banks, and literally hundreds of newspapers and periodicals. It contains more institutions of higher learning than any other city in the world. All this has affected temperament, in the sense of making it more plebeian. In a public lecture at the Woodrow Wilson Center, veteran scholar Gregory Henderson reacts conservatively, perceiving a threat of decadence:

> Where sedateness, quiet and even immobility were once valued, has come explosive hustle, uncurbed noise. A street pattern of disputaciousness has broken all ideals of calmness in human intercourse. Abruptness of manner and even tinges of pugnaciousness, certainly of ruggedness, seem to replace the ceremonial politeness of *yang-ban* Haltung, often even in offices. The dark, low-keyed rooms with sparse furnishings and a lack of pretension give way to an overlit, frequently gaudy and contrived ambience. The old is torn down or removed from daily life, museumized. The Olympic image is of victories in sweaty wrestling and boxing matches; diving, swimming, sailing, fencing, equestrian events go

uncontested. . . . Tŏ-gye would have thought boxing and wrestling not only un-Korean but disturbing to harmony and the sports' proper ethos: lower class. . . . The Confucians esteemed sedateness and order; Kim Il Sŏng and Ch'ŏn Du-hwan, for other reasons, prize the same. But only Kim, through drastic measures, can achieve it.

Henderson paints a slightly exaggerated profile of Seoul with its "unrestrained jostling (and) searing noise, including voices whose cadence would have wrenched the Confucian soul." He calls it the "broken beehive effect." He complains that modesty is no longer inculcated in children, who are encouraged by their parents to "boast and perform." Has upper-class Confucianism failed to percolate down? Why is the Korean nation different from Japan or Confucian Singapore?

For Henderson, Koreans are now a "hard-working, deep-drinking, high-risk-taking, hard-swinging, not very squeamish, vibrant society totally unrelated to the *yang-ban* pattern or the observations and predictions made of it seventy to one hundred years ago by all visitors." He attributes the "economic miracle" and the Korean colonization of American retail stores to this change of character.

But perhaps much of what seems different is simply more externalized—for instance, the attitude to government, which Henderson describes well:

> What one has for central power is far from love, it is not even respect, nor is it by any means always fear or even apprehension. It is a kind of chronic consciousness often heightening the preoccupation with a force with which one has almost constantly to cope. Nor is its presence confined to taxation, passports, law-abidingness or political activity. It is deeply involved in ed-

ucational and career choices, and bank loans, and it is not infrequently involved, above the lower social levels, in choosing the friendship circles (as formerly of living sites), marriage, whom one calls, whom one writes to, sometimes even whom one asks after, and the degree of enthusiasm with which one—outside the family—relates to other people. . . . Contrary to what both Korean regimes hope, Koreans are basically a highly political people.

But a strong measure of authoritarianism prevails, and "South Korea lives the irony of being a fervently anti-communist and free-trade country which, at the same time, has many characteristics of a socialist state."

This preoccupation with authority diminishes when Koreans emigrate to societies where government is less omnipresent. Unfortunately, this adaptability often leads to expatriate Koreans losing the qualities of their culture more quickly than the Chinese and Japanese. Similarly, public sycophancy toward "leaders" swiftly turns to disparagement after their fall or death, as with President Yi Sŭng-man and the despotic but brilliant and intensely nationalistic Pak Chung-hi, and as seems about to happen with Ch'ŏn Du-hwan. This characteristic has no doubt encouraged Kim Il-sŏng to promote his son as successor, fearing not only the posthumous fate of his South Korean counterparts, but that of friends and contemporaries like Josef Stalin and Leonid Brezhnev.

Some elements in Korean culture are overdue for reform. Until now, for instance, the law has not defended the sovereign citizen, but officialdom—the government. A detained person is still guilty until (rarely) proven innocent. "Lenient" judges have been rusticated. In the North, of course, justice is, in Henderson's apt phrase, "even more abject." If true tyranny is, as Antoine de Saint-Exupéry wrote, not when the individual oppresses the mass but when the mass oppresses the individualist, there remains a measure of tyranny in Korea as in all Confucian societies. It is conceivable that one attraction of the Christian churches is their concern with justice for the individual; but they may also perhaps be held somewhat responsible for the more tiresome aspects of individualism on which Henderson was quoted earlier.

It is hard to see authoritarianism disappearing overnight while the role of the military remains so important. The peninsula is the most militarized region on earth, although, before the Japanese imperium, the hermit kingdom had been, in Henderson's words, "one of the least militarized polities." Its massive and successful industrialization is no less a reversal of roles for such a rural folk. In this regard, some observers have compared Korea's role reversal to Israel's, where a people have improbably excelled in militarism, the repression of minorities, and agriculture, while proving less than successful at a skill they practically invented—managing an economy.

The point should not be labored. If the country has a flourishing industrial class and an overabundance of soldiers, it also has an exceptionally large body of educators, and the scholar remains more highly respected than the tycoon. North Korea also places a heavy emphasis on education. Koreans worship learning at least as much as they venerate their departed spirits. They love their traditions, their *han-gŭl* script. They cry at their traditional music.

This is not as dichotomous as it might appear. Despite the *yang-ban* system, and royal and *yang-ban* patronage, most great Korean art was plebeian. Over three hundred thousand pieces of celadon and other ceramics have been lovingly preserved in the museums; yet, astonishingly, no one knows the name of a single master potter. A handful of the *yang-ban* literati put their chop to Zen paintings; but other artists did not, because the painters and master potters were not masters but slaves, whose proportion in the population was about twelve times greater than in China or Japan, until Japan abolished bondage in Korea in this century. It is true that, as Henderson says, "slaves tend to ape the culture of those who own them," and that the original concepts of Korean art presumably came from the art-purchasing aristocracy; but the fact is that Korea's art was, by definition, folk art. Even the great architects were mostly monks of the lowest caste.

Yet, as Laurel Kendall has underscored, Koreans are reluctant to recognize the plebeian contribution to their culture. "They want to be good Confucians, good *yang-ban*," she says. As Father Dennis McNamara has pointed out, in a Woodrow Wilson Center lecture, Koreans admire their past culture much as Europeans admire Ancient Greece. They tend to see the West as exotic, a little ridiculous, and Japan as barbaric—notwithstanding the fact that Japan has now surpassed not only Korea and China, but also the West, economically.

For Kendall, today's triumph of the underclass is an echo of the more openly important role played by women, the most numerous underclass of all. She is speaking not only of how the *mansin* came out of the closet once again after the assassination of President Pak, but of the rising economic and spiritual power of the woman in the home, where she handles the finances and the traditional household spirits, exorcisms and loans.

Henderson seems to agree:

> On the whole, judging from thirty-seven years of commentary heard from cognoscenti, the number of foreigners who think Korea a land of outstanding women exceeds those who deem it a land of exceptional men. For vibrancy, ambition for themselves and

their men, for commitment and energy, they have few equals in this world.

The Koreans are also, too often, unfortunate examples of the Peter Principle—that each person seeks to advance to his first level of incompetence. America is full of Korean emigrants who believed that anyone could succeed at business, just as Europe is full of Indians and Pakistanis who think that anyone can run a restaurant. Koreans are a polite but not inherently a modest people. They are assertive while often lacking the self-confidence to ask for advice and criticism. The late W. Averell Harriman once told this writer that you could recognize the truly capable person by how he insisted on his own incompetence, and the quintessential twit by his "can do" attitude. By this demanding standard, Koreans often fall short.

The *Far Eastern Economic Review*'s witty Welsh editor, Derek Davies, regularly publishes examples of fractured Asian English that surpass even those headlines of the Columbia Journalism Review's "Lower Case." The examples, however, come mostly from modest origins—the Malaysian roadside restaurant that accidentally makes a dish sound poisonous, the back-alley Indian pharmacy that unintentionally turns a medicine into something hilariously obscene. In Korea, bloopers are made at more august levels. Where but in Seoul could one find a soft-drinks firm investing millions of dollars in new products for the Olympic and tourist market and, having decided to give them "with-it" English names, goes about choosing them *itself*? Hence, if you're tempted, you can now swill Cool-Pis and Sweat, on the rocks.

Yet this full-speed-ahead-and-damn-the-torpedos approach also has its virtues. There seems little doubt that Koreans, especially women, do better at English than the shier and more self-conscious Japanese (and much better than Americans or

Europeans do at either Korean or Japanese) because of their willingness to take the plunge and risk mistakes.

Koreans are intrigued by the different and the unexpected. Much East Asian art at its best seems to have a "Zen" quality—an unfinished factor which suggests illusion and enables the viewer, listener, or reader to contribute his own illusion. Until modern times, probably no two *wadang*, or Korean roof tiles, were alike. Korean asymmetry is not always as successful as that of Japan, but this is in part because it is less conceived, more spontaneous.

To be understood, a nation has to be compared with others in its environment. Koreans tend to emphasize their cultural links to China, but emotionally reject any cultural association with Japan except when it puts Japan in the role of the historic inferior. The Koreans can be tiresome in their putdown of Japan, in their unconsciously self-deprecating attempts to assert their Korean superiority. The prejudices are based, not so much on history, as on Korea's miseries under Japanese administration.

To be just, the Korean attitude reflects a phenomenon which Westerners of the World War II generation can both condemn and understand, because the attitude is so common among armchair warriors of the West's postwar generation. In any era of history, those who actually go into combat are only too aware that they find themselves on one side rather than the other because of a geographical accident of birth. They could equally well have been born on the other side—the "wrong" one. The term "war crimes" refers to those committed by the side that lost. (In the case of the Pacific War, for instance, Hiroshima and Nagasaki don't count, because those responsible were winners.) It is difficult to imagine Korean resistance veterans seeing Japanese veterans as anything more than youthful victims of *in-yon*. Inevitably, however, a later generation has copied Western armchair warriors in vicariously refighting

World War II against the innocent descendants of former enemies. Much of the blame must lie with the prejudice which is encouraged by the history curriculum in Korean schools. Then again, all countries teach their own history with about as much objectivity as Jean Chauvin, and perhaps one only really learns the truth about one's own country in foreign books.

Some of the blame must also rest with the Korean personality. Across the board, Koreans seem to have difficulty distinguishing between perseverance and obstinacy. Henderson complains that they have "great difficulty in compromise, in yielding." Korea's outdated attitude toward Japan may well be the most fundamentally demeaning aspect of this shortcoming. To quote Henderson again:

> Part of the Korean profile consists of its maintaining the longest and bitterest public facade of accusation against the former colonial master of any former colonial people.

Indeed, the Algerians and the Portuguese Africans and the Indonesians would seem to have as much right to be traumatized by past brutalities, but they have avoided this self-indulgence. One imagines that a future Palestine and a future Azania may well come to terms with Israelis and white South Africans. As Henderson further notes: "Almost no other colonial people is ethnically as close to its former master." For him, this is an irony; but has it, one wonders, helped to create the intensity, even to a degree the absurdity, of the trauma?

All this is not to decry, of course, the cause and the courage of Korean resistance to Japanese occupation. As Churchill suggested, resistance to occupation may be the most honorable form of warfare. One of Korea's twentieth-century martyrs, Yi Yuk-sa, was executed by the Japanese for writing "subversive poetry"—surely a death which makes anyone in the writing profession green with envy.

Koreans, in their art and in their persona, remain torn between their two "national" creatures. One is the Siberian tiger, the tough but foolish failure-figure of the nation-founding legend. The other is the stork—the slender symbol of beauty, freedom, grace, and flight. Interestingly, in the Korean version of the tale of the tortoise and the hare, it is the trusting, initially careless, hard-running hare who catches up the ground lost and eventually beats the sly, calculating, too-clever-by-half tortoise.

Yet the Korean isn't only the driving force he aspires to be. His most popular songs are treaclelike in sentimentality. The best of Korean poetry shows both sadness and acceptance of the time play in which we conceive of our existences.

With its populist tradition, it is not surprising that one of the better television series that Seoul has produced in recent times concerned Hong Kil-dong, the country's (fictitious) Robin Hood. Based on the early eighteenth-century novel by Hŏ Kyun—and written, defiantly, in *han-gŭl* instead of Chinese ideographs—this is the saga of the son of a nobleman and a peasant girl, who survives by his mastery of the martial arts.

Unable to become a warrior because of his mother's humble background, considered a bit of a simpleton, he takes to the mountain paths, gathering together a fraternity he calls the *hwal-bin-dang*, or save-the-poor movement. There seems an obvious correlation with the antibourgeois, antibusiness, antiauthority "inverse snobbery" of Sakyamuni—or Jesus. Hong robbed the rich—including rich temples—to give to the impoverished. As with Robin Hood (and, in a way, Jesus) a price is put on his head. He is regularly reported to be in different places at the same time. He becomes the hero of the masses. The story ends happily with Hong creating a utopian kingdom on an island in the East Sea, or Sea of Japan. There is even a

Maid Marion, whom he rescues from a mythical monster. (In the television series, the monster is the grasping, Shylockian Chinese trader in Korea who employs her.)

Like that of the twelfth-century Hood, Hong's fictitious life spawned multiple legends, songs, and jokes. He was both a combat and a sexual athlete, a tragicomic figure of illiterate chivalry. In a sense, therefore, he prefigures the heroes of the Korean resistance under Japanese occupation. However, Hong also came to terms with political reality, helping the Korean establishment when it was in difficulty. This perhaps represents the best in the Korean political tradition. On the other hand, it is the confusion between perseverance and obstinacy, so contradictory in a Buddhist culture, that keeps the two Koreas from establishing an open border.

On the plus side, most Koreans seem to be aware of the problem, which the average citizen, with the exasperated attitude toward government to which Henderson refers, blames on "the politicians." This attitude is also not new. My favorite story from Korean folklore is one that any reporter condemned to Washington will appreciate:

In about 200 B.C., Emperor Yao went to visit Ch'ao Fu, a sage who lived in a windbreak which he had patched together in a tree. The emperor, with humility, offered the scholarly hermit his throne. Ch'ao Fu retorted testily that he must wash his ears in the river because the emperor had put such a vile proposal into them. Overhearing the conversation, a farmer pulled his cow from the stream, saying he did not want her milk poisoned by the washing of Ch'ao Fu's ears.

Korea today belongs, essentially, not to the names you read on page one of the *Washington Post* or the *Guardian* or *Le Monde* during an election, but to a leapfrog generation of younger Koreans—a nation-within-a-nation of students who resent the three-year draft into the police or the military, where the conditions match those of the Foreign Legion, and a nation of

A LIFE IN *MI-RAE*

emigrant empire builders. Koreans own or rent fifty-three percent of the grocery stores in Washington, for instance; but the cousins they left behind run the world's largest shipyards and produced a fifth-generation computer only six months after Cray Research of the United States and Fujitsu of Japan. Like Japan, Korea is spurred by its absence of natural resources. Qualities of the past persist and survive in Korea, but the nation is pointed firmly toward the future. In Buddhism, there is the Buddha of the past, Sakyamuni (Sŏk-ka-mo-ni in Korean), the Buddhas or bodhisattvas of the present, and the Buddha of the future—*Bul mi-ruk*. It is before the latter that the Koreans appear to be in contemplative zazen.

Of South Korea's forty-three million people, seven million are presently in primary school, three million in middle school, and two and a quarter million in high schools and technical schools. Of these, five hundred thousand, or nearly twenty-three percent, will go on to higher education, if one includes both four- and two-year institutions. (There are about five hundred of the latter.)

Formal education alone does not make revolutions. This is a media country. Even under the Japanese, the restless natives resisted in *han-gŭl*. Before 1941, when the Japanese finally silenced the press, the *Dong-a Il-bo* had been confiscated 489 times; publication was suspended sixty-three times. Under the generals, defiance has continued; in 1986, the magazine *Mal* (Words) revealed the extent of government censorship, which included ordering the placement and length of selected stories, especially those regarding the president. He became known behind his back as President Ch'ŏn O-nŭl ("President Ch'ŏn To-day"), because that was how the TV news and page-one stories always began. Arrested and tried, the editors of *Mal* were given only short sentences—which was taken to be a sign of independence by the courts—then acquitted on appeal.

Today, there are thirty-two daily papers, eight of them

national in circulation, one hundred forty-two weeklies, and over sixteen hundred other periodicals. Although, as in most countries, ownership of a color television set requires purchase of a license, virtually every family has one. As in America, it is primarily the press, rather than the constitution, which has kept the government fairly honest, and also helped to retain the country's unusual level of economic egalitarianism. Fifty percent of the wealth is divided among the country's most affluent forty percent, and the other half among the less fortunate sixty percent. There are fat cats, of course, with conspicuous hillside villas, chauffeurs, and maids, but the fraction is remarkably small. The sharing of wealth is even more remarkable than in Japan, much more so than in Europe, and immensely more impressive than in the United States. Among Communist countries, probably only Cuba has as good a record.

Today, the generational division in Korea, as in Western countries, is mostly reflected in the difference between city and countryside. In the hillside hamlets and fishing villages, wives still become servants of imperious mothers-in-law, and are especially reluctant to marry eldest sons because of the latter's preoccupation with filial duties toward ancestors. The cities, as in Japan and, a generation or so earlier, the Occident, have bred the nuclear family concept. Even so, selfishness is less excused in Korea than in America. The epicure is not necessarily, or even normally, a hedonist. As in Europe, an aged mother or father who is gravely ill would probably prefer death to impoverishing the family by expensive treatment, as America's elderly often do. Yet filial respect is much greater in Korea, including the Buddhist-shamanist equivalent of All Saints' Day, the "day of the dead" of the Catholic world. The name of a distinguished family elder may be preserved on a wooden tablet in a treasured box, where his spirit also resides. Dying at home remains all-important.

Perhaps nothing so well illustrated this and the revolutionary—presumably Marxist—challenge to it as when, in 1987, a solitary striker was killed in the rash of labor disputes. The unions wanted to take his coffin to Kwangju, the capital of the country's political opposition, to be carried at the head of a demonstration march. The family, of course, wanted him buried in their ancestral home, or *pon*. Finally, the police shamed the activists into giving the casket back to the family so that the young shipyard worker could rejoin his ancestors and become a reasonably contented spirit.

Not surprisingly, it is the needless traditions which are fading first. For instance, it is no longer required to remove one's glasses in the presence of an elder, although priests often still do so when they pray (that is, speak to God). Eye visibility, however, remains important, so sunglasses are still usually removed during any conversation.

Most of the Korean diet makes for less cholesterol and arteriosclerosis than the regimens of the West, but the heavy salt content of *kimch'i* encourages heart attacks. There are growing signs of popular awareness of such problems; the modest fad in Seoul for Western fast food, which tends to make cholesterol matters worse, has not so far spread to the provinces. A nation nearly one hundred percent literate seems likely to find ways of improving its traditional diet without destroying its essence.

In human affairs, not everything that affronts Western values is necessarily bad. Indeed, as a benchmark, Western values are irrelevant, although it is possible that some universal values exist. All Western writers discoursing on conservative cultures tend to sound stridently liberal. This author has tried, probably unsuccessfully, to be a little less ethnocentric than most. However, like all other Western writers on Korea, I am conscious of having placed a rather heavy stress on the issue of women in society. This is not because the conception of women's place in society is different in Korea from the conception in America and much of the West—which is irrelevant—but because the issue is basic to society, and more importantly because this is a live issue among Koreans themselves, including many prominent Korean men. In reality, since the Occidental cultures only gave the vote to women in living memory, and instituted many other aspects of inegalitarianism, the West is not well placed to criticize a culturally different set of questionable practices. Again, one can note that the role of the male in Confucian society is remarkably similar to that of the paterfamilias of Islam and Judaism or of the *chef de famille* under the Napoleon Code which prevails in France and many other countries. Certainly, any suggestion that Korean women are less contented than, say, American women would be unwarranted, and Korean women have a record for achieving their objectives with less combustion. All in all, one gets the impression that the need to reconcile equality with congenital difference seems to be proceeding in Korea at about the pace which the culture can handle without negative side effects. To say that Korean women want more independence, the right to eat with their husbands and not walk two paces behind, is fairly obvious, and those victories seem guaranteed. To imply from that that Korean women desire, any more than Japanese women, to mimic the women of the West would be to take an ethnocentric view. This is clearly a watershed season in the fabric of Korean social life. However, Koreans, men and women, see themselves as more realistic than Westerners, and they may be right.

Marriage remains an intensely family affair, surrounded by much of the old clan mystique. Brides still usually don't smile on their wedding day, out of superstition—they would expect to be afflicted by daughters, and therefore have no one to care for them in their old age. Few men or women would consider a life entirely bereft of marriage. The slang phrase for a spinster or a bachelor who shows no sign of getting wed means

A LIFE IN *MI-RAE*

"big baby." An American magazine said in a cover story a few years ago that American women who had reached the age of thirty-five without marriage still had a five percent chance of finding a husband; but in Asia, even more than in Europe or Africa or Latin America, such an opportunity would be unlikely. Even men, who are not hampered by the age cap on parturition, rarely postpone marriage beyond thirty, in Korea. Paul Crane, the medical missionary who is still the best-known chronicler of Korean mores in the English language, says that in his time (that is, until a decade or so ago) a widow's only source of consolation was her late husband's long-stemmed pipe. Even today, widow remarriage is even more of an exception than in the West; among other things, it would confuse the ancestors of both husbands. However, this must surely change in the near future.

On the other hand, divorce remains rare, occurring in less than five percent of marriages; even if it were not now widely known that the sex of the baby depends on the chromosomes of the father, it is unlikely that Korean wives would follow the fate of those of Henry VIII or the Shah of Iran and be displaced. Even in the days when a mother was blamed for not having sons, divorce or even infidelity to acquire a male heir was not widespread; more probably, the wife would suggest that her husband try for a son with a servant girl in their employ, thus ensuring that his fidelity to his marriage and household remained intact.

As in most societies, and certainly a little more than in the United States, the sexes seem to be most comfortable when they are segregated. Older women, for instance, can follow the precedent long set by their menfolk and get respectably drunk together.

Events have taken their toll on Korean culture: the rise of the *chaebol* and the Korean economy, and the role of the army in government, have threatened and could ultimately challenge the position of the scholar at the top of the caste pyramid. Will Koreans, like a few European countries—and even more like Japan and some other Asian nations—manage to overcome the gross materialism that almost inevitably develops in newly-affluent peoples? Japan has proved that even the greatest economic triumphs do not have to come at the cost of losing life's graces. But is there significance in the fact that the relatively poor in the Korean countryside are now more schooled in traditional politeness than are the theoretically more sophisticated toilers of the towns and cities?

What may perhaps survive, given the nature of the people, is the feeling of satisfaction, and indeed superiority, that comes with self-discipline. But this, as noted earlier, is also at risk, as Confucianism comes increasingly under challenge. There would seem to be a need, through education, to try to preserve the best of the ancient ethic. Modern Soviet scholars, headed by Nobari Simonia, have concluded, with Marx, that tradition informs the revolution more than ideology. The Confucian tradition, once seen as retarding modernization by preserving caste, and as especially hobbling to women, can now be seen as a sort of usefully demanding work ethic—however much some of the canon may be out of date or imperfectly expressed.

Significantly, the news anchorpersons on Korean television, both male and female, still gracefully end their broadcasts by thanking their audiences for listening, and then bowing—albeit from a seated position, but sufficiently for their features to drop out of sight. (A bow, by the way, is more than the polite inclination of the head, or nod, practiced in Europe. The most important part consists of trying to touch one's chin to one's neck, and keeping the back straight. The hands do not have to be clasped behind the back in the "at ease" position, as practiced in many Western countries, but neither should they hang simianly at the sides: they should be palmed tidily on the buttocks.)

Koreans are sui generis, and can sometimes be arrogant in their awareness of it. Where else could one find an arms manufacturer turned preacher who, surpassing every outrage of America's televangelists, proclaims himself the new Messiah? Mun Sŏn-myŏng (he of the "Moonies") has felt the eminently shamanist need, despite his age and girth, to be raptured by the Holy Ghost. Perhaps this is all of a pattern with Kim Kum-hwa becoming, despite her sex, all the generals of the five directions, and some client's late husband to boot. Why not?—the Korean, like the African, is possessed by spirits. Animism seems to have survived better on the peninsula than the Shinto equivalent in Japan, in spite of the latter's apparently Korean origins.

Despite Henderson's partly justifiable strictures about raised voices, disputaceousness, lack of modesty and the like, it seems likely that in such virtues as quiet-spokenness, devotion to privacy, neatness and cleanliness, and so many other things which are cardinal to civilization, probably only the Japanese surpass the Koreans as the world enters the Pacific age. And when who comes first ceases to count, the laurels for who tries hardest may well fall to the Koreans.

A GUIDE TO READING *HAN-GŬL*

CONSONANTS

ㄱ	g
ㄴ	n
ㄷ	d
ㄹ	{ r (initial) / l (final) }
ㅁ	m
ㅂ	b
ㅅ	s
ㅇ	{ -ng (final) / (no sound as initial) }
ㅈ	j
ㅊ	ch'
ㅋ	k'

VOWELS

Simple vowels

아	a
야	ya
어	ŏ (us)
여	yŏ (yummy)
오	o
요	yo
우	u
유	yu

Diphthongs

애	ae (am)
얘	yae (yam)
에	e (etch)
예	ye (yet)
외	oe (web)
와	wa
위	wi (wit)
워	wŏ (worry)

257

A GUIDE TO READING *HAN-GŬL*

ㅌ	t'	ㅇ	ŭ (full)	의	ŭi (full + it)
ㅍ	p'				
ㅎ	h	이	i (it)	왜	wae (wag)
				웨	we (wet)

ACKNOWLEDGMENTS

I am particularly indebted to Dr. Lee Du-hyun of Seoul National University for his patience and assistance and for his introductions to other Korean academics, and also to Dr. Laurel Kendall of the American Museum of Natural History for her help and kindness and introductions. I have quoted freely from the works of both these experts, and thank them for generously granting permission to do so.

For their willingness to share their knowledge of Korea's maritime communities, I am thankful to Dr. Han Sang-bok and Dr. Chun Kyung-soo, also both of Seoul National, and I express my gratitude to Kim Kum-hwa for allowing me to be present at some of her séances with the spirits.

As quotations in the text indicate, research materials which I have used to supplement my own experiences and observations include the books of Dr. Andrew Nahm, Dr. Peter Hyun, Halla Pai Huhm of the University of Hawaii, Dr. Paul S. Crane, Dr. Alan Carter Covell and his mother, Dr. Jon Carter Covell, and monographs, essays, and talks by Gregory Henderson of Harvard, Father Dennis McNamara of Georgetown, Dr. Martina Deuchler of the University of Zurich, Dr. Edward W. Wagner of Harvard, Dr. Mark Peterson of Brigham Young,

ACKNOWLEDGMENTS

the late Dr. Youngsook Kim-Harvey, Dr. Clark W. Sorenson of Vanderbilt, Dr. Cho Hae-joang of Yonsei University, Brian Wilson, Dr. David R. McCann of Cornell, Dr. Barbara E. Young, Dr. Hesung Chun Koh of Yale, Dr. Yi Kwang-rin, Dr. Richard Rutt, Dr. Pak Chi-wŏn, Dr. Kim Tong-wook, Dr. Kim Dŭk-ran of Kang-nŭng University, Gertrude Ferrar, Michael E. Macmillan, Ho-min Sohn, Grete Diemente Sibley, Tom Coyner, Gary Rector, Norman Thorpe, Cho Joong-ok, and others too numerous to mention.

Except where otherwise specified, the analyses are my own subjective ones, as are probably any or all mistakes.

———R.W.H.

SELECT BIBLIOGRAPHY

HISTORIES OF KOREA

Among the more accessible to the general reader are:

Covell, Jon Carter. *Korea's Colorful Heritage*. Seoul and Honolulu: Si-sa-yŏng-o-sa, 1985.

Hyun, Peter. *Koreana*. Seoul: Korea Britannica, 1984.

Nahm, Andrew C. *A Panorama of Five Thousand Years: Korean History*. Elizabeth, N.J., and Seoul: Hollym, 1983.

ANTHROPOLOGICAL AND CULTURAL STUDIES

Chun Kyung-soo. *Reciprocity and Korean Society*. Seoul: Seoul National University, 1984.

Chun Shin-yŏng, ed. *Upper-Class Culture in Yi-Dynasty Korea*. Seoul and Honolulu: Si-sa-yŏng-o-sa, 1982.

Covell, Alan Carter. *Folk Art and Magic*. Elizabeth, N.J., and Seoul: Hollym, 1986.

Covell, Jon Carter, *The Center Stage for Seventy Years: The Chosun*. Elizabeth, N.J., and Seoul: Hollym, 1984.

Crane, Paul S. *Korean Patterns*. Seoul: Royal Asiatic Society, 1967.

SELECT BIBLIOGRAPHY

Halla Pai Huhm. *Kut: Korean Shamanist Rituals.* Elizabeth, N.J., and Seoul: Hollym, 1980.

Han Sang-bok. *Korean Fishermen.* Seoul: Seoul National University, 1977.

Kendall, Laurel. *Shamans, Housewives and Other Restless Spirits.* Honolulu: University of Hawaii Press, 1985.

Kendall, Laurel and Mark Peterson, eds. *Korean Women: View From the Inner Room.* New Haven, Conn.: East Rock Press, 1983.

Lee Du-hyun. *Role Playing Through Trance Possession.* New York: Wenner-Gren Foundation for Anthropological Research, 1982.

Lee Kwan-jo. *Search for Nirvana.* Seoul: Seoul International Publishing House, 1984.

Morse, Ronald A., ed. *Wild Asters: Explorations in Korean Thought, Culture and Society.* Washington, D.C.: Woodrow Wilson International Center for Scholars, The Smithsonian Institution, 1986.

Ok Cho-joong. *Home Style Korean Cooking.* Tokyo: Shufunotomo, 1981.

GUIDEBOOKS

The best two are:

Korea. Hong Kong: Apa Productions; New York: Prentice Hall; London: Harrap; Australia: Lansdowne Press, 1984.

Facts about Korea. Seoul: Korean Overseas Information Service, 1985.

Others include:

Korea. U.S.: Fodor's Travel Guides; London: Hodder and Stoughton, annual.

Korea. Seoul: Korean National Tourist Corporation, annual.

Rucci, Richard B., ed. *Living in Korea.* Seoul: American Chamber of Commerce, 1984.

INDEX

Acheson, Dean, 62, 63
A-chik-ki, 111
Actors, 211
Acupuncture, 174, 175, 179–80
Adams, Will, 46
Adoption, 100
Air transport, 225
Alcohol consumption, 19, 179, 215–16, 222–25
Alcoholic beverages, 221–22, 225
   drinking etiquette, 223–25
Allen, Horace, 102, 186
Altaic nomads, 37–38
An-bang (women's inner room), 98–99, 193–94
Anchovy fishing, 153–54
An Chung-gŭn, 58
Anderson, Scott and Jon Lee, 118
Apartment rentals, 226
Aphrodisiacs, 174, 175, 176
Apothecaries, xxi, 5–6, 173–74
   fees of, 177
   items sold by, 173–74, 176
   medical consultations, 176–77, 178
   prescriptions from, 177–78
   Western interest in, 177
   window displays of shops, 175

Art
   brush-drawing, 195
   cabinetmaking, 196
   calligraphy, 72, 75
   celadon ceramics, 195, 196–97
   dance, 201–2
   film industry, 211–12
   folk art, 197–99, 203–4, 242–43
   literature and poetry, 75, 97–98, 228–29, 247
   music, 8, 137, 199–201, 204
   "natural" art, 195
   painting, 133–36, 197–99
   papermaking, 196
   plebeian nature of, 242–43
   religious art, 133–36, 198–99, 230, 231–32
   song, 98, 200, 202–3
Astronomy, 112
Attlee, Clement, 61

Baker, Kathleen Mary Drew, 160
Ballad singing, 202–3
Bamboo used as medicine, 178
Baseball, 209
Basketball, 209

263

Beer, 221, 224
Berneux, Siméon-François, 115
Bird, national, 36, 247
Birthdays, xxii
"Bodhisattva of mercy" sculpture, 120, 231–32
Bowing, 4, 7, 29, 254–55
Brekhmann, I. I., 184
Bribery
  in business, 90–91
  in government, 27–28
Brillat-Savarin, Anthelme, 213
Brush-drawing, 195
Buddhism
  bodhisattvas, 120, 121, 231–32
  branches of, 110
  Buddha figures, 120–21
  Buddha of the future, 249
  colorfulness of, 118–19
  common people, association with, 113
  funerals, 109
  God, lack of, 109–10
  history of Korea, role in, 39, 110–13
  holidays, 113
  Hwa-om (Flowering Splendor) school, 112, 121
  pacifist nature of, 114
  pictoral and sculptural art, 120–21, 199, 230, 231–32
  popular attitudes toward, 105–6
  reform movements, 43
  reincarnation cycle, 113
  shamanism, acceptance of, 110, 118–22
  Sŏn (Zen) Buddhism, 74, 110, 122
  syncretism of, 117
  temples, 118–20, 122, 199, 231
  Tripitaka Koreana (Buddhist canon), 44, 74, 122
Bul (Buddha figures), 120–21
Bulguk-sa (Buddha land temple), 122, 199

Busan, 63, 230
Bus travel, 225

Cabinetmaking, 196
Calligraphers, 75
Calligraphy, 72, 75
"Can do" attitude of Koreans, 244–45
Car rentals, 226
Catholicism, 114–16
Celadon ceramics, 195, 196–97
Censorship, 211, 212, 249
Ceremony, Koreans' love for, 30–31
Cespedes, Gregario de, 115
Chang Myŏn, 66
Ch'ao Fu, 248
Chesa (rites for ancestors), 171
Chiang Kai-shek, 61, 63
Chih Tsung, 175
Children
  adoption of, 100
  ceremonies regarding, 11
  games played by, 14
  gifts for, 92
  given names, referred to by, 87–88
  island children, 161
  naming of, 12–13
Ch'il-gŏ chi ak (Confucian doctrine), 21
Ch'il-song, 134
China
  history of Korea, role in, 38–39, 41, 112–13
  Korean War, 64, 65
Chindo dogs, 3, 36, 152
Chin-do Island, 36, 152
Chinese language, 78–79
Chinese pictographs, 10, 73–74, 79
Chi Tsu, Prince, 38
Ch'oe Che-u, 117
Ch'oe Mal-li, 80
Ch'oe Wŏn-chol, 232
Chogi p'asi (fish market), 154–55
Cho Hae-joang, 169, 170, 171–72

Ch'oi Hui-a, 136
Ch'ŏm-sŏng-dae observatory, 112
Ch'ŏn-do-gyo cult, 117
Ch'ŏn Du-hwan, 9, 66–67, 126, 240, 241
Chong-no bell, 101
Ch'ŏng-yol, King, 43, 205
Ch'ŏn Kyŏng-su, 159, 161, 162, 164
Chopsticks, 10, 220–21
Cho-rang-mal pony, 36
Christianity, 110, 242
    Catholicism, 114–16
    educational facilities, 116–17
    fundamentalists, 117, 118
    growth of, 116
    history of Korea, role in, 49, 55–56, 114–16
    persecution of Christians, 115–16
    popularity of, 18
    Protestant sects, 116
    resistance image, 18
    shamanism's influence on, 143–44
    women, appeal for, 100–101
Chu-ae, King, 40
Chuk-do Island, 164–65
Chung-sŏn boatmen, 153–54
Churchill, Winston, 61, 246
Chu-sŏk (harvest festival), 92
Civil service examinations, 9–10, 49, 51, 96
Clavell, James, 46
Climate and seasons, 34–35
Cloisonné artists, 6–7
Clothing
    traditional, 204–5
    Western, 206–7
Conflict, attitudes toward, 18–19
Confucianism, 107, 109
    conservatism of, 114
    divorce, rules regarding, 21
    government, impact on, 34, 100
    human relations and, 8–10, 81–82
    introduced to Japan, 112

    introduced to Korea, 41
    modern challenge to, 254
    religion, threat to, 108
    women, perspective on, 21, 100–101
"Country face," 205
Country festivals, 232–33
Countryside, nature preserved in, 34–36
Courtesans. *See Ki-saeng* hostesses
Cousins, Norman, 186
Covell, Alan, 122, 124, 132, 133, 135, 136, 137, 144
Covell, Jon Carter, 74, 97, 98, 102, 119, 123, 126, 193
Crane, Paul Shields, 19, 24–26, 28, 31, 92, 253
Crime, 30
Crying, 20
Curiosity of Koreans, 7–8

Daech'ŏn beach resort, 229–30
Dae-gu, 176
Dance, 201–2
Dang (witch's shrine), 133–36
Dang-je ceremony, 158–59
Davies, Derek, 244
the Dead
    ghost marriages, 164
    islanders' rites for, 157–58
    memorialization of, 109
    modern attitudes toward, 250–51
    shamanist beliefs about, 13–14
    spirits, contact with, 126–32, 137–38
    See also Funerals
Decadence, threat of, 239–40
Demilitarized Zone (DMZ), 36, 239
Denying a request, 91
Deuchler, Martina, 103
Dining etiquette, 93–94, 220–21
Divorce, 21–22, 99–100, 171, 253
Dragon festivals, 134
Drinking etiquette, 223–25

Driving, 3–4
Drug culture, 228

the Economy, 66–67
Education
　Christian schools, 116–17
　English, study of, 10
　for girls, 22, 102
　Han-gŭl alphabet and, 73, 74–75
　importance to Koreans, 242
　literacy rate, 80
　of the literati, 49–53
　pictographs, instruction in, 10, 73–74, 79
　university entrance exams, 10, 105
the Elderly, 13–14, 160–61
Emotion, expression of, 4
English, study of, 10
Entertaining of guests, 93–94
Etiquette
　dining etiquette, 93–94, 220–21
　drinking etiquette, 223–25
　social etiquette. *See* Human relations
Ewha Women's University, 102, 116
Exogamy, tradition of, 38–39, 96, 155
Expatriate Koreans, 241

Family life, xvii–xxiii, 15
Farmers' dances, 202
Ferryboat transport, 226
Fertility and birthing rites, 150–51
Film industry, 211–12
Fishing, 151–52, 153–54
　hae-nyŏ diving women, 152, 169–71
　illegal methods, 160
　squid harvesting, 165
Fish markets, 154–55
Flag of Korea, 26–27, 59, 110
Flattery and respect, 86–87, 88–89
Flora, 35–36
Flower, national, 36

Folk art, 197–99, 203–4, 242–43
Folk heroes, 247–48
Food and drink, 213–14
　alcoholic beverages, 221–22, 225
　an-ju ("something-to-eat-with-drinks"), 216, 224
　basic Korean meal, 218
　beer, 221, 224
　breakfast in the country, 4–5
　bulgogi beef dish, 218–19
　dietary changes in modern Korea, 251
　dining etiquette, 93–94, 220–21
　drinking etiquette, 223–25
　gujul-pan crepe, 219
　island cuisine, 168
　kimch'i, 127, 216–18
　kim-jang sauce, 217
　kung-jung chon-gol bouillabaisse, 219–20
　lunch as main meal, 218
　meat dishes, 218–19
　panch'an (side dishes), 221
　red pepper, 46, 115, 218
　restaurants, 220–21
　seafood, 219
　squid, live, 168
Football (soccer), 208, 209
Foote, Lucius, 56
Forestland, 35
Fortune-tellers, 142
Fulder, Stephen, 185
Funerals
　Buddhist funerals, 107–8, 109
　gifts brought to, 91
　island death rites, 157–58
　shamanist funerals, 139

Games, 14
Gaya Kingdom, 39–40
Generational division, 250
Genghis Khan, 43

# INDEX

Ghost marriages, 164
Gift giving, 90–92
Ginseng. *See In-sam*
Gluttony, 93
Golf, 210
Gori (shamanist dance), 138–39
Government
  bloated bureaucracy, 28–29
  bribes for officials, 27–28
  Confucianism's impact on, 34, 100
  government-in-exile during Japanese occupation, 60–61
  on the islands, 155–56
  opposition to, 30
  personal dossiers kept by, 28
  post-Korean War developments, 65–67
  public attitudes toward, 27, 240–41

Hae-in-sa (Sea Echo) monastery, 74, 122, 230
Hae-nyŏ diving women, 152, 169–71
Hae-un-dae beach, 230–31
Hairstyles, 205
Halla Festival, 233
Halla Pai Huhm, 126, 138, 139
Hal-lyŏ Waterway, 47, 230
Halsell, Grace, 143
Hamel, Captain Hendrik, 49
Han, definition of, 2
Han-bok dress, 7, 125, 198, 204, 207
Han-gang River, 2
Han-gŭl alphabet, 10, 22
  cosmological principles of, 77–78
  criticism of, 80
  education, importance to, 73, 74–75
  guide to, 257–58
  horizontal writing of, 76–77
  invention of, 45, 79–80
  Korean personality reflected in, 77
  letters of, 76, 77
  logic and simplicity of, 76

sounds represented by individual letters, 77
Han-gŭl calligraphy, 72, 75
Han-gŭl Day, 80
Han Sang-bok, 150–51, 153, 155, 156, 158, 159
Harriman, W. Averell, 244
Hasami Island, 159–60, 162–64
Hasuk chip (guest house), 226
Henderson, Gregory, 239–41, 242, 243–44, 246
Hermit Kingdom, 16, 33–34, 48–49, 55–56
History of Korea
  Altaic nomads, 37–38
  Americans, arrival of (1800s), 56
  Buddhism, role of, 39, 110–13
  China, trade with, 112–13
  Chinese rule, 38–39, 41
  Christianity, role of, 49, 55–56, 114–16
  Europeans, arrival of, 48–49
  Hermit Kingdom, 16, 33–34, 48–49, 55–56
  Japan, conquest of, 39–41
  Japanese invasions (1500s), 46–48
  Japanese occupation, 16–18, 20, 56–61, 113, 245–47
  Korean War, 34, 62–65
  Ko-ryŏ Kingdom, 42–43
  the literati, 49–54, 80
  Lyi's accession to power, 44–45
  medicine, history of, 45, 102, 174–75
  modern Korea, 65–67
  Mongols, influence of, 43–44, 166–67, 205
  origins of Korea, legendary, 36–37
  religion, role of, 108
  three kingdoms, 39–41, 110–11
  Unified Silla, 41–42, 111–12
  U.S.-Soviet trusteeship, 61–62
  World War II, 34, 60–61, 245–46
  written language, 73–75

Hodge, General John, 62
Hojuk dungbon (family registry), 16
Hŏ Kyun, 247
Honeymoons, 214
Hong Kil-dong, 247–48
Horoscopes, 142, 156
Hotels and hostelries, 4, 215, 226–27
Housing
   city houses, 15
   heating systems, 15, 35, 194
   roofs of buildings, 192–93
   traditional Korean home, 15, 193–95
Human relations
   conflict, avoidance of, 18–19
   in Confucian society, 8–10, 81–82
   denying a request, 91
   dignity of another, respect for, 82–83
   discourtesies of foreigners, forgiveness of, 89
   emotion, expression of, 4
   entertaining of guests, 93–94
   eye visibility, 251
   flattery and respect, 86–87, 88–89
   gift giving, 90–92
   greetings, 25
   loyalty in friendship, 9, 84
   masculine and feminine expressions, use of, 89
   names, correct use of, 84, 85–88
   negotiation style, 83–84
   privacy, 92–93
   strangers, meetings between, 83, 84–85
   titles, use of, 82, 86–87
   trust between people, 93
Human rights, 29–30
Humility of Koreans, 82–83
Humor of Koreans, 8
Hwa-dan, 97
Hwan-gap ceremony, 12
Hwang Chi-ni, 97
Hwan-in, 36
Hwan-ung, 36, 174
Hyun, Peter, 125, 210

I-Ching (book), 142
Id, Korean, 17
Ideographs, 10, 73–74, 79
Idu (clerical learning), 79
Ik-chong, Prince, 201, 202
Inch'ŏn, MacArthur's landing at, 63–64
Income equality, 250
Independence Club (political party), 58
Inkyo, 175
In-sam (ginseng), xvii
   commercial industry, 182–83, 184–85
   curative effects, claimed, 185–86
   history of, 183
   popularity of, 174
   scientific analyses of, 185
   wild *in-sam*, hunt for, 181–82
   worldwide trade in, 183–84
In-sam-ju (ginseng wine), 225
Inside the League (Anderson), 118
In-yon (fate), xxi, 6, 113, 114
Islam, 110, 117
Islands
   death rites, 157–58
   farmer-fishermen (crofters), 159–60
   fertility and birthing rites, 150–51
   fishing by islanders, 153–55, 160
   food and drink, 168
   ghost marriages, 164
   government, 155–56
   hae-nyŏ diving women, 152, 169–71
   kye clubs, 161
   legal systems, 161–62
   marriage, 155, 163–64, 171–72
   marriage ceremonies, 156–57, 162–63
   men in *hae-nyŏ* communities, 171–72
   Mongol influences, 166–67
   polygyny, 163–64, 171–72
   punishment for offenses, 156
   seaweed farming, 155, 160
   shamanism, 150–51, 152, 156–59, 163
   social relationships, 160–61

squid harvesting, 165
tourism, 167–68
village ceremonies, 158–59
widows, treatment of, 164, 171
wildlife, 36
See also specific islands
Ito Hirobumi, 58

Jaisohn, Philip, 58
Japan
  Confucianism introduced in, 112
  Korean conquest of, 39–41
  Russia, war with (1904), 57–58
  shamanism in, 111
the Japanese, 3, 7
  Korean attitude toward, 17–18, 245–47
Japanese invasions (1500s), 46–48
Japanese occupation
  colonization, 59–61
  government-in-exile, 60–61
  legacy of, 16–18, 20, 245–47
  resistance to, 59–60
  Shintoism imposed on Korea, 113
  takeover process, 56–59
Jeju Island, 36, 126, 152, 165–69, 233
Jesuits, 46, 55, 114–15
Jin-gu, Princess, 40
Jip (retail outlets), 222
Jip-hyŏn-jŏn academy, 79–80
Job titles, 82
John Paul II, Pope, 116

Kaesŏng, 42, 43
Kagŏdo Island, 150–51, 153–56, 158–59
Kang-hwa Island, 37
Kangnŭng, 232
Kendall, Laurel, 103, 127, 128, 130–31, 136, 243
Ki (vital life force), 179–80
Ki-bun (mood), xviii, 18, 25, 84, 93, 161

Ki-ja, Chief, 38
Kim, K. I., 141
Kimch'i (National dish), 127, 216–18
Kim Chŏng-hui, 75
Kim Ch'un-ch'u, 209
Kim Dae-jung, 66
Kim Dae-song, 122
Kim Dŭk-ran, 141
Kim Il-sŏng, 12, 108, 214, 240
  accession to power, 62
  shamanism, interest in, 65, 123, 124–25, 143
  successor for, 241
Kim Jae-kyu, 66
Kim Jong-il, 12–13
Kim Kum-hwa, 108, 126, 128, 136, 255
Kim Kwang-yel, 141
Kim Kyung-ship, 177
Kim Man-jung, 98
Kim Ok-kyun, 26
Kim Pa-chin, 175
Kim Sat-kat, 75
Kim Su-ru, King, 111
Kim Tae-gŏn, 115, 140
Kim Tong-wook, 49–53
Ki-saeng hostesses, 95–96, 113, 223
  modern-day hostesses, 229
  poetry by, 97–98
Ki-saeng houses, 96–97, 152, 216
Knife-dancing, 138–39
Ko-gu-ryŏ Kingdom, 39, 41, 111
Kojong, Emperor, 56, 57, 58, 59, 115
Konishi, General, 114–15
Koreana (Hyun), 125
Korean Fishermen (Han), 150–51, 153, 155, 156, 158, 159
Korean language, 73, 75–76
  Chinese, different from, 78–79
  masculine and feminine expressions, 89
Korean Patterns (Crane), 24–26, 28, 31, 92
Korean War, 34, 62–65
  casualties, 65

Korean Women (anthology), 98, 99, 169
Ko-ryŏ Kingdom, 42–43
Kung-fu, doctrines of, 39
Kut ceremony, 107, 138–39, 222
  cost of, xx
  descent into hell, 123–25
  spirits, involvement of, 127–31
Kwiju, battle of, 43
Kwŏn-dang (strike), 53
Kye clubs, xxii, 23, 104, 161
Kyejo-am grotto, 232
Kyong-ae, King, 223
K'yŏng-bok Palace, 95
Kyŏngju, 33, 41–42, 231
Kyŏng-p'o-dae pavilion, 231

Lao-tzu, 39, 110
Lee Du-hyun, 139–40, 141
Lee Tong-kol, 179–80
Legal system, 29–30
  on the islands, 161–62
Literacy rate, 80
the Literati
  daily life, 53–54
  education of, 49–53
  Han-gŭl alphabet, acceptance of, 80
  See also Yang-ban
Literature and poetry, 75, 97–98, 228–29, 247
Low, Frederick, 56
Loyalty of Koreans, 9, 84
Lunch as main meal of the day, 218
Lyi Sŏng-gye, General, 44–45

MacArthur, General Douglas
  Korean War, 63–64
  as shamanist god, 131–32
McCann, David, 97–98
McNamara, Dennis, 243
Makkŏlli (alcoholic beverage), 222, 225
Mal (magazine), 249

Mansin (witches), 103, 104, 137
  kut ceremony, 123–25, 127–31
  sin-byŏng (possession sickness), 104, 126, 132, 138, 140–41
Marriage
  arranged marriages, 11–12, 16
  child-bride marriages, 99
  East-West marriages, 81–82
  exogamy, 38–39, 96, 155
  ghost marriages, 164
  honeymoons, 214
  husband's and wife's names for each other, 87–89
  islanders' marriages, 155, 163–64
  modern attitudes toward, 252–53
  polygyny, 163–64, 171–72
  re-marrying, 22
  spouse-hunting, 105–7, 227–28
Marriage ceremonies, 16, 107
  gifts from guests, 90, 91
  of islanders, 156–57, 162–63
Martial arts, 207, 210
Mask dances, 202
Medicine
  acupuncture, 174, 175, 179–80
  bamboo used as, 178
  history of, 45, 102, 174–75
  in-sam (ginseng), xvii, 174, 181–86
  medical manuals, 45, 48, 175
  pharmacies, 173, 175
  saunas and massage, 178–79
  skin pressure techniques, 174, 178
  Western and Oriental medicine, comparison of, 186–87
  See also Apothecaries
Meditation, 106
Midinettes ("girls of noon"), 227–29
Min, Queen, 56, 57, 102, 143
Minstrels, 203
Miura Goro, 57
Mongol influence in Korea, 43–44, 166–67, 205
Mosques, 117

Mŏt (taste), 8, 19, 201
Mount Gaya Park, 230
Mudang (witches), 11, 24, 40, 103, 104, 108, 125
  apothecaries, work with, 173–74
  courtships, assistance with, 106–7
  in-sam hunt, role in, 181–82
  male *mudang*, 126
  number of, 125–26
  picture galleries of, 133–36
  popularity of, 143–44
  psychiatrists' perspectives on, 141
  rites of, 138–40
  training of, 126
Mun-mu, King, 134
Mun Sŏn-myŏng, 118, 255
Music, 8, 199–201, 204
  shamanist music, 137
Musical instruments, 137, 200
Myŏng-jong, King, 53

Nag-ji octopi, 168
Nagsan-sa temple, 112, 231–32
Nak-hwa-am hermitage, 230
Names
  of children, 12–13, 87–88
  etiquette regarding use of, 84, 85–88
  family names, 12
  given names, 12–13, 86, 87–88
  husband's and wife's names for each other, 87–89
  nicknames, 89
  of women, 13
"National" creatures, 36, 247
Negotiation style of Koreans, 83–84
Network (film), 94
Newspapers, 249–50
Night life, 215–16
Nihon Shoki (Japanese chronicle), 40
Non-gae, 229
Nong-ak (farmers' dances), 202
Noodle shops, 220

North Korea
  creation of, 62
  Korean War, 62–65
  as security threat to the South, 238–39
  shamanism in, 122–23
  travel restrictions, 214–15
Numerology, 134–35, 142–43
Nun-ch'i (intuition), 17, 24

Olympic Games of 1988, 2, 208–9, 210
Ondol heating system, 15, 35, 194
O Su-na, 105–7

Paekche Kingdom, 39, 40, 41, 111
Painting, 133–36, 197–99
Pak Byung-Ro, 72–73, 77, 78, 80
Pak Chae-yon, 177
Pak Chi-wŏn, 53–54
Pak Chong-yang, 56
Pak Chung-hi, 66, 126, 143, 241
Paksa (doctor), 87
Pak Yŏng-hyo, 26
P'ansori ballad singing, 202–3
Papermaking, 196
Pari Kong-ju, 123–24
Patience of Koreans, 31
Peterson, Mark, 100
Pharmacies, 173, 175. *See also* Apothecaries
Philippines, 59
Physiognomies of Koreans, 3
Pictographs, 10, 73–74, 79
Pin-dola, 134
Poetry, 75, 203, 247
  by *ki-saeng*, 97–98
Police corps, 3–4, 29–30
Politicians, respect for, 86
Polman daejung kyung. See Tripitaka Koreana
Polo, Marco, 183

Polygyny, 163–64, 171–72
Pomun Lake resort, 231
Printing technology
  movable metal type, 44, 73
  wooden blocks, 74
Privacy, importance to Koreans, 92–93
Prostitution, 227, 228
Pu-dok (female virtue), 22
Puyŏ, 33
P'yŏng-yang, 33, 37, 64

Reagan, Nancy, 206
Rector, Gary, 200, 202
Red pepper, 46, 115, 218
Reischauer, Edwin, 45
Religion
  Confucianism as challenge to, 108
  historical perspective on, 108
  shamanism, relation to, 107–9
  See also specific religions
Religious art, 133–36, 198–99, 230, 231–32
Restaurants, 220–21
Reunification of the Koreas, 67
Rhee, Syngman. *See* Yi Sŭng-man
Rhi Bu-yong, 141
Ridel, Father, 116
Ridgway, General Matthew, 64
Rocking Rock, 232
Roofs of buildings, 192–93
Roosevelt, Franklin D., 61
Royal Asiatic Society, 24
Russo-Japanese War (1904), 57–58

Sadness of Koreans, 8, 19–20
Saint-Exupéry, Antoine de, 241–42
Sam-sin (goddess of life), 150, 151
San-sin (mountain spirit), 133
Saunas and massage, 178–79
Schweitzer, David, 180
Seafaring tradition, 14–15
Seafood, 219
Seaweed farming, 155, 160

Security forces, 238–39
Sejo, King, 80
Sejong, King, 22, 45, 73, 79–80, 201
Seoul
  apothecary's shops, 175–76
  capital, selection as, 45
  as decadent city, 239–40
  driving in, 3–4
  growth since 1954, 1–2
  as international city, 2–3
  Korean War, 63, 64
  Myŏng-dong section, 30
  name, meaning of, 2
  outskirts, 2
  population, 1
  transportation in, 225
Seoul National University, 72
Set-bang (room rental), 226
Sexuality of Koreans, 26
Shamanism
  Buddhism, influence on, 110, 118–22
  children, ceremonies for, 11
  Christianity, influence on, 143–44
  clothes of the dead used in rituals, 137–38
  daily life, role in, 106–7
  the dead, beliefs about, 13–14
  divination ceremonies, 127–28
  fans used in ceremonies, 137
  as female imperium, 122
  fertility and birthing rites, 150–51
  funerals, 139
  institutionalization of, 143
  islanders' practice of, 150–51, 152, 156–59, 163
  in Japan, 111
  knife-dancing, 138–39
  as Korean phenomenon, 110
  in modern society, 144–45
  music in, 137
  in North Korea, 122–23
  origins of, 136
  popularity of, 107
  religions, relation to, 107–9

religious art, 133–36, 198–99
sexual aspects, 132–33
spontaneity of, 131
symbols of, 136–37
trance possessions, 139–40
Trinity concept in, 134–35
See also Kut ceremony; *Mansin;*
Mudang; Spirits
Shellard, E. J., 185
Shintoism, 40, 113
Shirokogoroff, S. M., 141
Shōgun (Clavell), 46
Sibley, Grete Diemente, 119, 120
Siddhārtha Gautama, 109–10
Sightseeing
by Koreans, 214–15, 232
places of interest, 229–33
Si-jo poetry, 97, 98, 203
Silla Kingdom, 39, 41–42, 111–12
Simonia, Nobari, 254
Sin-byŏng (possession sickness), 104, 126, 132, 138, 140–41
Sin Yun-bok, 97, 203–4
Sir-hak (practical learning), 74–75
Skiing, 210
Skin pressure, 174, 178
Social rank
breakdown of the system, 96–97
castes of various ranks, 94–95
examinations to determine, 9–10, 49, 51, 96
flexibility in modern Korea, 25–26
hereditary nature of, 95–96
history of ranks, 42
human relations, role in, 81–82
importance of, 9
the literati, 49–54, 80
lower orders, 95
yang-ban (gentry), 10, 13, 42, 43, 55, 94–95, 242
Sŏ family, xvii–xxiii
Sŏ-hak (Western learning), 115, 117
So-ju (alcoholic beverage), 221, 225
Sŏkkuram hermitage, 122, 199

Sŏlag-san national park, 232
Sŏl Ch'ong, 79, 112
Sŏn Buddhism, 74, 110, 122
Song, 98, 200, 202–3
Song-gyun-gwan Academy, 49–53, 96
Sŏng-myŏng, King, 111
Sŏn Ki-chŏng, 208
Spirits, 123
contact with, 126–32, 137–38
pictoral representations of, 133–36
Sports and fitness, 207–11
Spouse-hunting, 105–7, 227–28
Squid, eating live, 168
Squid harvesting, 165
Ssirum wrestling, 203, 210, 211
Stalin, Josef, 61, 64
Strangers, meetings between, 83, 84–85
Students, foreign, 226
Sun-jong, 58
Superstition. *See* Shamanism
Swastika, Korean, 196
Swimming, 208, 210
Syncretistic cults, 110, 117–18

Taegam (housekeeper spirit), 128
Tae-guk-ki (Korean flag), 26, 59, 110
T'ae-jong-gyo cult, 117–18
T'aekwŏndo (martial art), 4, 207, 210
Tae-won-gun, 56
Takeshiuchi, 40
T'alch'um (mask dances), 202
Tale of Ch'un-hyang (Hwang), 97
Tan-gun, 37, 133
Tano Che festival, 152
Taoism, 110
Tastefulness of Koreans, 19
Taxis, 225
Team spirit of Koreans, 31
Television, xix, xxi, 14, 24, 212
Temples, Buddhist, 118–20, 122, 199, 231
Tennis, 209

Tipping, 90
Titles, Koreans' love of, 82, 86–87
Tokugawa, Shōgun, 46
Tol ceremony, 10
Tong-daeg-jip restaurants, 220
Tong-hak (popular revolution), 57
Tong-il Church, 118
Topography, 35
Tourism
  on the islands, 167–68
  sightseeing on the mainland, 229–33
Toyotomi Hideyoshi, 26, 46, 47, 48
Traditions, changes in, 251
Train travel, xxii, 225, 226
Trance possessions, 139–40
Transportation around Korea, 225–26
Tripitaka Koreana, 44, 74, 122
Truman, Harry S, 61
Trust between people, 93
Turtle ships, 46–47
Tyranny in Korea, 241–42

Ŭi-sang, 112, 231
U Island, 169–72
Ŭlrin Mirŭk (thousand-year-old Buddha), 230
Ul-rŭng Island, 164–65
Unification Church, 118
University entrance exams, 10, 105
U.S. influence in Korea, 30–31, 56
U.S.-Soviet trusteeship, 61–62

Vacations, 81
Visiting cards, 83, 84–85
Volleyball, 209

Wang-in, 111
Wang Kŏn, 42, 43
Weltevree, Jan Janse, 48
Westerners in Korea, 81–82

Widows, 22, 100–101, 164, 171, 253
Wildlife, 36
Witches. *See Mansin; Mudang*
Women
  attractiveness to Westerners, 20–21
  child-bride marriages, 99
  Christianity's appeal for, 100–101
  clothing worn by, 204–7
  Confucianism and, 21, 100–101
  drunkeness of husbands, reaction to, 224
  education for girls, 22, 102
  in the 1980s, 23–24
  emotionalism permitted to, 84
  equality reforms, 22–23, 252
  family, role in, 101
  family finances, management of, xix, xxii, 23
  female anatomy, Korean obsession with, 102
  hae-nyŏ diving women, 152, 169–71
  in-law relationships, xviii-xix, 22
  ki-saeng hostesses, 95–96, 97–98, 113, 223, 229
  "Korean miracle," role in, 24
  kye clubs, xxii, 23, 104, 161
  "mother" name for, 87, 88
  names of, 13
  origins of, legendary, 36–37
  social and spiritual power of, 103–4, 243–44, 251–52
  sports participation, 209
  spouse-hunting, 105–7, 227–28
  subservience to males, traditional, 21–22
  Westerners' perceptions of, 251–52
  widows, 22, 100–101, 164, 171, 253
  witches. *See Mansin; Mudang*
  working women, 81, 227–29
Won-bul-gyo cult, 117
Wŏn-hyo, 111–12
World War II, 34, 60–61, 245–46

INDEX

Wrestling, 203, 210, 211
Writing
   Chinese characters used in, 79
   history of, 73–75
   Koreans' love for, 72–73
   poetry, 75, 97–98, 203, 247
   See also Han-gŭl alphabet

Yak. See Apothecaries
Yak-chung kol-mok ("herb street"), 176
Yang-ban (gentry), 10, 13, 42, 43, 55, 94–95, 242. *See also* the Literati
Yangban chŏn (Pak), 53–54
Yangmin (lower classes), 42
Yang-yang, 232
Yao, Emperor, 248
Yatsu Mitsuo, 180
Yi Kwang-rin, 49

Yin and yang symbol, 26–27, 198
Yi Sŭng-hun, 115
Yi Sŭng-man (Syngman Rhee), 22, 60, 61, 62, 65–66, 126, 143, 241
Yi Sun-shin, Admiral, 46–48
Yi Yuk-sa, 246–47
Yŏbo (expression), 86
Yŏ-gwan inns, 4, 215, 220, 226–27
Yŏ-in-suk (guest houses), 4, 226
Yong-wang (Dragon King), 133–34
Yonsei University, 116–17
Yo-sŏk, Princess, 111–12
Young, Barbara, 142
Youngsook Kim-Harvey, 99, 141
Yu Kwan-sun, 60
Yun Ch'i-o, 206
Yu Tae-u, 180

Zen Buddhism. *See* Sŏn Buddhism